✔ KU-198-763

Microsoft®
Internet Explorer 4

At a Glance

Microsoft®*Press*

Published by **Microsoft Press**
A Division of Microsoft Corporation
One Microsoft Way
Redmond, Washington 98052-6399

Copyright © 1997 Perspection, Inc.

All rights reserved. No part of the contents of this book may be reproduced or transmitted in any form or by any means without the written permission of the publisher.

Library of Congress Cataloging-in-Publication Data
Microsoft Internet Explorer 4 at a Glance / Perspection, Inc.
    p.   cm.
   Includes index.
   ISBN 1-57231-740-X
   1. World Wide Web (Information retrieval system)   2. Microsoft Internet Explorer.   I. Perspection, Inc.
TK5105.883.M53M534 1997
005.7'13769--dc21
                                      97-37610
                                      CIP

Printed and bound in the United States of America.

1 2 3 4 5 6 7 8 9 QEQE 2 1 0 9 8 7

Distributed to the book trade in Canada by Macmillian of Canada, a division of Canada Publishing Corporation.

A CIP catalog record for this book is available from the British Library.

Microsoft Press books are available through booksellers and distributers worldwide. For futher information about international editions, contact your local Microsoft Corporation office, or contact Microsoft Press International directly at fax (206) 936-7329.

Microsoft, Microsoft Press, Microsoft Internet Explorer, Microsoft Internet Explorer logo, Microsoft Outlook Express, Microsoft FrontPage Express, Microsoft NetMeeting, Microsoft NetShow, Windows, and Windows NT are registered trademarks of Microsoft Corporation. Other product and company names mentioned herein may be the trademarks of their respective owners.

Companies, names, and/or data used in screens and sample output are fictitious unless otherwise noted.

For Perspection, Inc.
Writers: **Steven M. Johnson, Robin Geller, Cheryl Kirk**
Production Editor: **David W. Beskeen**
Developmental Editors: **Jane Pedicini, Mary-Terese Cozzola, Kathy Finnegan**
Copy Editor: **Jane Pedicini**
Technical Editor: **Nicholas Chu**

For Microsoft Press
Acquisitions Editor: **Kim Fryer**
Project Editor: **Saul Candib**

Contents

Learn about the
Internet Explorer Suite
See page 6

*"How do I
browse the Web
with Internet
Explorer?"*

See page 16

Research information
on the Internet
See page 32

View Active Channels
See page 44

Download files from the Web
See page 52

"How do I change my home page?"

See page 68

"How do I listen to the radio from the Internet?"

See page 96

View streaming audio and video with NetShow
See page 108

Compose an e-mail message
See page 120

Read messages
from a newsgroup
See page 142

Communicate with
audio and video
See page 168

*"What a funny
comic strip!"*

See page 178

"How do I create my own Web Page?"

See page 186

Work with paragraph lists
See page 210

Create a marquee
in your Web page
See page 216

Insert ActiveX controls
See page 230

Use the Internet Explorer
logo in your Web page
See page 239

Download Internet Explorer
See page 244

Acknowledgments

The task of creating any book requires the talents of many hard-working people pulling together to meet impossible deadlines and untold stresses. We'd like to thank the outstanding team responsible for making this book possible: the writers, Steve Johnson, Robin Geller, and Cheryl Kirk; the editors, Jane Pedicini, Mary-Terese Cozzola, and Kathy Finnegan; the copy editor, Jane Pedicini; the technical editor, Nicholas Chu; the production team, David Beskeen and Gary Bedard; and the indexer, Michael Brackney.

At Microsoft Press, we'd like to thank Kim Fryer for the opportunity to undertake this project, Saul Candib for project editing and software liason expertise, and Lucinda Rowley for helping to create and fine tune the Microsoft At a Glance series.

Perspection

Perspection

Perspection, Inc. is a technology training company committed to providing information to help people communicate, make decisions, and solve problems. Perspection writes and produces software training books, and develops interactive multimedia applications for Windows-based and Macintosh personal computers.

Microsoft Internet Explorer 4 At a Glance incorporates Perspection's training expertise to ensure that you'll receive the maximum return on your time. With this staightforward, easy-to-read reference tool you'll get the information you need when you need it. You'll focus on the skills that increase productivity while working at your own pace and convenience.

We invite you to visit the Perspection World Wide Web site. You can visit us at:

http://www.perspection.com

You'll find a description for all of our books, additional content for our books, information about Perspection, and much more.

About
At a Glance

Microsoft *Internet Explorer 4 At a Glance* is for anyone who wants to get the most from their computer and their software with the least amount of time and effort. We think you'll find this book to be a straightforward, easy-to-read reference tool. With the premise that your computer should work for you, not you for it, this book's purpose is to help you get your work done quickly and efficiently so that you can get away from the computer and live your life.

No Computerese!

Let's face it—when there's a task you don't know how to do but you need to get it done in a hurry, or when you're stuck in the middle of a task and can't figure out what to do next, there's nothing more frustrating than having to read page after page of technical background material. You want the information you need—nothing more, nothing less—and you want it now! And it should be easy to find and understand.

That's what this book is all about. It's written in plain English—no technical jargon and no computerese. There's no single task in the book that takes more than two pages. Just look up the task in the index or the table of contents, turn to the page, and there's the information, laid out step by step and accompanied by a graphic that adds visual clarity. You don't get bogged down by the whys and wherefores; just follow the steps, look at the illustrations, and get your work done with a minimum of hassle.

Occasionally you might want to turn to another page if the procedure you're working on has a "See Also" in the left column. That's because there's a lot of overlap among tasks, and we didn't want to keep repeating ourselves. We've also scattered some useful tips here and there, and thrown in a "Try This" once in a while, but by and large we've tried to remain true to the heart and soul of the book, which is that information you need should be available to you at a glance.

Useful Tasks...

Whether you use Internet Explorer 4 for work, play, or some of each, we've tried to pack this book with procedures for everything we could think of that you might want to do, from the simplest tasks to some of the more esoteric ones.

...And the Easiest Way To Do Them

Another thing we've tried to do in Internet Explorer 4 At a Glance is to find and document the easiest way to accomplish a task. Internet Explorer often provides many ways to accomplish a single result, which can be daunting or delightful, depending on the way you like to work. If you tend to stick with one favorite and familiar approach, we think the methods described in this book are the way to go. If you like trying out alternative techniques, go ahead! The intuitiveness of Internet Explorer invites exploration, and you're likely to discover ways of doing things that you think are

easier or that you like better. If you do, that's great! It's exactly what the creators of Internet Explorer 4 had in mind when they provided so many alternatives.

A Quick Overview

This book isn't meant to be read in any particular order. It's designed so that you can jump in, get the information you need, and then close the book and keep it near your computer until the next time you need it. But that doesn't mean we scattered the information about with wild abandon. If you were to read the book from front to back, you'd find a logical progression from the simple tasks to the more complex ones. Here's a quick overview.

First, we assume that Internet Explorer 4 is already installed on your machine. If it's not, the Setup Wizard makes installation so simple that you won't need our help anyway. So, unlike most computer books, this one doesn't start out with installation instructions and a list of system requirements. You've already got that under control.

Section 2 of the book covers the basics: starting the Internet Explorer program: connecting to the Internet; browsing the Web and your local hard drive; navigating basics; and using the Smart Toolbar.

Section 3 explores how to find and update information: searching for information on the Internet; creating and editing a Favorites list; viewing and maintaining a History list; subscribing to a Web site; subscribing to a channel; and obtaining information from Microsoft.

Section 4 describes tasks that allow you to save information: downloading files from the Web; copying and saving text and graphics; saving a Web page, setting up a Web page; and printing a Web page.

Section 5 examines tasks for personalizing Internet Explorer: personalizing the start page; changing the window appearance, choosing security zones; shopping on the Internet; improving performance; changing colors, fonts, languages, and advanced settings.

Section 6 describes tasks for expanding the functionality of Internet Explorer: understanding and installing add-ons and viewers; finding and using add-ons, plug-ins, and viewers; broadcasting audio and video with NetShow; playing sounds and videos; finding and using ActiveX and Java programs; and controlling ActiveX and Java content.

Sections 7 and 8 examine tasks for working with e-mail and newgrounps using Outlook Express: creating and sending e-mail; adding contacts to the address book; adding attachments to e-mail; reading and replying to e-mail; working with multiple accounts; configuring the newsreader; reading news; finding and subscribing to a newsgroup; and posting your own messages.

Section 9 describes tasks for communicating using NetMeeting: making and receiving a call; starting a conference; using NetMeeting chat; sending and receiving files; chatting for fun; and changing your chat character.

Sections 10 and 11 describe tasks for creating Web pages using FrontPage Express: creating a Web page using wizards; adding and modifying Web pages; inserting and modifying images; creating and editing hyperlinks; creating a bookmark, printing Web pages; creating and formatting tables; using WebBots; working with forms; and inserting ActiveX controls, Java applets, and plug-ins.

Section 12 describes tasks for working with Internet Explorer tools: getting online support; publishing a Web page; setting up a personal Web server; downloading, installing and removing Internet Explorer; getting updates to Internet Explorer; administering to Internet Explorer users; getting free software; and working with beta software.

A Final Word (or Two)

We had three goals in writing this book, and here they are:

◆ We want the book to help you do all the things you want to do.

◆ We want the book to help you discover how to do things you didn't know you wanted to do.

◆ And, finally, we want our book to help you enjoy doing your work with Internet Explorer 4. We think that would be the best gift we could give you as a "thank you" for buying our book.

We hope you'll have as much fun using Internet Explorer 4 At a Glance as we've had writing it. The best way to learn is by doing, and that's what we hope you'll get from this book.

Jump right in!

2

Browsing the Web with Internet Explorer

Microsoft Internet Explorer 4 is more than a traditional Web browser program. It is a flexible tool you can use to navigate your computer, network, or intranet, as well the Internet. By integrating Internet Explorer with your desktop, it turns your desktop into a personal home page, called the *Active Desktop*, from which you can:

◆ Connect to the Internet

◆ Jump directly to your favorite Web sites

◆ Obtain specialized content on Active Channels

◆ Open a document on your hard disk drive

Learn One Method to Work Efficiently

With the Active Desktop installed, your computer will look a little different, but you need to remember only one set of navigational skills to move around. With the Smart Toolbar and the Address bar, you can open documents on your hard disk in the same way that you access Web sites on the Internet. To help ease the transition to this new method of working on your computer, you can also open and close programs in the traditional way.

Getting Started with the Internet Explorer Suite

The Internet Explorer Suite is a variety of programs that work together to provide you the simplest and most efficient way to create and view content, as well as to communicate with others. Each program serves a distinct purpose, but their features all function similarly, so learning the entire suite is easy. The Suite includes:

Internet Explorer—A browsing program for exploring content on the World Wide Web, a network or an intranet, and your Active Desktop (if you have installed the Web Integrated Desktop). With Internet Explorer, you can view Web content online or offline, and protect yourself and your computer with features such Microsoft Wallet, Security Zones, and the Content Advisor.

Outlook Express—A messaging program based on the e-mail and newsgroup communications tools of Outlook 97. Outlook Express accesses and manages multiple e-mail and newsgroup accounts, provides offline reading and composing capabilities, and offers security options.

NetMeeting—A program that combines your PC with the Internet to allow you to communicate and collaborate with people around the world through phone and video conferencing, and through data conferencing using a shared white board or chat features.

NetShow—A program that enables you to broadcast multimedia shows across the Internet or an intranet. NetShow integrates audio and video letting you synchronize sound with moving pictures and illustrations.

FrontPage Express—A WYSIWYG HTML editor based on the Web authoring and management tools in Microsoft FrontPage. FrontPage Express walks you through creating new Web pages and editing existing HTML documents.

Active Channels—A feature that turns your desktop into a virtual television for Web sites. Channels feature specialized content developed especially for Internet Explorer that you can display full screen, as Web pages, and as a screen saver on the Active Desktop. For any Web page to which you subscribe, Internet Explorer downloads new content to you as it's available.

Active Desktop—A feature that turns your desktop into a home base for starting programs, switching files, and getting information from the Internet, an intranet, or a network. The Active Desktop allows you to open any document and browse your hard drives, network, intranet, and the Internet with the same navigational tools. Internet Explorer uses a *Smart Toolbar* that recognizes the difference between directory paths and Web addresses, so it always displays only the buttons you need for the current document; its *Address bar* provides the same surfing tools whether you are working in My Computer, Windows Explorer, or on the Active Desktop itself.

Viewing the Internet Explorer Active Desktop

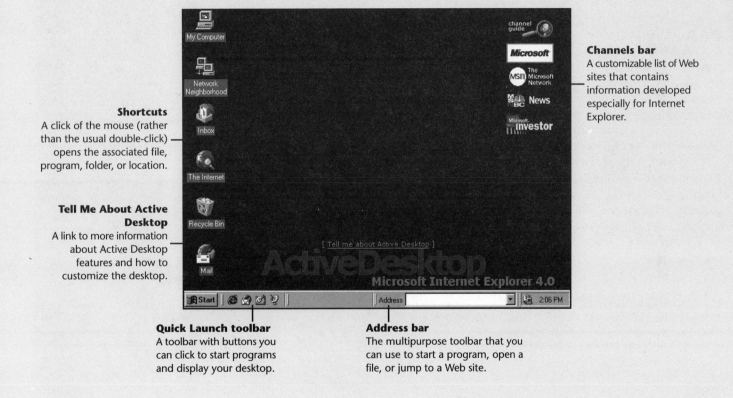

Shortcuts
A click of the mouse (rather than the usual double-click) opens the associated file, program, folder, or location.

Tell Me About Active Desktop
A link to more information about Active Desktop features and how to customize the desktop.

Channels bar
A customizable list of Web sites that contains information developed especially for Internet Explorer.

Quick Launch toolbar
A toolbar with buttons you can click to start programs and display your desktop.

Address bar
The multipurpose toolbar that you can use to start a program, open a file, or jump to a Web site.

Using the Active Desktop

If you like the single-click advantage that you get when browsing the Web, then the Active Desktop is for you. The Active Desktop looks and functions more like a personalized Web page. You can add an Address bar to your taskbar or desktop so you can browse folders and even run programs without using the Start button or opening My Computer or Windows Explorer. Global Favorites give you quick access to your favorite Web sites and to the files, documents, and projects you work on most.

TIP

Show the desktop quickly.
To see the desktop without closing or minimzing windows, click the Show Desktop button on the Quick Launch toolbar.

Access the Web from the Start Menu

1 Click the Start button on the taskbar.

◆ Point to Favorites and then click a favorite to start Internet Explorer and display your favorite Web site.

◆ Point to Find, and then click On The Internet to start Internet Explorer and perform a Web search.

◆ Click Run and then enter a URL to start Internet Explorer and display the Web site.

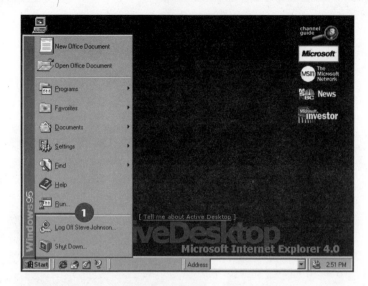

Add or Remove an Active Desktop Toolbar

1 Right-click the taskbar.

2 Point to Toolbars.

3 Click the toolbar you want to add or remove.

4 If you want, drag the toolbar to the Active Desktop.

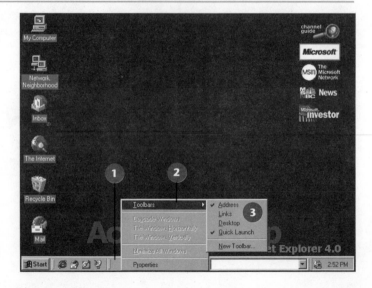

TIP

Move Start menu items. *To change the location of files on your Start menu, drag them to a new location in any folder on the menu.*

Show or Hide the Active Desktop

1 Right-click the Desktop.

2 Point to Active Desktop.

3 Click View As Web Page.

A check mark next to the menu item indicates the Active Desktop is shown, while a blank indicates the Active Desktop is hidden.

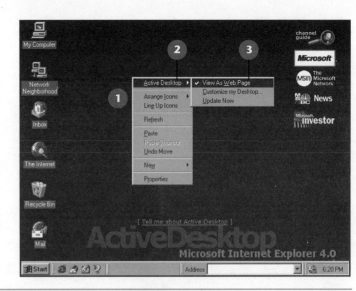

TIP

Drag files to the Start menu. *To add files and programs to your Start menu, drag them to the Start button on the taskbar.*

Show or Hide Web Items on the Active Desktop

1 Right-click the Desktop.

2 Click Properties.

3 Click the Web tab.

4 Click the item you want to show or hide. Select the item to show it or deselect the item to hide it.

5 Click OK.

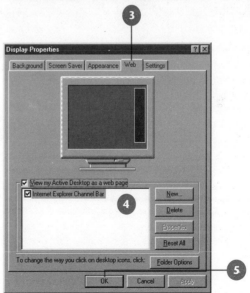

Customizing the Active Desktop

With Internet Explorer, you can bring live Web content to your desktop. You can place pieces of Web pages or HTML-based code directly on your Active Desktop. For example, you can add Web content to continuously display weather information on your desktop. To use Web items, you must be running Internet Explorer with the Active Desktop turned on. You can check out the cool Web items in Microsoft's Desktop Gallery. You can also activate a Web screen saver that cycles through a series of Web pages. The Web screen saver is created with a screen saver channel. The screen saver uses the full screen view of Internet Explorer.

Add Web Items to Your Active Desktop

1. Right-click the Desktop, and then click Properties.

2. Click the Web tab.

3. Click New.

4. Click Yes to close the Display Properties dialog box and connect to the Active Desktop Gallery Web page.

5. Click Continue.

6. Read the Active Desktop Gallery Web page.

7. Click the down scroll arrow, and then click a link to an Active Desktop item.

8. Click Add To My Desktop.

9. Click OK to subscribe.

10. Click the File menu, and then click Close.

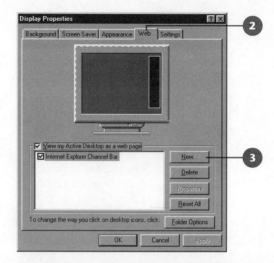

Sample Web item

TIP

Select channel screen saver channels and display time. *Open the Display Properties dialog box, click the Screen Saver tab, click Settings, select the channels you want to use, set the display time, and then click OK.*

Create a Channel Screen Saver

1. Right-click the Desktop, and then click Properties.

2. Click the Screen Saver tab.

3. Click the Screen Saver drop-down arrow, and then select Channel Screen Saver.

4. If you want, click Preview.

5. Click OK.

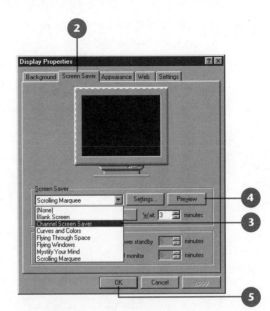

SEE ALSO

See "Modifying the Internet Explorer Window" on page 72 for information about using the full screen view.

Add a Web Background

1. Right-click the Desktop, and then click Properties.

2. Click the Background tab.

3. Click Browse.

4. Click the Files Of Type drop-down arrow, and then select HTML Document.

5. Locate the HTML document you want to use as a background, and then double-click the file.

6. Click OK.

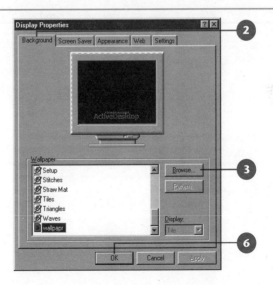

Connecting to the Internet

Sometimes connecting your computer to the Internet can be the most difficult part of getting started. The Connection Wizard simplifies the process, whether you want to set up a new connection using an existing account or you want to select an Internet service provider (ISP) and set up a new account. You might need to obtain connection information from your ISP or your system administrator. If you are on a corporate intranet, you might need to use a *proxy server*, which provides a secure barrier between your intranet and the Internet and prevents other people from seeing confidential information on your intranet. Or you can configure Internet Explorer with a settings file supplied by your corporate system administrator.

Get Connected Using the Internet Connection Wizard

1 Click the Start button on the taskbar, point to Programs, point to Internet Explorer, and then click Connection Wizard.

2 Read the Get Connected information. Click Next to continue.

3 Click the option button for the setup you want to use. Click Next to continue.

4 Read the information in each wizard dialog box, and then enter the required information. Click Next to continue.

5 In the final wizard dialog box, click Finish.

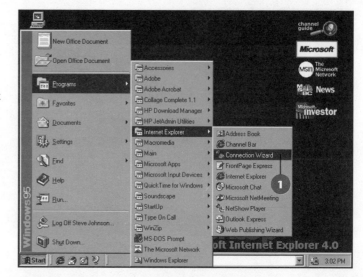

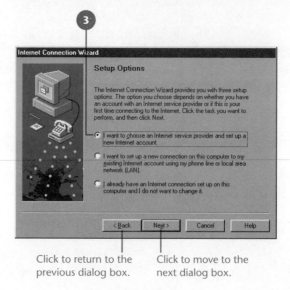

Click to return to the previous dialog box.

Click to move to the next dialog box.

TRY THIS

Learn more about your setup options. *Click the Help button and then click a setup option with the Help pointer to read about the selected option.*

TIP

Connect first. *Before you can configure your computer to use a proxy server or automatically configure Internet Explorer on a corporate system, your computer must be connected to a local area network.*

SEE ALSO

See "Administering to Internet Explorer Users" on page 250 for information on getting the Internet Explorer Administration Kit.

Configure Your Computer to Use a Proxy Server

1 In the Internet Explorer Window, click the View menu, and then click Internet Options.

2 Click the Connection tab.

3 Click the Connect Using A Proxy Server check box to select it.

4 Click Advanced, enter the proxy server addresses.

5 Click OK.

6 Click OK.

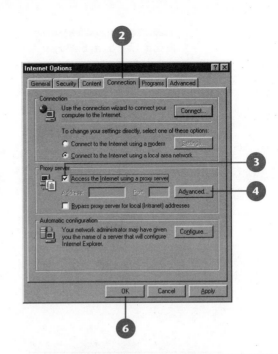

Configure Internet Explorer on a Corporate System

1 In the Internet Explorer window, click the View menu, and then click Internet Options.

2 Click the Connection tab.

3 Click Configure.

4 Type the address or file and location supplied by your system administrator.

5 Click Refresh.

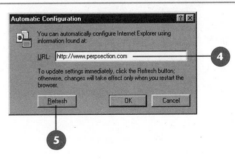

2

Starting Internet Explorer

Once you are at your computer's desktop, you can start Internet Explorer just as you would any other program you have installed on your system. If your desktop is visible, the quickest way to start Internet Explorer is with The Internet icon on the desktop. If any other programs are open, it's easier to use the Start menu or the Quick Launch toolbar on the taskbar on your Active Desktop.

TIP

Password required. *If you have an account with an Internet Service Provider (ISP), you might need to type your user name and password before Internet Explorer will connect to the Web.*

Start Internet Explorer from the Start Menu

1 Click the Start button on the taskbar.

2 Point to Programs.

3 Point to Internet Explorer.

4 Click Internet Explorer.

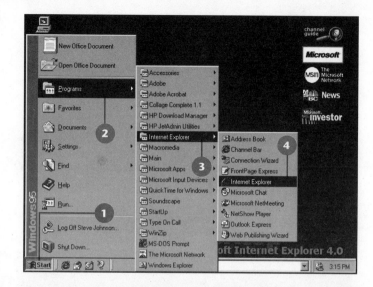

Start Internet Explorer from the Quick Launch Toolbar

1 Click the Launch Internet Explorer Browser button on the Quick Launch toolbar.

2 Click Start for a quick tour Internet Explorer.

3 Click the Close button.

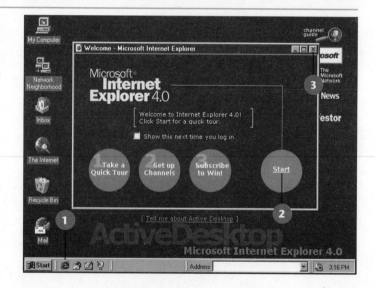

Viewing the Internet Explorer Window

Menu bar
Contains all the commands you need to access and move around Web pages, customize Internet Explorer, and get Help.

Title bar
Displays the program name, Microsoft Internet Explorer, preceded by the name or address of the Web page you are viewing.

Standard toolbar
Provides buttons to access and move around Web pages, and to work in Internet Explorer.

Links toolbar
Contains buttons to link to several Microsoft Web sites.

Address bar
Displays the address of the current document or Web page; lets you type a new filename or Web page address or search for other files or Web sites.

Browser pane
Displays the current document or Web page.

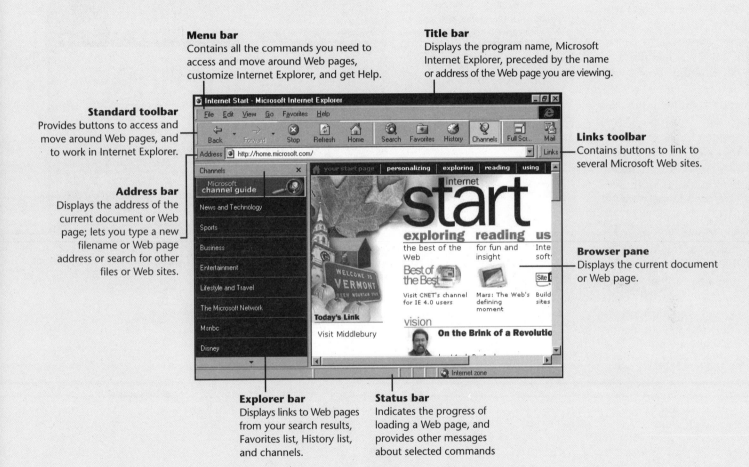

Explorer bar
Displays links to Web pages from your search results, Favorites list, History list, and channels.

Status bar
Indicates the progress of loading a Web page, and provides other messages about selected commands

Browsing the Web

With Internet Explorer, you can browse sites on the Web with ease by entering a Web address or by clicking a link. Each method is better at different times. For example, you might type an address in the Address bar to start your session. Then you might click a link on that Web page to access a new site. With Internet Explorer, you can find Internet addresses faster with AutoComplete. When you type an Internet address in the Address bar, Internet Explorer tries to find a recently visited page that matches what you've typed so far. If Internet Explorer finds a match, it automatically fills in the rest of the address.

View a Web Page

Use any of the following methods to browse Web pages:

◆ In the Address bar, type the Web page address, and press Enter or click the Address bar drop-down arrow and select a Web page address you've opened this session.

◆ Click the File menu, click Open, type the Web page address, and then click OK.

◆ Click any link, such as a 3-D image, a picture, or colored, underlined text on a Web page.

Type a Web page address here, and then press Enter.

Click the Address bar drop-down arrow, and then select a Web page address.

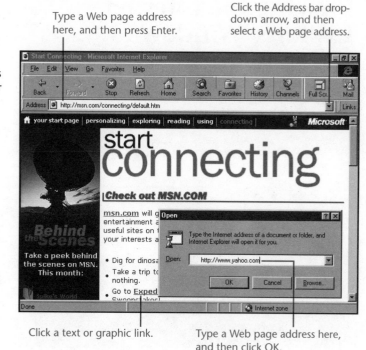

Click a text or graphic link.

Type a Web page address here, and then click OK.

TIP

Select an address from the Address bar. *Click the Address Box drop-down arrow, and then select an address.*

TRY THIS

Open a Web page in a new window. *Click the File menu, point to New, click Window, and then type a Web address in the Address bar of the new Internet Explorer window.*

TIP

Internet Addresses and URLs. *Every web page has a uniform resource locator (URL), an Internet address in a form your browser program can decipher. Like postal addresses and e-mail addresses, each URL contains specific parts that identify where a Web page is located. For example, the URL for Microsoft's Web page is http://www.microsoft.com/, where "http://" shows the address is on the Web and www.microsoft.com shows the computer that stores the Web page. As you browse various pages, the URL includes their folders and filenames.*

Enter an Address Using AutoComplete

1. Begin to type an address that you have recently entered.

   AutoComplete remembers previously entered addresses and tries to complete the address for you. The suggested match is highlighted.

2. If necessary, continue to type until the address you want appears in the Address bar.

3. When correct address appears, press Enter.

Turn off AutoComplete

1. Click the View menu, and then click Internet Options.

2. Click the Advanced tab.

3. In the Browsing area, click the Use AutoComplete check box to deselect it.

4. Click OK.

Browsing Your Local Hard Drive

Internet Explorer isn't only for viewing Web pages. You can also use it to browse folders on your local hard drive and run programs in the same way that you access and browse Web pages on the Internet—from the Address bar. You can add an Address bar to My Computer, Windows Explorer, the Active Desktop, and the taskbar, as well as to the Internet Explorer window. You have the option to change the way your folders display. You can have your folders and computer act like the Web or work in the classic Windows method, or you can choose your own settings.

TIP

Mind your slashes. *To open a file on your computer, type \folder\filename; to open a Web page, type /Web site. Internet Explorer knows the difference between \ and /.*

Browse My Computer

1. Click the My Computer icon on the Active Desktop.

2. Point to any icon to display properties information.

3. Click any icon to open that drive or folder.

4. Continue clicking icons until you open the file or program you want.

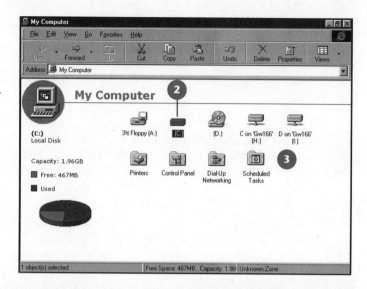

Open Folders or Files and Run Programs from the Address Bar

1. Type the hard drive, folder, or file in the Address bar you want to open or run, and then press Enter. For example, "C:" or Letter.doc.

2. If you want, click the Views button drop-down arrow on the Standard toolbar, and then select the view option you want to use.

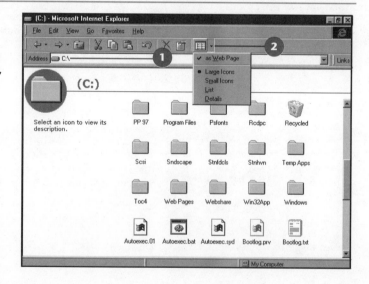

TIP

Sort drive or folder lists alphabetically. *When you view your hard drive or folders by List or Details, click the Name column header to sort the list alphabetically.*

TIP

Customize a folder. *Select the folder you want to customize, click the View menu, click Customize This Folder, click the customize option you want, and then follow the Customize This Folder Wizard instructions to complete the task.*

TIP

Access Folder Options quickly. *Click the Start button on the taskbar, point to Settings, and then click Folders & Icons.*

SEE ALSO

See "Changing Advanced Options" on page 89 for information on browsing in a new process with Internet Explorer.

Change the Folder Display

1 Type the drive or folder name in the Address bar.

2 Click the View menu, and then click Folder Options.

3 Click the General tab.

4 Click one of the Windows Desktop Update option buttons:

  ◆ Web style

  ◆ Classic style

  ◆ Custom

5 Click OK.

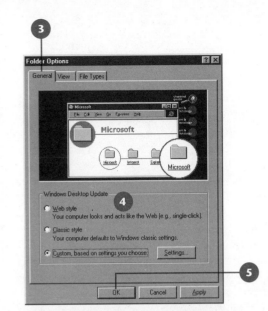

Change the Folder Display Settings

1 Type the drive or folder name in the Address bar.

2 Click the View menu, and then click Folder Options.

3 Click the View tab.

4 Click any of the Advanced Settings option buttons you want to change.

5 Click OK.

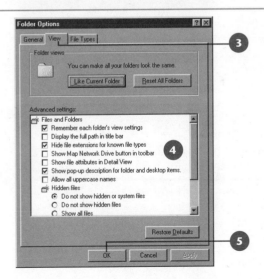

Working Offline

Working offline (disconnected from the Internet) minimizes the time your phone line is busy and reduces your connect time. This way, you use resources only to gather information, not to read it. Internet Explorer remains in Offline mode until you switch to Online mode. While offline, you can view subscribed sites and any pages stored on your hard disk in your History folder or your *Temporary Internet Files* folder, a cache of Web pages you have viewed recently. If you return to those sites, Internet Explorer opens these temporary pages instead of reloading the pages. Increasing the space on your hard drive for these cached pages enables you to open them more quickly.

SEE ALSO

See "Improving Performance" on page 86 for more information about using temporary Internet files.

Work Offline or Online

1 Click the File menu.

2 Click Work Offline.

A check mark appears to the left of the menu command to indicate that the feature is activated. Click Work Offline again to remove the check mark.

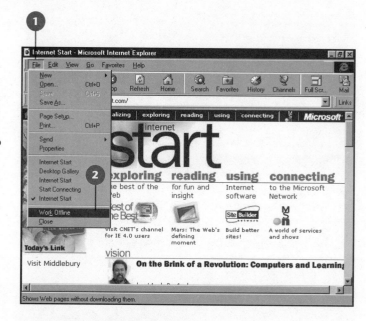

Open Recently Viewed Pages Faster

1 Click the View menu, and then click Internet Options.

2 Click the General tab.

3 Click Settings.

4 Drag the Amount Of Disk Space To Use slider to the right to create more space to store pages temporarily.

5 Click OK.

6 Click OK.

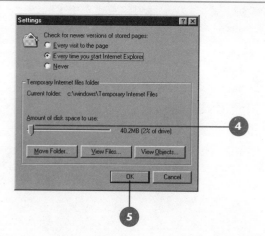

Navigating Basics

As you browse the Web or your local hard drive, you might want to retrace your steps and return to a Web page, document, or hard drive you've recently visited. You can move backward and then forward one location at a time, or you can jump directly to any location from the Back list or Forward list, which shows locations you've previously visited in this session. This way you can quickly jump to a recently visited location without having to click through them one by one. After you start the jump to a Web page, you can stop the jump if the page opens, or *loads*, slowly, or if you decide not to access it. If a Web page loads incorrectly or you want to update the information it contains, you can reload, or *refresh*, the page.

Move Back or Forward

◆ To move back or forward one Web page or document at a time, click the Back button or Forward button on the Standard toolbar.

◆ To move back or forward to a specific Web page or document, click the Back or Forward button drop-down arrow on the Standard toolbar, and then select the Web page or document you want to visit.

Back button

Forward button

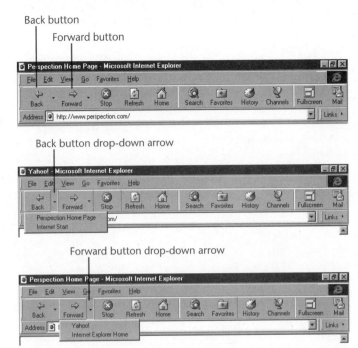

Back button drop-down arrow

Forward button drop-down arrow

Stop an Unwanted Load

1. Click the Stop button on the Standard toolbar.

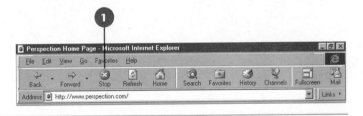

Refresh a Web Page, Document, or Drive

1. Click the Refresh button on the Standard toolbar.

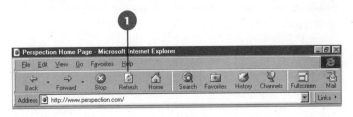

Using the Smart Toolbar

The toolbar buttons on the Standard toolbar, also known as the Smart Toolbar, provide shortcut methods for accessing the most common commands. Sometimes, a command opens a menu, the Explorer bar, or a dialog box so you can make further selections. As you open and move between files, locations, programs, and documents, the Smart Toolbar recognizes the difference between folder paths and Web addresses, and displays only the buttons related to the type of file currently open. Web buttons appear in the Standard toolbar when a Web page is displayed, while document buttons appear in the Standard toolbar when a document, hard drive, or folder is displayed.

Navigate with Web Buttons

Clicking a toolbar button will do one of the following things:

◆ Immediately perform an action.

◆ Open a menu containing more options.

◆ Display the Explorer bar or change its contents.

◆ Open a dialog box.

WEB BUTTONS	
Button	Action
	The Back button moves you to the previous page. Click the drop-down arrow to select a page from a History list.
	The Forward button moves you to the next page. Click the drop-down arrow to select a page from a History list.
	The Stop button stops loading the current page.
	The Refresh button reloads the current page.
	The Home button jumps you to your start page.
	The Search button searches for a page containing a keyword you type in the Explorer bar.
	The Favorites button adds to or accesses your personal collection of favorite pages.
	The History button displays a list of previously accessed pages in the Explorer bar.
	The Channels button displays a list of available channels in the Explorer bar.
	The Full Screen button hides the title bar and menu bar from view.
	The Mail button starts Outlook Express or your default mail server.
	The Print button prints the current page or active frame.

TRY THIS

Watch the Smart Toolbar change. *Click the Internet Explorer icon on the Active Desktop, type C: in the Internet Explorer Address bar and press Enter. Type Desktop in the Address bar and press Enter. Click the My Documents folder, and then click any document. Use the Back and Forward buttons to move among the open programs and files. Watch the Smart Toolbar!*

SEE ALSO

See "Modifying the Internet Explorer Window" on page 72 for information on displaying and hiding the Internet Explorer toolbars.

Navigate with Document Buttons

Clicking a toolbar button will do one of the following things:

◆ Immediately perform an action.

◆ Open a menu containing more options.

◆ Open a dialog box.

DOCUMENT BUTTONS

Button	Action
	The Back button moves you to a previous document. Click the drop-down arrow to select a document from a History list.
	The Forward button moves you to the next document. Click the drop-down arrow to select a document from a History list.
	The Up A Level button displays the next higher folder or drive.
	The Cut button removes selected material from the screen and places it on the Clipboard.
	The Copy button places a copy of selected material on the Clipboard.
	The Paste button copies selected material from the Clipboard to the insertion point location.
	The Undo button reverses your last action.
	The Delete button moves selected files or folders to the Recycle Bin.
	The Properties button opens a dialog box with file type and creation information.
	The Views buttons switches the view to large or small icons, or a simple or detailed list.

2

Getting Help and Web Training

Help is always just moments away in Internet Explorer. If you want to know what a particular feature is or how it works, that information is easily accessible from the Help screens, which you can search by category from the Contents tab or by keyword from the Index. The Help topics are conveniently hyperlinked so that one click displays a related Help screen. More extensive help is available on the Microsoft Web site, various pages that you can quickly access from the Help menu. If you are new to the World Wide Web, complete the Web Tutorial, which walks you through the basics of online browsing.

Get Help Using Help Contents

1. Click the Help menu, and then click Contents And Index.

2. Click the Contents tab.

3. Double-click a category in the left pane.

4. Double-click any topic to open it.

5. Read the Help information in the right pane.

6. When you're finished, click the Close button.

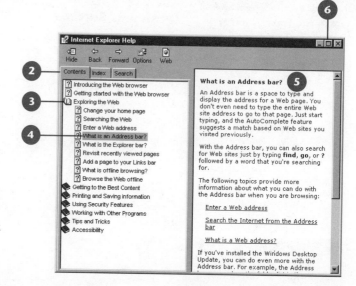

Search the Help Index

1. Click the Help menu, and then click Contents And Index.

2. Click the Index tab.

3. Type the topic about which you want more information. Notice that the index list scrolls as you type each character.

4. Double-click the topic name or click Display.

   Some topics display a dialog box with several topics to choose from.

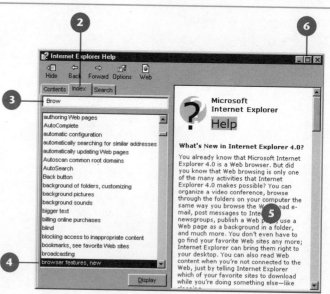

TIP

Hide Help until you need it. *To hide the Help window without closing it, click the Minimize button in the upper right corner of the window. Next time you need it, just click the program button in the taskbar.*

TIP

Get Help in a dialog box. *Click the Help button in the upper right corner of a dialog box. The mouse pointer changes to the Help pointer. Then click the element for which you want to see a ToolTip. A brief description appears and remains displayed until you click the dialog box again.*

4 When the topic you want appears in the list, double-click it. If necessary, double-click a more specific topic.

5 Read the Help information in the right pane.

6 When you are finished, click the Close button.

Complete the Web Tutorial

1 Click the Help menu, and then click Web Tutorial.

2 Click a link and read more about that topic.

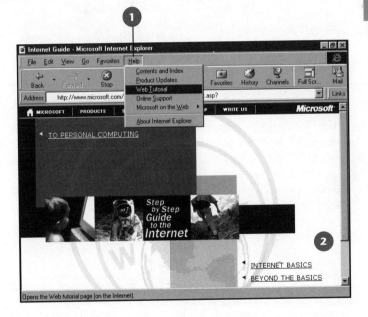

Working with Dialog Boxes

After selecting a menu command that is followed by an ellipsis, clicking its corresponding toolbar button, or pressing its assigned keyboard shortcut, a dialog box will appear. A *dialog box* is a special window that provides additional options and settings connected to a command. Related options within a dialog box are often grouped together on *tabs*. To make your choices, you might need to type text, select from drop-down lists, and click option buttons or check boxes.

TIP

Make a speedier selection.
Often you can select an option and close a dialog box at the same time by double-clicking your selection.

Select Dialog Box Options

A dialog box can contain one or more of the following elements:

◆ Tabs

◆ Text boxes

◆ Drop-down lists

◆ Check boxes

◆ Option buttons

A dialog box usually contains an OK button and a Cancel button. Some dialog boxes also contain an Apply button.

◆ Click OK to apply your selections and close the dialog box.

◆ Click Cancel to close the dialog box without applying your selections.

◆ Click Apply to display the results of your current selections without closing the dialog box, enabling you to modify your choices as needed.

Text box
Click in the box and type the value or text you want.

Drop-down list
Click the drop-down arrow and select an option from the list.

Option buttons
Click the option you want to select. Click a selected option button to deselect it.

Check box
Click one or more check boxes to select the options you want. Click a selected check box to remove the x.

Closing Internet Explorer

When you have finished browsing the Web, reading news, searching for information, and so forth, you need to exit Internet Explorer. When you close Internet Explorer, it disconnects you from the Internet (unless you are working offline, in which case you are already disconnected).

TIP

Internet Explorer remembers your status. *If you are working offline when you close Internet Explorer, the next time you start Internet Explorer you will still be working offline.*

SEE ALSO

See "Working Offline" on page 20 for more information about working offline and switching between Offline and Online modes.

Exit Internet Explorer Using the File Menu

1 Click the File menu.

2 Click Close.

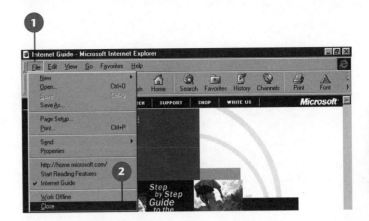

Exit Internet Explorer Using the Close Button

1 Click the Close button in the upper right corner of the Internet Explorer window.

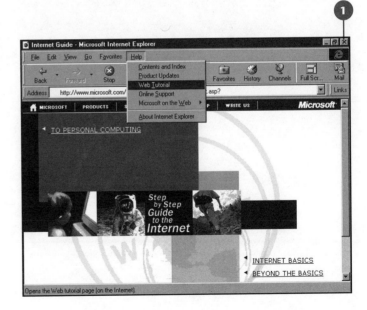

Finding Information with Internet Explorer

Microsoft Internet Explorer 4 offers several new features that allow you to:

◆ Search a wide list of search engines and directory listings for Web sites that match your criteria

◆ Easily find technical information about the Internet and Internet Explorer

◆ Use the Favorites folder to save and organize pointers to your favorite Web sites

◆ Keep track of the sites you browsed today, yesterday, or even last week

◆ Get information from a wide variety of sources delivered directly to your desktop

Finding Information on the Web

Internet Explorer offers some exciting new features to find and collect information, and to automatically receive information from Web sites on the Internet. Two new search features offer you direct links to the major search engines and information directories. Through the new Channels feature, you can now have information delivered directly to you in the form of a Web page or directly to your desktop from Web sites you subscribe to.

Understanding Search Sites, Favorites, and Channels

Internet Explorer provides a direct link to major search engines, your favorite Web sites, and lists of sites you visited previously. It also gives you the ability to subscribe to sites and have information sent directly to your desktop.

Search engines, like AltaVista, HotBot, and Lycos, gather their information mainly by using "robots," or special programs, to collect links to Web pages. These robots then simply list the sites in the search engine's databases. Little, if any, human intervention occurs. The goal of any good search engine is to seek out and find as many Web pages on the Internet as possible and create a quick reference to their locations. You ask the search engine which Web pages on the Internet contain keywords you are looking for, and its robot returns a list of sites from its huge collection of Web sites. The more general your request is, the more likely it is that the resulting list will be long; the more specific your request, the fewer the number of sites in the results.

Search directories differ from search engines in that a person actually looks at every link placed in the search directories' database. And that person decides which category, be it sports, news, weather, and so forth, a site should be cataloged under. This means not every Web page on the Internet is contained in this database of links. Only those sites that have been tested are listed in the database—not by the words that appear on the Web page, but by the category under which it falls.

When you use a search directory to search the Web, you'll get far fewer choices than if you used a search engine, but those choices will be more in tune with your search request, particularly if you are looking for sites that fall under broad categories. Because search directories don't index every single site in their database, they are not the place to go to find hard to find information such as the name of a particular person. Search engines are what you would use for hard to find information.

If you want to save the results of your searches, you can easily add them to your Favorites folder. *Favorites* are pointers to your favorite Web sites, which you can immediately access at any time from the Favorites menu.

Instead of visiting your favorite sites, you can have the sites come to you through the use of channels. When you subscribe to a *Channel*, which is a Web site that has opted to offer its content to Internet Explorer Channel subscribers, the content of that site—sports scores, financial information, movie reviews, and so on—comes directly to your desktop. No longer do you have to seek out Web sites to see if information on them has changed. When you subscribe to a channel, the Web site tells you when it changes.

Besides subscribing to channels, you can subscribe to individual Web sites using *Subscriptions* in Internet Explorer. It's like subscribing to a newspaper, but without the cost.

Finding Information on a Web Page

When you want to find information fast, but you don't have time to scroll through a Web page looking for the exact information you need, you don't have to. Internet Explorer lets you search not just the Web, but also individual Web pages for the information you want.

TIP

Use the keystroke shortcut to find information within a page. *Press Ctrl+F to display the Find dialog box.*

TIP

Copy and paste into the Find dialog box. *You can copy and paste text in the Find dialog box from other sources such as Microsoft Word documents. Copy the text, and then press Ctrl+V to paste it in the Find dialog box.*

Search a Web Page

1 Open the Web page in which you want to search for text on the page.

2 Click the Edit menu, and then click Find (On This Page).

3 Type the word or phrase you want to find.

4 If you want to find the whole word instead of words that might contain a part of the word, click the Match Whole Word Only check box.

5 If you want to match the word based on uppercase or lowercase spelling, click the Match Case check box.

6 Click the Up or Down option button to specify the direction in which to search the page.

7 Click Find Next to move through the page stopping to highlight the word as it's found.

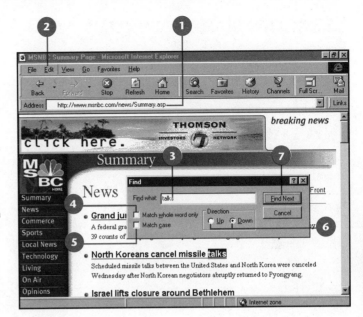

Searching for Information on the Internet

Sometimes the Web is just too overwhelming; there is too much information to plow through. Internet Explorer makes it easy for you to quickly access the most popular search engines and directories with the click of a button. Whether you need a full-powered search engine such as AltaVista, or you prefer a search directory, such as Yahoo, all you have to do is point and click. An All-In-One Search Web page contains links to all the popular search engines, making it easy to search for all the information you need from a single page.

Search the Internet Using the Search Button

1 Click the Search button on the Standard toolbar.

2 Click the Select Provider drop-down arrow, and then select the search provider you want to use.

The search window changes to display the search options for the selected provider.

3 Type the keyword you want to use for the search, and then click the Search, Find, or Seek button. (Each search provider labels its search button differently.)

The results are listed in the right-hand frame.

4 Click the link for the entry you want to view.

5 When you are finished, click the Close button or click the Search button on the Standard toolbar.

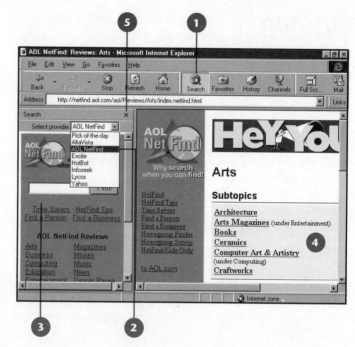

TIP

Be specific in your search.
To find the information you want, be as specific as possible when searching the Internet. If you want to know what the weather is like in Alaska, type "weather Alaska" or "what is the weather like in Alaska?" instead of just the word "weather" or "Alaska."

TIP

Get ToolTips when you search. *To get a description of a Web site returned by a search without clicking its link, move the cursor over the link in the Search window pane and hold it there. A ToolTip appears, listing the Internet address, URL, and other relevant information about the Web page—if the search engine supports this feature.*

Search the Internet Using Microsoft's All-In-One Page

1 Click the Go menu, and then click Search The Web.

2 Click the category for the information you want to search.

The pane on the right changes to display the search directory options.

3 Enter your search request.

4 Press Enter.

The results are listed in the search window.

5 Click a link to view the contents of a page found in the search.

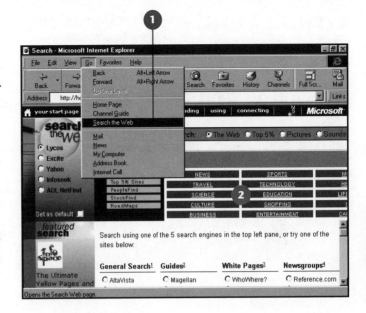

Creating and Organizing Your Favorites List

How about creating a permanent pointer to your favorite Web site? You can with the help of Internet Explorer's Favorites feature. You can create a list of your favorite Web sites by using the Favorites menu option or by clicking the Favorites button on the Standard toolbar, then dragging your favorite site to one of the folders in the Favorites pane.

TIP

Drag and drop favorites.
You can add a favorite site to your list by clicking the Favorites button on the Standard toolbar, and then dragging the page icon of the currently displayed page, located in the Address bar, to the folder of your choice in the Favorites pane located on the left side of your browser window.

Create a Favorites List

1 Open the Web site you want to add to your Favorites list by either typing its Internet address in the Address bar or using the Search button.

2 Click the Favorites menu, and then click Add To Favorites.

3 Type the name for the site or use the default name supplied.

4 If you want, click Create In to add the site to a folder within the Favorites folder.

5 Click OK to add the site to your Favorites folder.

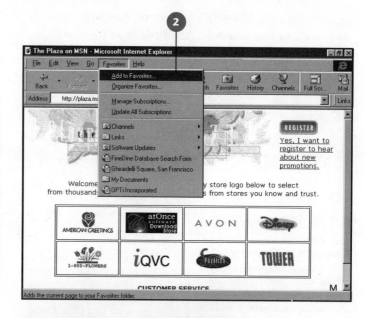

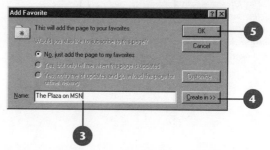

TIP

Right-click to add a favorite. *You can right-click anywhere in the background of a Web page, and then click Add To Favorites on the shortcut menu. The Web page is automatically added to the Favorites list.*

TIP

Drag and drop to organize favorites. *You can drag and drop sites into the folders of your choice while the Organize Favorites dialog box is open.*

TRY THIS

Display information about your favorites. *Right-click an empty area of the Organize Favorites dialog box, click View on the shortcut menu, and then click Details to view your favorites by name, size, type, and date modified.*

Organize Your Favorites List

1 Click the Favorites menu, and then click Organize Favorites.

2 Click the Web site you want to move, rename, or delete.

3 Click Move to move the site to another folder within the Favorites folder; click Rename to rename the site; or click Delete to remove the site from your list of favorites.

4 When you are finished, click Close.

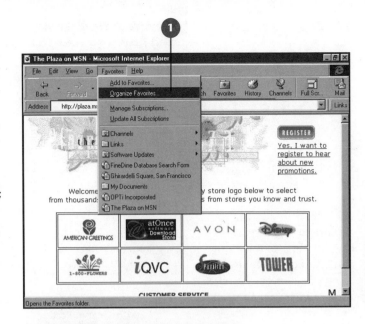

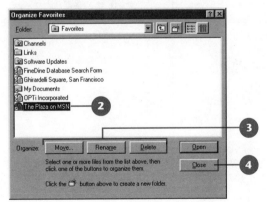

Viewing and Adding to Your Favorites List

To make it easier to view your Favorites list, you can click the Favorites button on the Standard toolbar or select Favorites on the Explorer Bar to display your Favorites in a split window pane. You click a folder to display its contents, or click a file or Web page to open it. The split window pane works the same way it does in Windows Explorer. In addition to creating a Favorites list of Web pages, you can add folders, drives, and even files that you access frequently to your Favorites list. Adding folders, drives, and files to your Favorites list gives you instant access to your computer to manage and open files quickly from Internet Explorer.

View Your Hard Drive and Add it to Your List of Favorites

1 Display the contents of your hard drive. For example, type *C:* in the Address bar.

2 Click the View menu, point to Explorer Bar, and then click Favorites.

The window splits to display your Favorites list in the left pane.

3 Drag the hard drive icon from the Address bar to the Favorites pane.

As you drag, the hand pointer changes to an insert pointer indicating where the new favorite will be added to the list.

4 Click the Close button in the upper right corner of the Favorites pane.

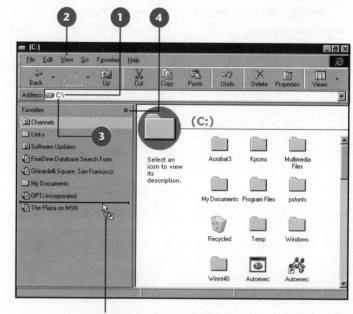

This is the location where the new favorite will be added to the list.

TIP

Scroll the list of favorites.
If your list of favorites is very long, directional arrows appear in the middle of the favorites pane. To scroll down or up the Favorites list, click the down arrow or up arrow.

TRY THIS

Close the Favorites pane.
Right-click the Favorites title bar, and then click Close on the shortcut menu.

Favorites button

View a File and Add it to Your List of Favorites

1 Type the location path and name of the file you want to add to your Favorites list and then press Enter.

The file is displayed in the Internet Explorer window.

2 Click the Favorites button on the Standard toolbar.

The window splits to display your Favorites list in the left pane.

3 Drag the icon of your file from the Address bar to the Favorites pane.

As you drag, the hand pointer changes to an insert pointer indicating where the new favorite will be added to the list.

4 Click the Close button in the upper right corner of the Favorites pane.

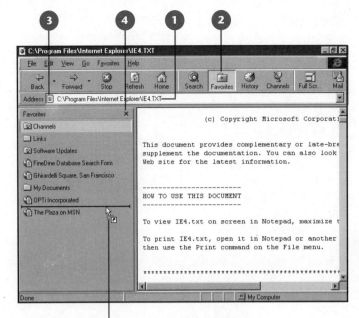

This is the location where the new favorite will be added to the list.

Viewing and Maintaining a History List

Sometimes you run across a great Web site and simply forget to add it to your Favorites list. With Internet Explorer there's no need to try to remember all the sites you've visited. The History feature keeps track of where you've been for days, weeks, or even months at a time. Because the History list can grow to occupy a large amount of space on your hard drive, it's important that you control the length of time visited Web sites are retained in the list. Internet Explorer will delete the History list periodically based on the settings you specify. You can also delete individual listings in the History folder as needed.

History button

View a Web site from the History List

1 Click the History button on the Standard toolbar.

2 Click a week or day to expand or compress the list of Web sites visited.

3 Click the folder for the Web site you want to view, and then click a page within the Web site.

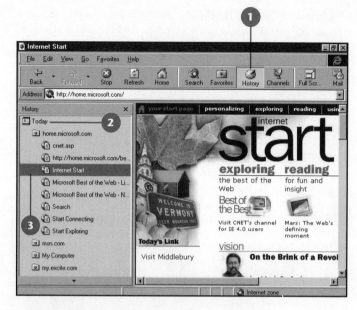

Clear the History File

1 Click the View menu, and then click Internet Options.

2 Click the General tab.

3 Click Clear History.

4 Click OK.

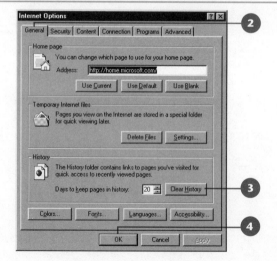

TIP

Delete an individual history entry. *Click the History button to display the list of visited sites, right-click the link you want to delete, and then click Delete History Item.*

TIP

Close the history list. *Click the History button on the Standard toolbar again or click the Close button on the Explorer bar.*

Configure Your History Folder

1 Click the View menu, and then click Internet Options.

2 Click the General tab.

3 Specify the total number of days you want to keep links listed in the History folder.

4 Click OK.

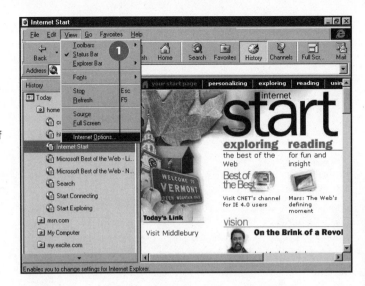

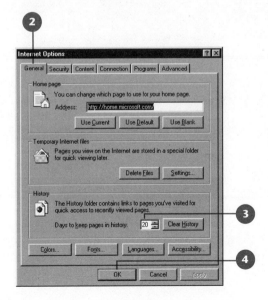

Subscribing to a Web Site

Many Web sites, such as MSNBC, CNN, ABC News, and USA Today, offer daily updates of news, weather, and sports. Other Web magazine sites, such as the Atlantic Monthly, Slate, and Salon1999, update their Web pages weekly or monthly. You can choose to be notified of changes to a Web site automatically, without having to browse the site manually, through the use of Web page subscriptions. Internet Explorer can notify you automatically via e-mail when a page changes, download the page for you so you can read the latest information offline. When you subscribe to a Web site you are guided through the subscription options via the Web Site Subscription Wizard. When you are done, a gleam is added to the upper left corner of the Web page icon in your Favorites list.

Subscribe to a Web Site

1 Open the Web site you want to subscribe to.

2 Click the Favorites menu, and then click Add To Favorites.

3 If you want, enter a new name for the page.

If you do not want to customize the subscription, you can click OK.

4 Click Customize to open the Web Site Subscription Wizard.

5 Click the Yes or No option button to be notified in an e-mail message.

6 Click Next to continue.

7 Enter a user name and password only if the site requires it, and then click Finish.

8 Click OK.

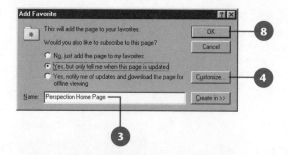

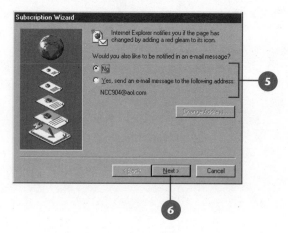

Subscribing to a Channel

Active Channels are Web sites that deliver information to you in a variety of ways: through a Web page, via e-mail, as a screen saver, or directly to your desktop. With channels you choose the delivery option that works best for you by subscribing to the channel of your choice. Unlike cable channels on TV, there are no costs involved for subscribing to Internet Explorer channels. There are hundreds of channel partners ready to deliver content to your desktop, including MSNBC, Computer Weekly, Better Homes & Gardens, Disney, and CBS SportsLine to name a few. More are added every day.

TIP

Subscribe to a channel quickly. *Right-click the channel you want to subscribe to, click Subscribe, and then click OK.*

Subscribe to a Channel

1 Click the Channels button on the Standard toolbar or click the View Channels button on the Quick Launch toolbar.

2 Click a channel or click the Channel Guide button to display a list of channels.

3 If necessary, click the category of channel and Web site you want subscribe to.

4 Click the Add Active Channels button found on the web site.

5 Click the subscription option to want.

6 Click OK.

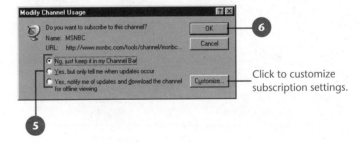

Click to customize subscription settings.

Managing Your Subscriptions

If you subscribe to several sites, you might need to modify the way Internet Explorer notifies you of any changes or sends new information from a Web site to you. If you haven't been receiving any new information for a site you've subscribed to, you will have to alert Internet Explorer to update that subscription and seek out the new information. Or perhaps a site now requires that you supply a username and password. By managing your subscriptions, you can easily make changes to the way you receive your subscriptions. You can set options to notify you by e-mail when a subscription is updated or to schedule a time to automatically update a subscription.

Modify a Subscription

1. Click the Favorites menu, and then click Manage Subscriptions.

2. Right-dlick the Web site for the subscription you want to modify, and then click Properties.

3. Click any of the following tabs to change properties settings for the selected subscription:

   ◆ Use the Subscription tab to unsubscribe to a subscription or review subcription summary information.

   ◆ Use the Receiving tab to set subscription notification by e-mail and download options.

   ◆ Use the Schedule tab to specify when you want to update a subscription.

4. Click OK.

5. Click the File menu, and then click Close.

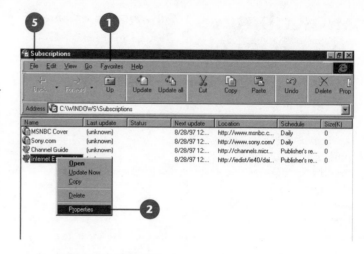

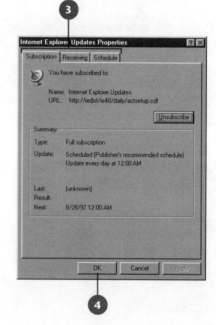

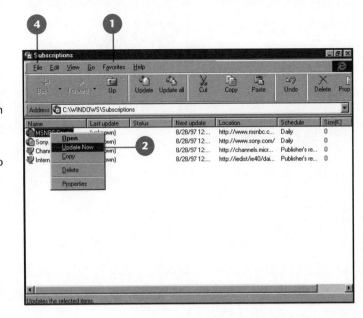

TIP

Update all subscriptions.
Click the Favorites menu, point to Subscriptions, and then click Update All.

TIP

Unsubcribe to a Web site.
Open the Subscriptions window, right-click the subscription you want to unsubscribe to, click Properties, click the Subscription tab, click Unsubscribe, click Yes, and then click OK.

TIP

Browse while you sleep.
Open the Subscriptions window, right-click the subscription you want to schedule, click Properties, click the Schedule tab, click New, specify a time, click OK, and then click OK.

Update Subscription Web Site Information

1 Click the Favorites menu, and then click Manage Subscriptions.

2 Right-click the subscription you want to update, and then click Update Now.

3 If you want, click Details to monitor the update process.

4 Click the File menu, and then click Close.

3

Viewing Channels

Before you can view a channel, you need to display the Channels bar with a listing of the channels currently avaiable on the Web. If you haven't started Internet Explorer, you can start Internet Explorer and display the Channels bar by clicking the View Channels button on the Quick Launch toolbar or clicking a specific channel on the Channels bar on the Active Desktop. If you have already started Internet Explorer, you can display the Channels bar by clicking the Channels button on the Standard toolbar. You can view a channel by simply clicking a channel category and then clicking the channel you want to view.

View Channels button

Start Internet Explorer and Display the Channels Bar

1 Click the View Channels button on the Quick Launch toolbar.

Internet Explorer starts in full screen mode and displays the Channels bar.

Channels Bar

Active Channel information

Click Next to continue.

Start Internet Explorer and View a Channel

1 Click a channel in the Channels bar on the Active Desktop.

Internet Explorer starts in full screen mode and displays the channel you selected.

The selected channel is displayed.

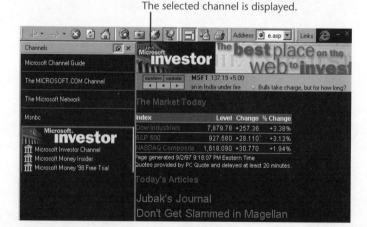

SEE ALSO

See "Subscribing to a Channel" on page 41 for information on subscribing to a channel.

TIP

Delete a channel from the Channels bar. *Right-click the channel you want to delete, and then click Delete.*

Channels Bar on
the Active Desktop

View a Channel from Internet Explorer

1 Click the Channels button on the Standard toolbar.

2 Click a channel to view the channel or click a category to expand that category.

3 If the channel offers multiple Web pages from which to choose, click the channel to display the list of other pages, and then click the channel you want to view.

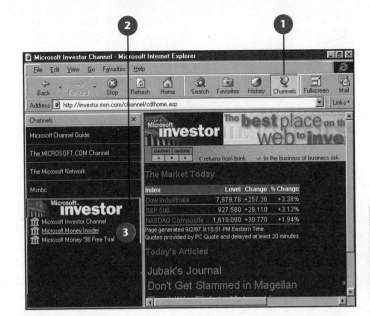

Working with Channels

The information that a channel displays can be automatically or manually updated and sent to your desktop. You can even schedule when you want the update to occur. If you no longer want to subscribe to a channel, you can unsubscribe to it at any time. You can also arrange the channel listing to place channels in the various channel categories.

SEE ALSO

See "Subscribing to a Channel" on page 41 for information on subscribing to a channel.

Channels button

Update a Channel

1 Click the Channels button on the Standard toolbar or the Quick Launch toolbar.

2 Right-click the channel you want to update, and then click Properties.

3 Click the Schedule tab.

4 To update the channel now, click Update Now.

5 To schedule an update, click the Schedule option button, and then click New or Edit. Click OK to continue.

6 Click OK

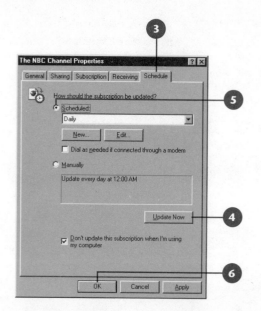

Unsubscribe to a Channel

1 Click the Channels button on the Standard toolbar or the Quick Launch toolbar.

2 Right-click the channel you want to unsubscribe to, and then click Properties.

3 Click the Subscription tab.

4 Click Unsubscribe.

5 Click OK.

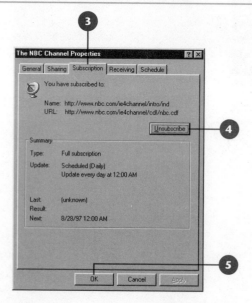

TIP

Update all Web site and channel subscriptions quickly. *Click the Favorites menu, and then click Update All Subscriptions.*

TIP

Create a custom schedule for a channel. *Click the Favorites menu, click Manage Subscriptions, select the channel you want to customize, click the View menu, click Custom Schedules, select the schedule options you want, click OK, click the File menu, and then click Close.*

SEE ALSO

See "Viewing Channels" on page 44 for information on viewing the Channels Bar and viewing a channel.

Arrange Channels

1. Click the Channels button on the Standard toolbar or click the View Channels button on the Quick Launch toolbar.

2. Click the channel and drag it on top of the category.

   The channel appears in the category in which you have placed it.

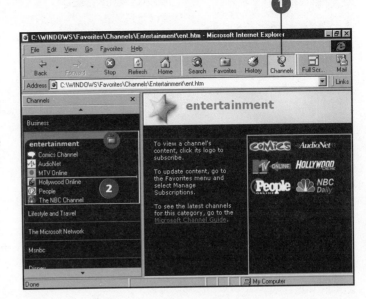

Obtaining Information from Microsoft

Do you need a question about Internet Explorer answered quickly? Or maybe you're interested in knowing how other people are using Internet Explorer to make their Web browsing experience easier. Internet Explorer offers direct links to Microsoft Web sites offering everything from a list of frequently asked questions to free software you can download.

SEE ALSO

See "Getting Help and Web Training" on page 24 for information about the World Wide Web tutorial.

Access Microsoft on the Web

◆ Click the Help menu, point to Microsoft On The Web, and then click the Web page you want to view.

MICROSOFT'S WWW SITE	
Web Page	Description
Free Stuff	Download the latest components, enhancements, and add-ons for Internet Explorer.
Get Faster Internet Access	Learn about the latest technology for speedier downloading.
Frequently Asked Questions	Read the most commonly requested information.
Internet Start page	Connect to Microsoft's Internet Explorer Start page.
Send Feedback	Tell Microsoft what you think about its product.
Best Of The Web	Visit highly rated Web sites.
Search The Web	Find specific links and Web pages.
Microsoft Home Page	Connect to Microsoft's Web page.

4

Handling Information with Internet Explorer

From time to time you will need to handle various types of information coming from the Internet. With Internet Explorer you can:

◆ Copy text and graphics from a Web site to a document stored on your computer

◆ Download programs, games, and other files to your computer

◆ View and listen to a variety of media clips including movies, audio, and MIDI music clips

◆ Create style sheets that override Web page settings, making it easier to view any page on the Internet

◆ Print virtually any Web page you see

◆ Save entire Web pages for later viewing

Understanding Common Error Messages

Trust Murphy and his law—if things can go wrong, they will, especially on the Internet. Because you are connecting to so many different systems, which in turn are connected to so many different networks, you'll no doubt run into your share of problems on the Web. Sometimes you won't be able to connect; other times you might have problems printing, saving, or even displaying Web pages. Knowing how to decipher error messages and fix problems will help to make your Internet experience easier.

The most common error message you'll run into while surfing the Web is "404 – File Not Found." This error simply means that either the address you supplied did not point to an actual file stored on the Web server you are connecting to, or the file no longer exists on that server because someone has deleted it or moved it. Double check your spelling and try again. Or try shortening the address to include just the domain name instead of the full path and filename.

The second most common error is "403 – Forbidden Access or Access Denied or Connection Refused by Host." This message indicates that you are trying to connect to a server that requires a login name and password. Either

you didn't supply a name, or you didn't type your password correctly. If you don't know what login name or password you should be using, consult the webmaster of the server you are trying to connect to. This person should have login information handy.

When downloading files, you might run into this error message: "The request to the host has taken longer than expected" or "Server Busy." This means that the site you are trying to connect to is overloaded with requests from other users. The best thing to do is wait until the network traffic jam subsides, and then try again. Peak download hours on the Internet are from 4:00 p.m. to 11:00 p.m., so it's best to avoid downloading during those hours.

Another frequently displayed error message is "DNS Lookup Failed" or "The server does not have a DNS entry." This usually means you've misspelled the domain name for the site you are trying to access. However, it could also indicate that your network settings are not correct. Check the TCP/IP settings available from the Network option of the Control Panel or from the Dial-Up Network settings, and make sure you have the right IP address for the DNS server supplied in the DNS configuration.

Avoiding Viruses

When you start downloading files to your computer, you must be aware of the potential for catching a computer virus. A *virus* is an executable program whose sole purpose is to cause havoc to your computer. A virus might simply display an innocuous warning on a particular day, such as Friday the 13th, or it might cause a more serious problem, such as wiping out your entire hard disk. Viruses are found in executable (.EXE and .COM) files, along with Microsoft Word and Microsoft Excel macro files.

Viruses can be annoyances that not only take up your time, but also ruin valuable data and programs on your hard drive. The Internet can expose your computer to a wide variety of viruses through e-mail, file transferring, and even possibly through Java and ActiveX, which are both programming languages used to enhance Web pages.

You can't catch a virus from a simple e-mail message, but you can catch a virus from a file attached to an e-mail. And even though most viruses take the form of executable programs, data files that have macros or Visual Basic code attached to them, such as Word or Excel files, can also be infected with viruses.

Although it's more likely that you'll catch a virus through sharing diskettes than by downloading files, there are a few things you can do to keep your system safe from the infiltration of viruses.

First, make sure you are using the most up-to-date virus checking software. Companies such as MacAfee, Norton, and Symantec offer shareware virus checking programs available for download directly from their Web sites. These programs will monitor your system, checking each time a file is added to your computer to make sure it is not in some way trying to change or damage valuable system files.

Second, be very careful from where you download files. Major file repository sites, such as FileZ, Download.com, or TuCows, regularly check the files they receive for viruses before posting such files to their Web sites. Don't download files from Web sites unless you are certain that they check their files for viruses.

Third, make sure you activate macro virus checking protection in both Word and Excel. To do so, click the Tools menu, click Options, click the General tab, and then make sure the Macro Virus Checking option is selected. And always elect not to run macros when opening a Word or Excel file that you received from someone who might not be using proper virus protection.

Finally, make sure you keep your virus checking software up to date. New viruses and more virulent strains of existing viruses are discovered every day. Unless you update your virus checking software, new viruses can easily bypass outdated virus checking software.

4

Downloading Web Site Files

There are thousands of sites on the Internet offering all sorts of files you can download to your computer, from recipes to the latest solitaire game. Internet Explorer even offers a direct link to the Microsoft Web site offering updates and programs to download. Whether it's the Microsoft Web site or another, you can download files from any Web site by simply finding the file you want, selecting the link, and telling Internet Explorer where you want to save the file. Then let Internet Explorer do the rest. Internet Explorer will connect to the appropriate file server and then transfer the file to your computer.

Download a File from Microsoft's Products Download Page

1 Click the Help menu, click Microsoft On The Web, and then click Free Stuff.

2 Click the Download link for the product you want to download.

3 Read the instructions for downloading the product, scroll down and locate the link to download the file, and then click the link.

4 Select the version of the product you want to use. Click Next to continue.

5 Select the language, and then click Next.

6 Click the link closest to you to download the file. The File Download Wizard will open.

7 Click the Save This Program To Disk option button, and then click OK.

8 Select the directory in which you want to save the file, and then click Save.

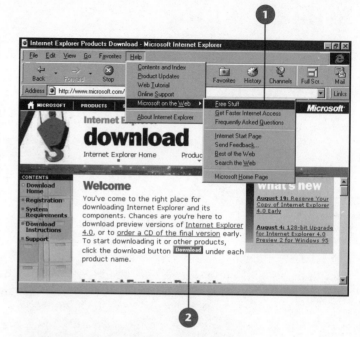

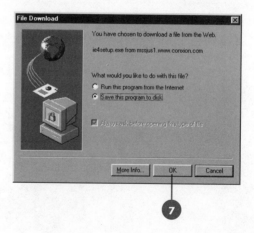

TIP

The Free Stuff Download Page might have changed. *Some of the options shown on the Free Stuff Download Page or some of the steps to access it might be slightly different from the way they're shown in this book.*

TIP

Download files during off-peak hours. *Transfer rates can vary widely. Try downloading during off-peak hours—that is, in the early morning or late at night.*

TIP

You can stop the download process at any time. *If you want to stop the file transfer process during downloading, simply click Cancel.*

TRY THIS

Access a site with lots of files to download. *Try accessing the site www.download.com to find plenty of files to download.*

Download a File from a Web Page

1 Locate the Web page from which you want to download a file.

2 Right-click the link pointing to the actual file, and then click Save Target As on the shortcut menu.

3 Click the directory in which you want to save the file.

4 Click the Save button.

The File Download dialog box will display the estimated time to download the file, along with the estimated transfer time.

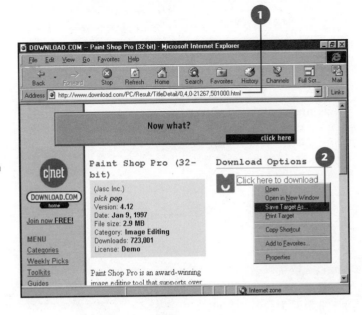

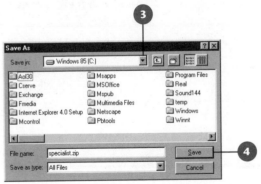

Downloading Files from an FTP Site

Sometimes you'll need to connect directly to a File Transfer Protocol (FTP) site to download a file. Internet Explorer allows you to easily access and download files from any FTP site, public or private. FTP servers do not offer fancy graphical interfaces, but they do offer quick point-and-click access to files stored in directories on the server. Most public FTP sites allow you to access files without requiring that you have an account on the server, offering instead what is called *anonymous login*. With anonymous login, all you have to do is supply the location of the FTP site; otherwise you'll need to supply a login name and password. You can also use the familiar Windows Explorer interface to connect to and transfer files from FTP sites.

Download a File from a Public FTP Site

1 In the Address bar, type the URL for the public FTP site.

2 If the site offers it, click the link to the /pub directory to display the list of files you can download.

3 Click the link for the file you want to download.

4 Click the Save This File To Disk option button, and then click OK.

5 Select the local folder in which to save the file, and then click Save.

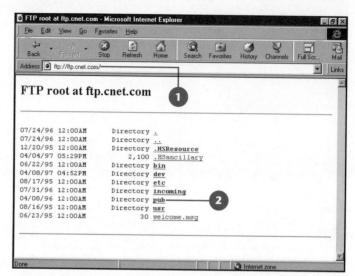

Download a File from a Private FTP Site

1 In the Address bar, type the URL for the private FTP site. Include your username and password in the URL.

2 Press Enter. The private FTP server should list the directory you specified.

3 Click the link for the file you want to download.

4 Select the folder in which to save the file, and then click Save.

5 Click OK.

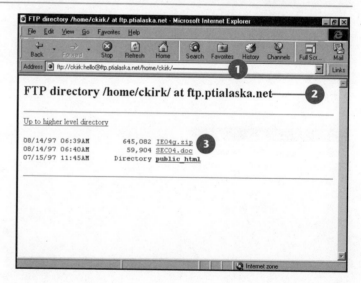

TIP

You must include your login and password in the URL for a private FTP site. *Internet Explorer does not offer an option to prompt you for your login and password. You must supply your login name and password in the URL for a private FTP site. The correct syntax to use is: ftp:// username:password@ftp.server/ directory.*

TIP

Some files display automatically when you try to open them. *By default, files with the extension .HTML, .GIF, .JPG, or .ASP will automatically display in a browser window when you open them. If you want to save one of these types of files, or if you are having problems saving any file, right-click the link, and then click Save Target As on the shortcut menu. Then select the location in which to save the file and click Save.*

TIP

Access files at a public FTP site. *Most public FTP sites will either display a list of directories or take you directly to the publicly accessible directory. This /pub directory is usually the location where publicly accessible files are stored.*

Download a File from an FTP Site Using Windows Explorer

1 Click the Start button on the taskbar, point to Programs, and then click Windows Explorer.

2 In the Address bar, type the URL for the FTP site, and then press Enter. Internet Explorer will connect to the site and display the FTP directory in the right pane of the Explorer window.

3 Click the link for the file you want to download.

4 Click the Save This File To Disk option button.

5 Click OK.

6 Select the folder in which to save the file.

7 Click Save.

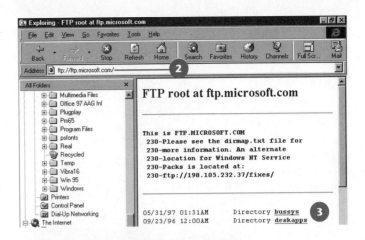

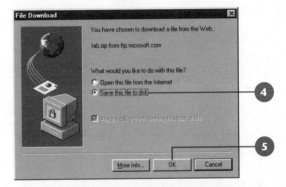

Copying and Saving Graphics

Using Internet Explorer, you can save just about any graphic you see on a Web page to your computer's hard drive. You can also save the background images many sites include on their pages. With the exception of many photographs, which are usually stored in JPEG format and can occupy up to 200 KB, most Internet graphics are relatively small in size, occupying no more than 50 KB, and are saved in GIF format. GIF and JPEG files can be opened with a wide variety of graphics programs, such as Microsoft Photo Editor, Image Composer, Adobe Photoshop, or Microsoft FrontPage.

Copy and Paste a Graphic

1. Open the Web page containing the graphic you want to copy.

2. Right-click the graphic, and then click Copy on the shortcut menu.

3. Open the application or document in which you want to paste the graphic.

4. Position the insertion point where you want to place the graphic.

5. Click the Edit menu, and then click Paste.

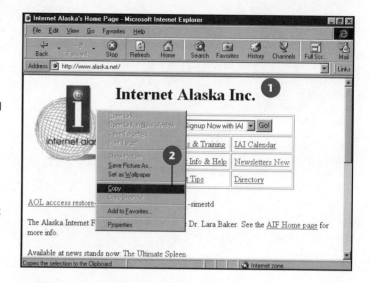

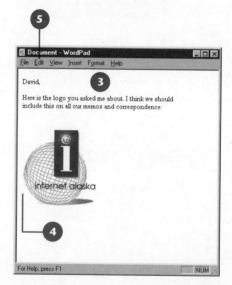

TIP

It's easy to copy just about anything on the Internet. *But sometimes it's not legal. Before you copy any text or before you include text on your own Web page, make sure you have permission from the original author of the text. If the original copyright holder finds you have violated the copyright, you could have a costly legal problem on your hands.*

TIP

Find out how much space the graphic file will occupy. *Right-click the graphic, and then click Properties on the shortcut menu. The size of the graphic will be displayed in the Properties dialog box.*

Save a Graphic

1 Right-click the graphic you want to save, and then click Save Picture As on the shortcut menu.

2 Select the folder in which you want to save the graphic.

3 Click the Save As Type drop-down arrow, and then choose to save the graphic as a GIF or Bitmap file.

4 Click Save.

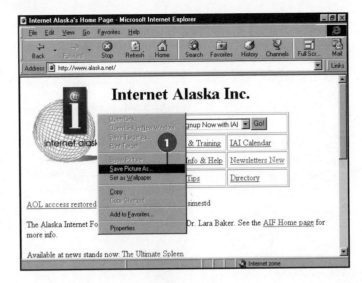

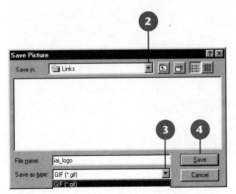

Copying and Saving Background Images

Using Internet Explorer, you can save the background images many Web sites include on their pages. A background image can appear tiled—as consecutive images displayed across a Web page—or individually. When you save or copy a tiled background image, only a single image is saved or copied. When you copy a background image, you can paste the image into another document or Web page. When you save a background image, you can choose the file format in which you want to save the image, and then open the file in a graphics program.

Copy and Paste a Background Image

1. Open the Web page containing the background graphic you want to copy.

2. Right-click the background of the Web page, and then click Copy Background on the shortcut menu.

3. Open the application or document in which you want to paste the image.

4. Position the insertion point where you want to place the background image.

5. Click the Edit menu, and then click Paste.

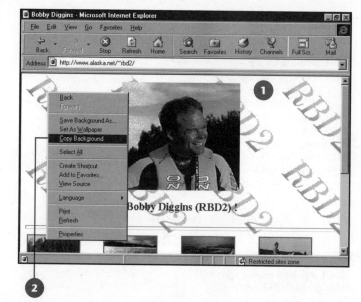

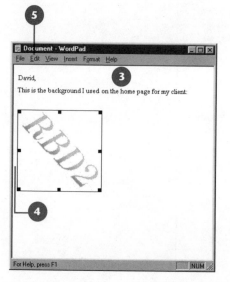

TIP

Open a graphic that you saved. *Internet Explorer and FrontPage Express can open files saved in the GIF format. If you saved a graphic as a Bitmap file, use Paint to open and edit the file.*

TRY THIS

Turn a favorite background into a desktop pattern. *Right-click the graphic, and then click Set As Wallpaper on the shortcut menu. The background will now be your desktop wallpaper pattern. Right-click an empty area on your desktop, click Properties, and then click Settings to change whether the image is tiled or centered.*

Save a Background Image

1 Right-click the background of the Web page, and then click Save Background As on the shortcut menu.

2 Select the location in which to save the file.

3 Type the filename for the image.

4 Click the Save As Type drop-down arrow, and then select a file type.

5 Click OK.

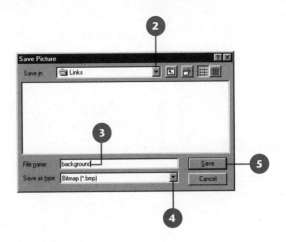

Copying and Pasting Text from a Web Page

Maybe you've found an interesting story or a great joke on the Web that you'd like to pass along to your friends and relatives. Using Internet Explorer, you can easily copy information from a Web page into an e-mail message or a Word, Excel, or PowerPoint document with a few clicks of the mouse button. When you select a range of text that includes a graphic, only the text within the selection can be copied. Text and graphics are independent elements.

TIP

You can select and copy all the text on a Web page. *Right-click an empty area of the Web page, click Select All on the shortcut menu, right-click the selected text, and then click Copy on the shortcut menu.*

Copy and Paste Text from a Web Page

1 Open the Web page containing the text you want to copy.

2 Use the mouse to highlight the text you want to copy.

3 Click the Edit menu, and then click Copy.

4 Open the application or document in which you want to paste the text.

5 Click to position the insertion point at the location where you want to place the copied text.

6 Click the Edit menu, and then click Paste.

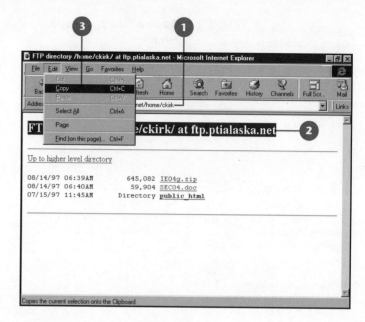

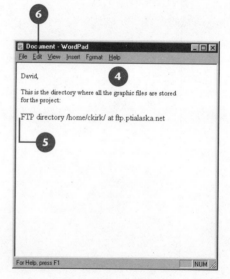

Getting Media Clips from the Web

You can find and download images and sound from the Workshop Gallery available on the Microsoft Web site or from other Web sites on the World Wide Web. Once you have connected to the Web site with the graphics and multimedia files you want to download, click a link to the file to save the file to your computer. You can use the files to create your own Web page or include them in other documents.

Find and Download a Media Clip

1 In the Address bar, enter the following address: *http://www.microsoft.com/ gallery/default.asp.*

2 Click the images or sounds link.

3 Click a link to the image or sound file you want to download.

4 Click the Save This Program To Disk option button, and then click OK.

5 Select the folder in which you want to save the file, and then click Save.

Creating and Using Style Sheets

Using style sheets is a convenient way to make Web pages more readable, regardless of the formatting used by the original Web page designer. A style sheet allows you to override the settings of the Web pages you browse with settings of your own, so that you can view pages in the format you prefer. Style sheets give you control over the layout of Web pages you browse. With style sheets, you can specify font styles, text sizes, text colors, text alignment, indentation, and other layout information. When you activate the Internet Explorer style sheet option, all Web pages you view will be displayed using the features defined in your style sheet.

Create a Style Sheet

1. Open the Web page you want to use as a style sheet.

2. Click the View menu, and then click Internet Options.

3. Click the General tab.

4. Click Colors, select the colors to be used for the text and links, and then click OK.

5. Click Fonts, select the fonts to be used for the style sheet, and then click OK.

6. Click OK.

7. Click the File menu, and then click Save As to save the page to your local hard drive.

   You can now use the settings saved with the page as a style sheet to format all Web pages you view with Internet Explorer.

8. Select the folder in which you want to save the style sheet.

9. Type the filename for the style sheet.

10. Click Save.

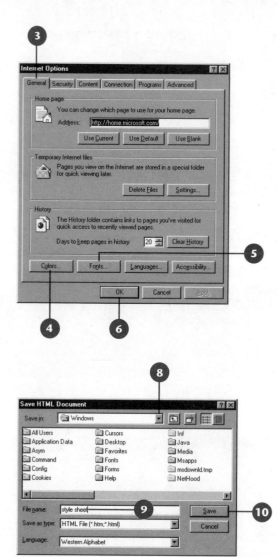

TIP

A style sheet does not affect the size of graphics. *Only the text, background color, and font sizes of text on a Web page are affected by the use of style sheets. Any graphics on the page are not affected.*

TRY THIS

Use style sheets developed by Microsoft. *Connect to Microsoft's Site Builder Workshop Gallery at http:// www.microsoft.com/gallery/ default.asp, click the Sytle Sheets link, and then click a style sheet link to download.*

TIP

Use style sheets from your Microsoft Office documents. *If you have certain styles already defined in a Word document, you can use the document as a style sheet.*

Use a Style Sheet

1 Open a Web page in the Internet Explorer window.

2 Click the View menu, and then click Options.

3 Click the General tab.

4 Click Accessibility.

5 In the Formatting area, click to select the three check boxes for ignoring colors, font styles, and font sizes used on Web pages. If the author of the original page used different color and text settings, the settings specified in your style sheet will override the author's.

6 Click the Format Documents Using My Style Sheet check box to select it.

7 Click Browse.

8 Locate the file you saved as a style sheet on your local hard drive, and then double-click the file to use it as the style sheet.

9 Click OK.

10 Click OK.

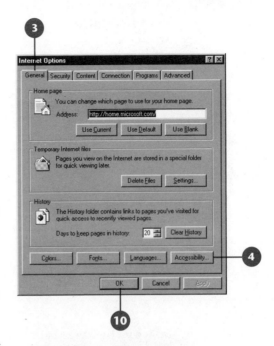

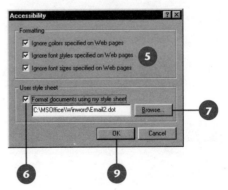

4

Printing a Web Page

Web pages are designed to be viewed on a computer screen, not printed on paper. Nevertheless, Internet Explorer provides many options for printing Web pages. On framed Web sites, you can print the page just as you see it or you can elect to print a particular frame. You can even use special page setup options to include the date, time, or window title on the printed page. To print a Web page, first set up Internet Explorer so that it prints the Web page as it is displayed on your screen. This involves making sure that pictures and graphics on the site are displayed, and that the option to print the background pictures and colors is activated.

Set the Printing Options

1. Open the Web page you want to print.

2. Click the View menu, and then click Internet Options.

3. Click the Advanced tab.

4. In the Multimedia area, make sure that the Show Pictures check box is selected.

5. In the Printing area, click the Print Background Colors And Images check box to select it.

6. Click OK.

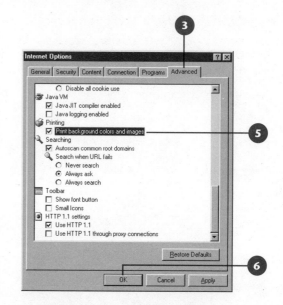

Specify the Page Setup

1. Click the File menu, and then click Page Setup.

2. Do one or more of the following:

    ◆ Click the Size drop-down arrow, and then select a paper size.

    ◆ Enter a header and/or footer in the Header and/or Footer box.

    ◆ Click the Landscape or Portrait option button.

    ◆ Specify the margins.

3. Click OK.

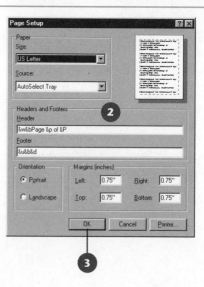

Change header and footer options. *The following are the variables you can enter in either the Header box or Footer box displayed in the Page Setup dialog box:*
&w – prints the window title
&u – prints the page address
&d – prints the short date
&D – prints the long date
&t – prints the time
&T – prints the time in 24-hour format
&p – prints the page number
&P – prints the total number of pages
&& - prints a single ampersand symbol

Make sure of your print options. *In the Print dialog box, don't select the Print All Linked Documents option unless you know only a few documents are linked. Otherwise, you might end up printing more than you expected.*

What is a frame? *A frame is a separate Web window within a Web page. Frames gives you the ability to show more than one Web page at a time.*

Print the Current Page

1. Click the File menu, and then click Print.

2. Click the Name drop-down arrow, and then select the printer you want to use.

3. Set any additional options, such as the Print Range and Number Of Copies.

4. Click OK.

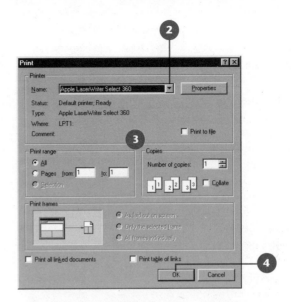

Print the Contents of a Frame

1. Open the Web page, and then click the frame to select it.

2. Click the File menu, and then click Print.

3. In the Print Frames area, click the Only The Selected Frame option button to select it.

4. Set any additional options, such as the Printer Name, Print Range, and Number Of Copies.

5. Click OK.

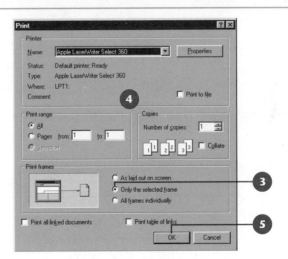

4

Saving a Web Page

Unlike word processing or desktop publishing documents, Web pages don't include actual graphics themselves. Instead, the HyperText Markup Language (HTML) used to create the Web page simply points to the locations on the Web server where the graphics are stored. When you save a Web page, Internet Explorer saves the text of the page, either formatted in HTML or as text only.

Save a Web Page

1. Open the Web page you want to save.

2. Click the File menu, and then click Save As.

3. Specify the folder or drive in which to save the file.

4. Type the name you want to assign the file.

5. Click the Save As Type drop-down arrow, and then specify to save the file as HTML or as text.

6. Click Save.

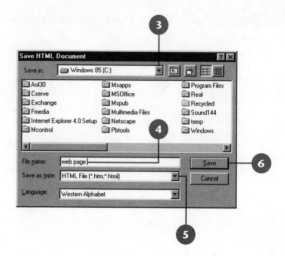

Personalizing Internet Explorer

Microsoft Internet Explorer is fully customizable. You can change a wide variety of options to make Internet Explorer work in the best way for you. Some of the ways you can personalize Internet Explorer include:

◆ Creating your own personalized home page

◆ Configuring the Links toolbar to contain the items you use the most

◆ Selecting what external programs, such as e-mail and newsgroup readers, will work with Internet Explorer

◆ Creating security zones so site contents can be checked for information that could potentially damage your computer

◆ Setting security options so important information is relayed only to those sites you allow

◆ Setting rating options that prevent children from seeing inappropriate sites

◆ Changing the colors, fonts, and languages used while you browse the Web

◆ Changing the language character set so fonts are displayed properly

Specifying Your Home Page

Your *home page* is the Web site that you want Internet Explorer to display whenever you launch the program or any time you click the Home button on the Standard toolbar or select Home Page from the Go menu. You can specify your home page either within Internet Explorer or through the Internet option on the Control Panel. You can choose one of the millions of Web pages available through the Internet as your home page, or, instead, you can have Internet Explorer automatically open to a particular file on your hard drive.

TIP

Specify your home page from the Control Panel. *Click the Start button on the taskbar, point to Settings, click Control Panel, and then click the Internet icon. Set your home page in the General tab of the Internet Properties dialog box, and then click OK.*

Specify Your Home Page

1 Click the View menu, and then click Internet Options.

2 Click the General tab.

3 Do one of the following:

♦ In the Address box, type the URL of the Web site to use as your home page.

♦ In the Address box, type the full pathname, including drive and folder of the file you want to use as your home page.

♦ Click the Use Current button to specify the current page as the home page.

♦ Click the Use Default button to specify the Microsoft Home Start Page as your home page.

4 Click OK.

Customizing the MSN Start Page

The MSN Start Page is the default page displayed as your home page when you click the Home button on the Standard toolbar. You can customize the MSN Start Page, choosing what items you want displayed, such as the day's top headlines, stock quotes, financial news, and so on. You can also specify what links you want to access directly from this page. Customizing the MSN Start Page takes just a few minutes, and you can change options at any time.

TIP

The MSN Start Page might look different. *The Microsoft Network folks are always fine-tuning their web site. The Custom link might be located in a different spot on the MSN Start Page you see.*

Customize the MSN Start Page

1. Make sure you are connected to the Internet. Customizing the Start Page will only work while you are online.

2. Make sure the default page (MSN Start Page) is specified as your home page.

3. Click the Home button on the Standard toolbar.

4. Click the Personalizing link on the Start Page.

5. Click the topic you want to customize in the Step 1 frame.

6. Click the information provider in the Step 2 frame.

7. Click Next to select from another category and another information provider.

8. When you have selected all the options to customize, click Finish.

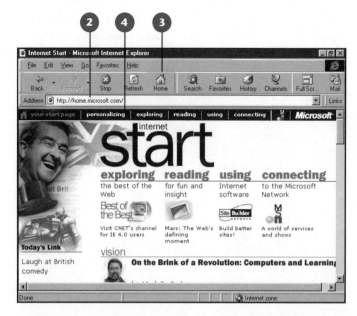

Modifying the Links Toolbar

The *Links toolbar* provides you with access to your favorite web sites at the click of a button. You can modify the toolbar to suit your needs. For example, you can add items for new sites to the toolbar so that you can click the item's icon to display the site quickly, or you can remove items you no longer want quick access to. You might also need to modify the properties of different items on the toolbar. For example, you can update the URL for an item or change the icon displayed for the item on the toolbar.

> **SEE ALSO**
>
> *See "Modifying the Internet Explorer Window" on page 72 for information on how to display the Links toolbar.*

Add an Item to the Links Toolbar

1. Open the Web page you want to add to the Links toolbar.

2. Drag the Web page icon in the Address bar onto the Links title on the Links toolbar.

3. Release the mouse button to position the new item.

Delete an Item from the Links Toolbar

1. On the Links toolbar, right-click the item you want to delete.

2. Click Delete on the shortcut menu.

3. Click Yes to confirm the deletion.

TRY THIS

Rearrange items on the Links toolbar. *Click and drag an item to the left or right of another. The item will be placed in the location where you release the mouse button.*

TRY THIS

Add a site from your Favorites folder to the Links toolbar. *Click the Favorites button on the Standard toolbar. Click and drag a favorite Web site link from the Favorites pane onto the Links title on the Links toolbar, and then release the mouse button.*

TRY THIS

Create a desktop shortcut for an item. *You can create a desktop shortcut for any Links toolbar item so that you can access a site right from your desktop. Simply right-click the item, point to Send To, and then click Desktop As Shortcut.*

Change the Properties of an Item

1. Right-click the item whose properties you want to change.

2. Click Properties on the shortcut menu.

3. Click the Internet Shortcut tab.

4. Do one or more of the following:

   ◆ In the Target URL box, type a new URL for the site.

   ◆ In the Start In box, specify the folder that contains the original files for the site.

   ◆ Click in the Shortcut Key box, and then press the keystroke combination you want to assign to the item.

   ◆ Click the Run drop-down arrow, and then select the type of window in which to display the site.

   ◆ Click the Change Icon button, select a new icon for the item, and then click OK.

5. Click OK.

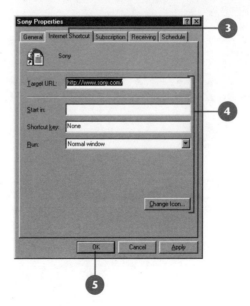

Modifying the Internet Explorer Window

There are many options you can select to customize the appearance of the Internet Explorer window. Some options provide you with more space on the screen to display Web site information, whereas others allow you to display or hide the status bar and the different toolbars. You can even move the toolbars around to reposition them in whatever arrangement works best for you.

Activate and Turn Off Full Screen Mode

1 Click the View menu, and then click Full Screen.

The menu bar, window title bar, Address bar, and Links toolbar will disappear. Also, a black status bar will appear at the top of the screen.

2 Click the Full Screen button on the toolbar at the top of the screen again.

The screen will return to normal view.

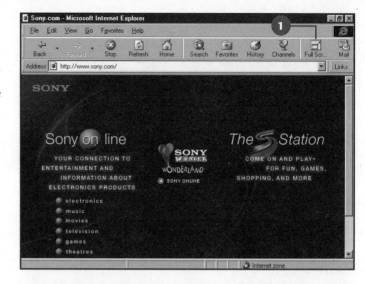

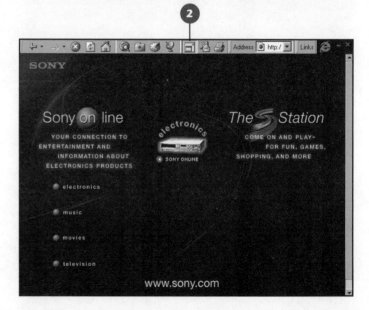

TIP

Use Microsoft Office-like toolbar buttons. *Click the View menu, click Internet Options, and then click the Advanced tab. Scroll down to the Toolbar area, and then click the Small Icons check box to select it. Click OK. The buttons on the Standard toolbar will change to look like those used in Microsoft Office.*

Display or Hide Toolbars

1 Click the View menu, point to Toolbar.

2 Click the toolbar you want to show or hide.

A displayed toolbar has a check mark to its left.

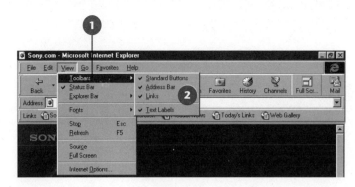

TRY THIS

Right-click to display the toolbars. *Right-click any empty area or toolbar title to access a list of toolbars to display or hide.*

Display or Hide Toolbar Text Labels

1 Click the View menu, point to Toolbar.

2 Click Text Labels to display or hide the text below the Standard toolbar icons.

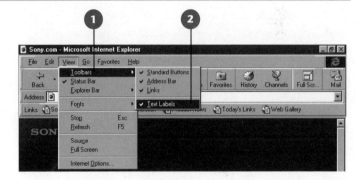

Show or Hide the Status Bar

1 Click the View menu, and then click Status Bar.

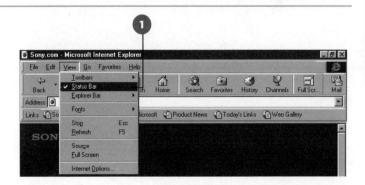

5

Understanding Security
on the Internet

No other Web browser offers as many customizable features as Internet Explorer does, particularly advanced security features that are built into the program. To understand all the Internet Explorer security features, you first have to learn about security on the Internet in general.

When you send information from your computer to another computer, the two computers are not linked directly together. Instead there could be several or even hundreds of computers in between responsible for passing your information along. Any one of these computers could intercept your data.

In addition, on the Internet it's relatively easy to masquerade as someone else. E-mail addresses can be forged, domain names of sites can easily be misleading, and so on. You need some way to protect not only the data you send, but also yourself from sending data to the wrong place.

Furthermore, there is always the potential that a site could infiltrate your computer system with files of its own, possibly deleting, renaming, or simply copying valuable information from your system without your knowledge.

Security Zones

Through the use of *Security Zones* you can easily tell Internet Explorer which sites you trust to not damage your computer and which sites you simply don't trust. In your company's intranet you would most likely trust all the information supplied on Web pages through your company's network, but on the Internet you might want to be warned first of potential dangers a site could cause your system. You can set up different levels of security based on different zones.

Certificates

When shopping on the Internet, you want to do business with only those companies that offer a certain level of security and promise to protect your buying information. In turn those companies want to do business with legitimate customers only. A *Certificate* (also called *digital IDs*) provides both the browser and the company with a kind of guarantee confirming that you are who you say you are, and that the site is secure and genuine, not a fraud or scam.

An independent company, called a *credentials agency*, issues three types of certificates: Personal, Authorities, and Publishers. A Personal certificate identifies you so that you can access Web sites that require positive identification such as banks that allow online transactions. You can obtain a Personal certificate from a credentials agency called VeriSign using the Security tab of the Options dialog in Outlook Express. An Authorities certificate insures that the Web site you are visiting is not a fraud. Internet Explorer automatically checks site certificates to make sure that they're valid. A Publishers certificate enables you to trust software, such as ActiveX controls, that you download.

Internet Explorer maintains a list of software companies whose certificates are valid and trustworthy. You can view your certificate settings in the Content tab of the Internet Options dialog box.

Content Advisor

The Internet is a reflection of society. Of course, parents might not want to subject their children to some of these reflections, such as strong language, violence, and other adult themes. However, most parents cannot spend every online minute with their children, censoring sites that are objectionable. In such cases you can employ Internet Explorer's *Content Advisor* to screen out inappropriate sites, preventing youngsters from seeing things they shouldn't.

The Content Advisor works with different rating bureaus, such as the Recreational Software Advisory Council (RSAC), to rate sites within certain ranges. The RSAC's rating system is based on research that compiled a rating system to reflect different levels of violence, strong language, and so on. You decide exactly what kind of sites can be accessed, what ratings systems are used, which ranges are available to users within those sites, and whether users of your computer can see unrated sites.

You can also assign a password to allow mature users to view such sites. As long as the user supplies the supervisor password you initially create when setting up the content rating systems, the user can then view sites where the material rates above the level chosen. At any time you can turn off the Content Advisor, opening up all sites on the Internet to be viewed by anyone without having to enter a password.

In order for the rating system to work, sites must subscribe to the system so that their ratings are passed to your computer when you access the sites. Most sites that want to offer quality information for children, and those adult sites interested in making sure only individuals 18 years old or older are accessing their sites, subscribe to rating systems like the RSAC. A site that voluntarily rates itself usually displays the RSAC logo on its main page. This logo is your indication that the site has properly rated itself and offers only materials that are appropriate to its rating.

Content Advisor dialog box

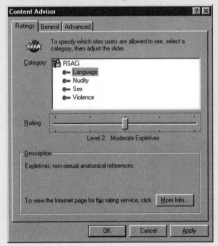

Creating Security Zones

Internet Explorer lets you create security zones based on where information comes from. For example, you might want to restrict access to Web pages that can be viewed from the Internet, but don't want any restrictions applied to those sites within your company's intranet. You can specify the level of security for each of the four available zones: Local Intranet, those sites within your company's network; Trusted Sites, which are sites you know and trust; Restricted Sites, which are sites you don't trust or that need high security; and Internet, which by default is anything not assigned to any other zone.

Select a Security Zone and Level

1 Click the View menu, and then click Internet Options.

2 Click the Security tab.

3 Click the Zone drop-down arrow, and then click the zone to which you want to assign the security options.

4 Click the option button for the level of security you want to apply to the selected zone.

5 Click OK.

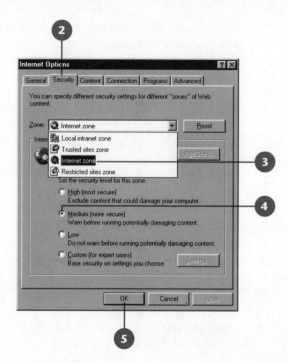

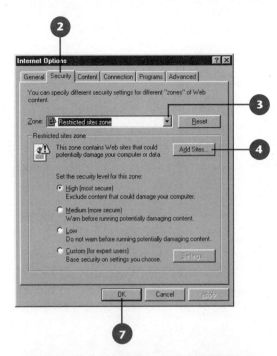

TIP

Remove a site from your Restricted Sites zone. *Click the View menu, click Internet Options, and then click the Security tab. Click the Zone drop-down arrow, click Restricted Sites Zone, and then click the Add Sites button. In the Web Sites area, click the site you want to remove, and then click Remove. Click OK twice.*

Add Sites to Your Restricted Sites Zone

1. Click the View menu, and then click Internet Options.

2. Click the Security tab.

3. Click the Zone drop-down arrow, and then click Restricted Sites Zone.

4. Click Add Sites.

5. In the Add This Web Site To The Zone box, type the full URL for the site.

6. Click OK.

7. Click OK.

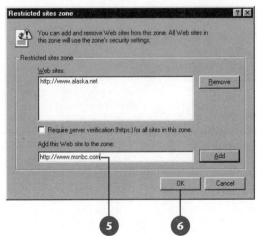

5

Setting Ratings Using the Content Advisor

If you have children who surf the Internet and you don't want to subject them to strong language, violence, or sexually explicit material, you can use the Content Advisor to restrict their access to inappropriate sites. By activating the Content Advisor and then setting up a supervisor password, you can prevent young eyes from seeing things they shouldn't see. If a rated site matches your ratings configuration, the site can be viewed. If the site is rated above the level you've set, or if the site is not rated and you've restricted access to unrated sites, the site can only be viewed when the supervisor password is supplied.

Set Content Advisor Ratings

1 Click the View menu, and then click Internet Options.

2 Click the Content tab.

3 Click the Enable option button to turn on the Ratings feature.

4 In the Password box, type a supervisor password, and then press Enter.

For security, an asterisk (*) appears for each character you type.

5 In the Confirm Password box, retype the password, and then click OK.

6 Click the category for which you want to set the rating.

7 Move the Rating slider to the rating level you want.

8 Click OK, and then click OK to acknowledge that the Content Advisor has been activated.

All sites that are restricted by the Content Advisor will not display within your browser unless the supervisor password is supplied.

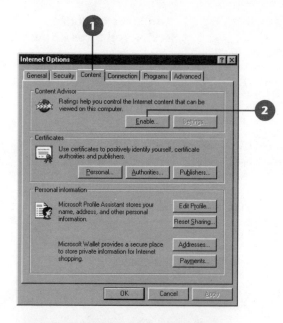

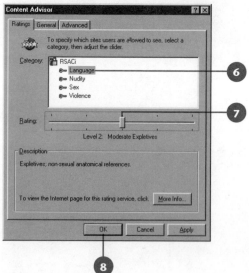

Storing Personal Information

Using Internet Explorer, you can store personal, home, business, and other information in a single location to make communicating and shopping on the Internet quick and easy. The *Profile Assistant* stores your name, address, and other important information. To make sure your information is safe and secure, Internet Explorer uses Microsoft Wallet. If you plan to shop over the Internet, you can securely store your personal information in a personal certificate to protect yourself from fraud.

SEE ALSO

See "Shopping on the Internet" on page 80 for information on using the Microsoft Wallet.

SEE ALSO

See "Getting a Personal Certificate" on page 154 for information on getting and installing a personal certifcate.

Enter Information Using the Profile Assistant

1. Click the View menu, and then click Internet Options.

2. Click the Content tab.

3. Click Edit Profile.

4. Click the tab you want to display.

5. Enter the appropriate personal, home, business, and related information in the boxes provided.

6. Click OK.

7. Click OK.

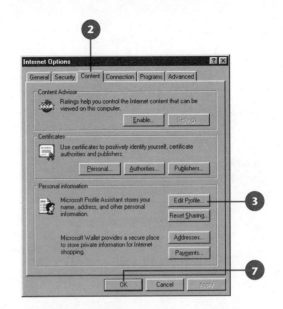

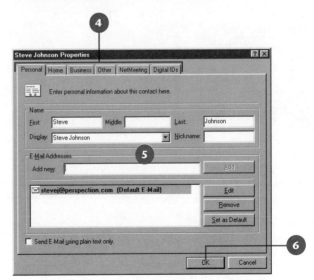

5

Shopping on the Internet

Microsoft Wallet offers a secure way to keep track of personal information related to Internet shopping, such as your credit card and billing information, so that when you shop online you don't have to worry about the information falling into the wrong hands. The Wallet makes online shopping easy—you only need to enter your address and payment information once, and then you can transmit it to Wallet-enabled Internet stores as you shop. The information is stored securely on the computer. You define a unique password for each payment method, so that only you can use it. You use the Wallet's Addresses option to store and access addresses that can be referenced for shipping and billing. You use the Payments option to store and access payment methods for your online purchases.

Add an Address to the Wallet

1 Click the View menu, and then click Internet Options.

2 Click the Content tab.

3 Click Addresses.

4 Click Add.

5 Enter the necessary information in the boxes.

6 Accept the default display name or enter a new one.

7 Click either the Home or Business icon.

8 Click OK.

9 Click OK.

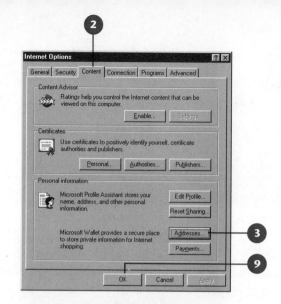

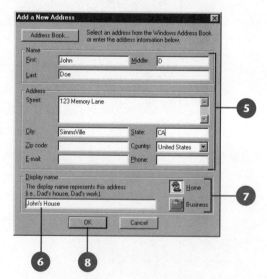

TIP

Disable a payment method. *You can uninstall any of the four payment methods—AMEX, Discover, MasterCard, or Visa. Click the View menu, and then click Internet Options. Click the Content tab, and then click Payments. Click Methods, click to deselect the method you don't want to use, and then click OK. That method will not show up in the list of available payment methods.*

SEE ALSO

See "Getting a Personal Certificate" on page 154 for information on sending information over the Internet securely.

Add a Payment Method to the Wallet

1 Click the View menu, and then click Internet Options.

2 Click the Content tab.

3 Click Payments.

4 Click Add, and then click the type of card you want to add as a payment method.

The Add A New Credit Card Wizard starts.

5 Click Next to continue.

6 Enter the name on the card, the expiration date, and the card number.

7 Accept the default display name shown, or enter a new one. Click Next to continue.

8 Enter the billing information for the card. Click Next to continue.

9 Supply a password for the card information so that only you can access the information to make changes.

10 Click Finish.

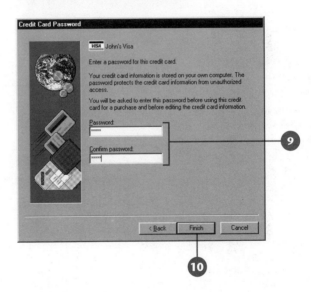

Changing Colors and Font Settings

Sometimes the color schemes and fonts of certain Web pages can make the information on the pages difficult to read. For example, the font might be too small or the color contrast too severe with the background of the Web page. In such cases, you can select the color, font size, background color, and even the character set used on the page. You can make these types of changes only if the default settings of the specific Web page can be overridden.

TIP

What's the difference between proportional and fixed-width fonts? *With a proportional font, the width of each character differs with the character's shape. For example, the letter "m" is wider than the letter "i." A fixed-width font gives the same amount of space to each character, like text typed on a typewriter.*

Change the Font Size

1 Click the View menu, and then point to Fonts.

2 Click the font size you want to use, either larger or smaller, for the text on the Web page.

The text will automatically change to the size you specified.

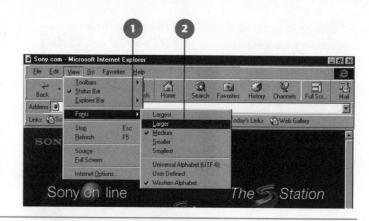

Change the Font Type

1 Click the View menu, and then click Internet Options.

2 Click the General tab.

3 Click Fonts.

4 Click the Proportional Font drop-down arrow, and then click the font you want to use for proportional text.

5 Click the Fixed-Width Font drop-down arrow, and then click the font you want to use for fixed-width (monospace) text.

6 Click OK.

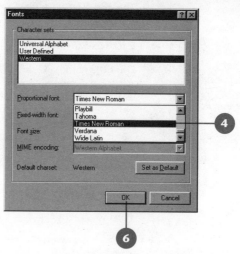

TIP

Use a combination of color and underlining for your links. *To make the hyperlinks on a Web page easy to find, you can apply underlining as well as color to the links. Click the View menu, and then click Internet Options. Click the General tab, and then click Colors. Make sure the Underline Links option is set to Always, select the colors you want for Visited and Unvisited links, and then click OK.*

Change the Color of Text

1 Click the View menu, and then click Internet Options.

2 Click the General tab.

3 Click Colors.

4 Click to deselect the Use Windows Colors check box.

5 Click the Text Color box to display the Color palette.

6 Click the color you want to use, and then click OK.

7 Click OK.

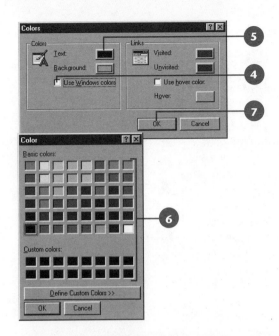

SEE ALSO

See "Changing Advanced Options" on page 89 for information on changing underlink links options.

Change the Color of Links

1 Click the View menu, and then click Internet Options.

2 Click the General tab.

3 Click Colors.

4 Click the Visited or Unvisited Color box to display the Color palette.

5 Click the color you want to use, and then click OK.

6 Click OK.

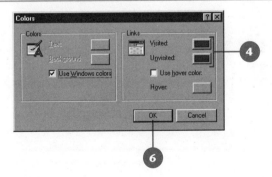

5

Adding a Language Character Set

In order to see Web pages written in a different language, you must first add the language character set to your Internet Explorer options. When you add a language character set, you enable Internet Explorer to display the correct characters for that language. This means that special characters, such as the tilde in Spanish, will be displayed properly on the page.

TIP

Add more language character sets. *You can add more language character sets from the Microsoft support Web site located at http:// www.microsoft.com. Use the search option on the Microsoft Web page to search for character sets.*

Add a Language Character Set

1 Click the View menu, and then click Internet Options.

2 Click the General tab.

3 Click Languages.

4 Click Add.

5 Select the language to add from the list of available languages.

6 Click OK.

7 Click OK.

8 Click OK.

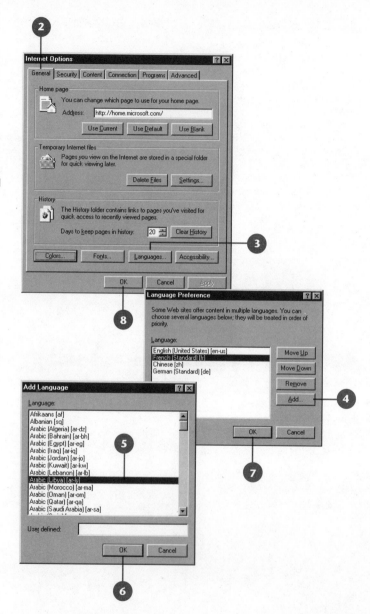

SEE ALSO

See "Getting Updates to Internet Explorer" on page 248 for information on installing the Multi-Language Pack for Internet Explorer.

Specify the Priority of Languages

1 Click the View menu, and then click Internet Options.

2 Click the General tab.

3 Click Languages.

4 In the list of languages, click the language you want to move, and then click the Move Up button or the Move Down button to change the position of the language in the list.

The language at the top of the list is used first.

5 Click OK.

6 Click OK.

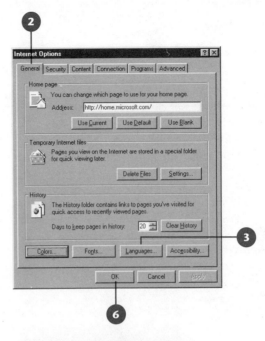

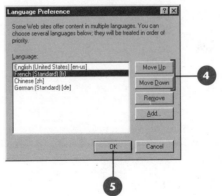

5

Improving Performance

Sometimes the Internet can be sluggish, especially if the site you are viewing is full of multimedia options like streaming video, sound files, or lots of images. Internet Explorer allows you to improve system performance by turning off options that can slow down your system. You can also improve performance by increasing the storage of temporary files on your computer so that Web pages don't have to be reloaded every time you go back to visit a site.

Turn Off Multimedia Options

1 Click the View menu, and then click Internet Options.

2 Click the Advanced tab.

3 In the Multimedia area, click to deselect the check boxes for:

- ◆ Show Pictures
- ◆ Play Animations
- ◆ Play Videos
- ◆ Play Sounds
- ◆ Smart Image Dithering

4 Click OK.

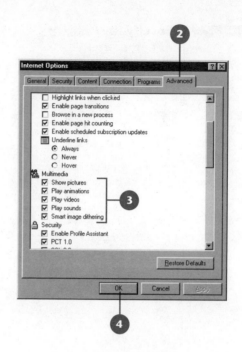

TRY THIS

View the temporary files stored on your computer.

Click the View menu, and then click Internet Options. Click the General tab, and then click Settings in the Temporary Internet Files section. Click View Files to view those files temporarily stored on your computer.

Increase the Storage of Temporary Internet Files

1 Click the View menu, and then click Internet Options.

2 Click the General tab.

3 Click Settings.

4 Click the Never option button so that Internet Explorer won't check each Web site visited for a newer version of the page.

5 Use the slider to increase the amount of hard disk space used to store temporary files.

6 Click OK.

7 Click OK.

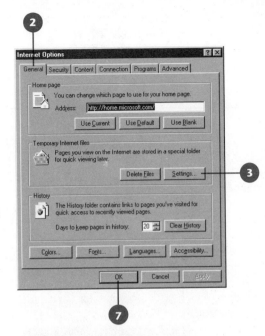

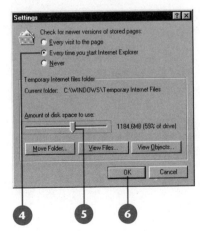

Choosing Programs to Use with Internet Explorer

Internet Explorer relies on other, external programs to provide you with connections to your e-mail, newsgroups, Internet telephones, calendars, and contact lists. You have full control over what programs are used for each option. Although Internet Explorer comes with a full suite of add-on programs—such as Outlook Express for reading e-mail and newsgroups, and Microsoft NetMeeting for conversing with others over the Internet using speakers and a microphone—you can choose other applications to provide you with the same options.

Choose Programs to Use with Internet Explorer

1 Click the View menu, and then click Internet Options.

2 Click the Programs tab.

3 Do one or more of the following:

◆ Click the Mail drop-down arrow, and then click the e-mail program you want to use.

◆ Click the News drop-down arrow, and then click the newsgroup reader program you want to use.

◆ Click the Internet Calls drop-down arrow, and then click the program to be used for Internet calls.

◆ Click the Calendar drop-down arrow, and then click the program to be used for scheduling.

◆ Click the Contact List drop-down arrow, and then click the Internet contacts or address book program you want to use.

4 Click OK.

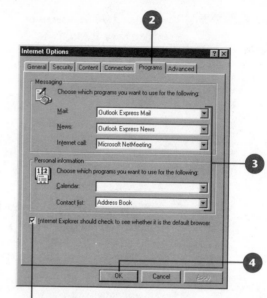

Click to have Internet Explorer check to make sure it's your default browser.

Changing Advanced Options

You can fine tune Internet Explorer to your liking by changing many of the advanced options. For example, you can have Internet Explorer inform you when a site tries to write information to your computer in the form of "cookies" files. You can turn Java logging on or off. You might want to make sure that background colors and images are included when you print Web pages. You can choose to run Internet Explorer in a *new process* so that it is the only program affected if you encounter an unstable program or Web page while you are browsing. These are just some of the advanced features you can take advantage of to further customize your Internet Explorer environment. The changes you make take effect immediately.

Change Advanced Options

1 Click the View menu, and then click Internet Options.

2 Click the Advanced tab.

3 Click to select or deselect the options you want to turn on or off.

4 Click OK.

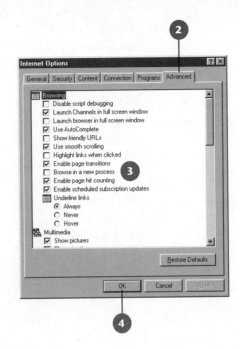

TIP

New process takes up memory. *Be aware that running in a new process requires more memory because Internet Explorer is no longer sharing resources, such as files and memory, with other programs on your system.*

TIP

What is a cookie? *A cookie is a file that a Web server stores on your computer. The most common use for cookies is to customize the way a Web page appears when you view it.*

Run in a New Process

1 Click the View menu, and then click Internet Options.

2 Click the Advanced tab.

3 In the Browsing area, click the Browse In A New Process check box to select it.

4 Click OK.

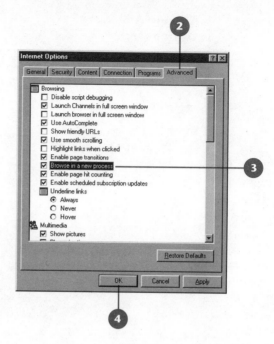

Expanding Functionality with Internet Explorer

The popularity of the Internet has resulted in an explosion of technology to deliver information to you in all forms—text, images, audio, and video. These new media types need to somehow use your Web browser to travel to your desktop. When you plug in and add on functions to support these exciting capabilities, Internet Explorer allows you to see information in a whole new light.

Multimedia adds another dimension to the Internet. Many Web sites include multimedia sound, video, and animation, in addition to text and graphics, to add interest and to attract viewers. Using Internet Explorer's built-in and add-on functionality, you can access the World Wide Web to listen to prerecorded or live radio programs, watch movies or videos, view the output of live video cameras, or play 3-D interactive animations and games over the Internet.

Understanding Add-Ons, Plug-Ins, and Viewers

Since no one is in charge of the Internet, no one is coordinating the development of all of the applications Internet users are demanding. The solution has been for the major Internet players (Microsoft and Netscape) to design their Web browsers to be *extensible*. An extensible program, like Internet Explorer, has specific functions that allow other computers programmers to add functionality to what it can already do. This means that companies can develop new Internet programs directly for Internet Explorer. Without an extensible browser, new Internet programs would have to run separately from the browser, making installation and operation more difficult.

The term *plug-in* was coined by Netscape to refer to programs that take advantage of Netscape Communicator's extensibility. Microsoft uses the term *add-on* to refer to programs that take advantage of Internet Explorer's extensibility.

A *viewer* is a particular type of add-on that allows you to read documents created by applications like word processors, spreadsheets, and presentation programs. For example, many companies have documents stored in Microsoft Word format that they would like to offer to people visiting their Web sites. Internet Explorer can read and display Word documents with a viewer for Word.

Microsoft offers viewers for Microsoft Excel and Microsoft PowerPoint also. Other companies, such as Adobe, offer viewers for their applications that you can view with Internet Explorer. Viewers are most useful for people who do not have the original application that created the document loaded on their computer.

Web page with add-on programs

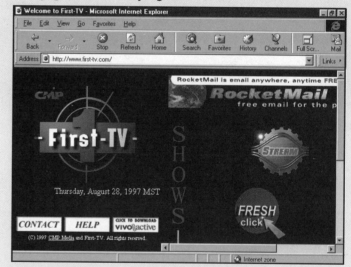

Finding Add-Ons, Plug-Ins, and Viewers on the Web

The best place to find add-ons, plug-ins, and viewers is the World Wide Web. Add-ons are available from several places on the Web, but the best place to go is to the company that created Internet Explorer—Microsoft. Microsoft's Web site contains add-ons and viewers on several different pages:

- http://www.microsoft.com/msdownload/
- http://www.microsoft.com/ie/download/
- http://home.microsoft.com/using/using.asp

You can also find add-ons, plug-ins, and viewers at software collection sites. These are Web sites that maintain large libraries of software available for downloading to your computer. Some popular sites are:

- http://www.shareware.com
- http://www.jumbo.com
- http://browserwatch.internet.com
- http://www.cooltool.com
- http://www.tucows.com
- http://www.download.com

Finally, many vendors that develop add-ons, plug-ins, and viewers offer their products for downloading from their own individual Web sites. For example, if you want the RealPlayer, you can go to http://www.realaudio.com, or if you want Adobe's PDF viewer, you can go to http://www.adobe.com.

Software collection Web site

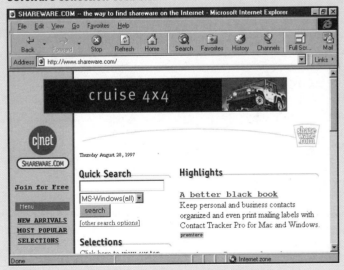

6

Installing Add-Ons and Viewers

Installing add-ons for Internet Explorer is a two-step process: download the program from the Internet, and then run the setup program to add the functionality. First, you need to locate the add-on's download site on the Web, and and click the appropriate link to initiate the download. The files that you download are typically setup programs. You can run these setup programs by double-clicking the setup file in Windows Explorer or by using the Run dialog box that you open from the Start menu.

SEE ALSO

See "Finding Add-Ons, Plug-Ins, and Viewers an the Web" on page 93 for Internet locations where you can find Internet Explorer add-ons, plug-ins, and viewers.

Install the RealPlayer Add-on

1 Create an empty folder in which to store the downloaded files.

2 Start Internet Explorer and connect to *http://www.realaudio.com.*

3 Read the Web page, and then click the link for downloading the RealPlayer add-on.

4 Click the Save This File To Disk option button.

5 Click OK, and then save the software setup files in your new folder.

6 Start Windows Explorer, and then double-click the RealPlayer setup file in your new folder.

7 Follow the instructions for installing the RealPlayer.

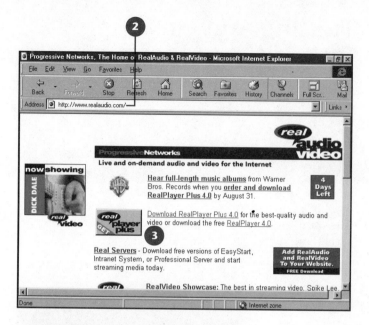

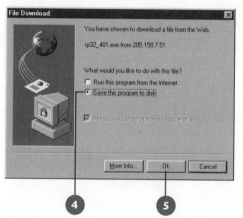

SEE ALSO

See "Using Add-Ons and Viewers" on page 96 for information about using Internet Explorer add-ons and viewers.

TIP

Install a plug-in. *To install a plug-in, you use the same procedure you use for installing an add-on.*

Install the Acrobat PDF Viewer

1 Create an empty folder in which to store the downloaded files.

2 Start Internet Explorer, connect to *http://www.adobe.com*, and then click links to the Adobe Acrobat Reader download Web page.

3 Read the Web page, and then click the link for downloading the Acrobat PDF viewer.

4 Click the Save This File To Disk option button.

5 Click OK, and then save the software setup files in your new folder.

6 Start Windows Explorer, and then double-click the Acrobat PDF viewer setup file in your new folder.

7 Click Yes to continue.

8 Follow the instructions for installing the Acrobat PDF viewer.

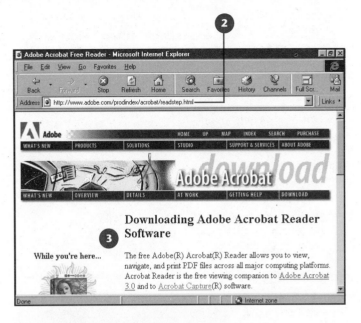

Using Add-Ons and Viewers

The common benefit of all add-ons and viewers is the ability to present information in a form that you couldn't take advantage of without the add-on or viewer. To take advantage of an add-on, all you have to do is visit a Web site that contains content that requires the add-on or viewer for proper delivery. Because the add-on or viewer becomes an integral part of Internet Explorer, you don't need to launch the add-on or viewer as a separate program. In most cases, viewers are also separate programs that can operate as stand-alone programs to view documents from places other than the Internet.

Play Streaming Audio and Video Using the RealPlayer Add-On

1 Start Internet Explorer and connect to a web site containing RealMedia sound or video.

Try connecting to *http://www.timecast.com* to locate a Web site with RealMedia.

2 Click a link to a web site with RealAudio or RealVideo.

3 Click a link to play RealAudio or RealVideo.

The RealPlayer is displayed.

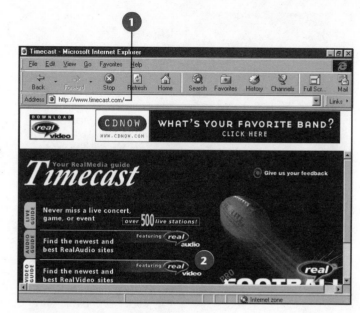

Play/Pause

Stop   Slider

Volume

Mute

Zoom

Compact Display

SEE ALSO

See "Installing Add-Ons and Viewers" on page 94 for information about installing Internet Explorer add-ons and viewers.

TRY THIS

Check out these RealAudio Web sites. *Connect to the following RealAudio Web sites: http://www.audionet.com or http://www.abc.com.*

TRY THIS

Check out these Acrobat PDF Web sites. *Connect to the following Acrobat PDF Web sites: http://www.latimes.com or http://www.wharton.upenn.edu.*

View a PDF Document with the Acrobat PDF Viewer

1 Start Internet Explorer and connect to a Web site containing an Acrobat PDF document.

Try connecting to *http://www.adobe.com* to locate a Web site with an Acrobat PDF document.

2 Click a link to open an Acrobat PDF document.

The Acrobat PDF document opens.

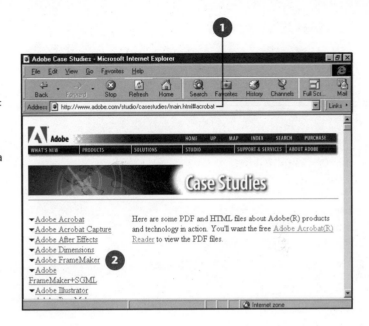

Understanding Java and ActiveX

Java is a computer language developed by Sun Microsystems that allows programmers to write interactive programs for Web browsers. Standard Web authoring tools limit to the activities and functions that are available from a Web page. With a complete programming language like Java, there are very few limits to the number of functions that a Web page can have. Here are a few of the things that Web programmers have been able to implement using the Java programming language:

◆ Scrolling stock tickers

◆ Photo e-mail directory

◆ Auto-rotating advertising banners

A Java program is called an *applet*. Applets are stored with the Web page on the Web server. When you visit a Web page containing Java enhancements, the Java applet is downloaded to your computer automatically along with the Web page—you don't have to do anything special. Internet Explorer knows how to run Java applications, so an applet begins to run as soon as it arrives at your computer. To keep your computer safe, Internet Explorer introduces a Java security model that allows you to run powerful, interactive Java applets without worrying about harming your computer or threatening your privacy.

Java information Web site

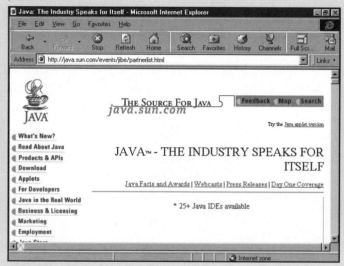

Microsoft likes to describes ActiveX as a set of technologies for creating interactive Web sites. Unlike Java, Microsoft's ActiveX is not a programming language, but a set of controls and programs that other programming languages (like Java) can use. Just as add-ons and plug-ins extend the capabilities of Internet Explorer, ActiveX extends the capability of Java.

Here are some applications that run inside Internet Explorer utilizing ActiveX:

◆ PowerPoint presentations

◆ Interfaces to corporate databases

◆ International clocks

◆ Interactive subway maps

ActiveX programs are called *controls*. Just like Java applets, controls are downloaded and run on your computer when you visit a Web page that contains ActiveX. In the lower left corner of Internet Explorer, you will see the words "Installing components while the ActiveX control is being downloaded." Sometimes, you might be presented with an on-screen certificate and asked if you would like the ActiveX control downloaded to your computer.

One big advantage that both Java and ActiveX have over plug-ins, add-ons, and viewers is that they work automatically. You don't need to go to the plug-in site, fill out a registration form, download a program, and run the installation program. Since Internet Explorer already has ActiveX and Java support installed, all you have to do is wait for the control or applet to automatically download; as soon as it arrives at your computer, it will begin executing.

ActiveX information Web site

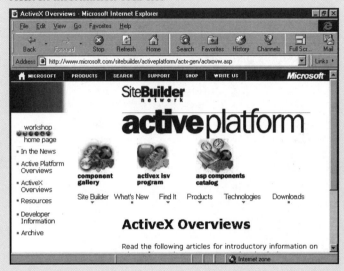

6

Using ActiveX Controls

ActiveX controls bring Web pages alive with effects such as live audio, scrolling banners, and much more. If you encounter a Web site that has an ActiveX control, Internet Explorer checks to see whether the control has been digitally signed. A digitally signed control has been independently certified to be free from computer viruses or destructive effects. You'll see a certificate indicating it's safe to install this software or a warning indicating it's not safe to continue.

SEE ALSO

See "Understanding Java and ActiveX" on page 98 for more information on ActiveX controls.

SEE ALSO

See "Controlling ActiveX and Java Content" on page 102 for information on security issues.

Use an ActiveX Control

1 Start Internet Explorer and connect to a Web page containing an ActiveX control.

Try connecting to *http://home.microsoft.com/exploring/exploring.asp* to locate a Best Of The Web site with an ActiveX control.

2 If necessary, click Yes to accept the ActiveX control.

The ActiveX control downloads and executes.

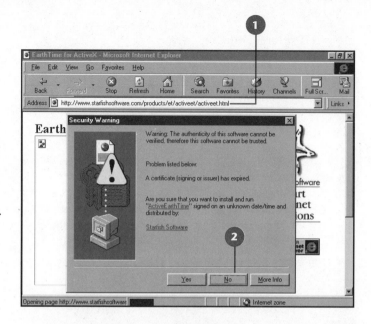

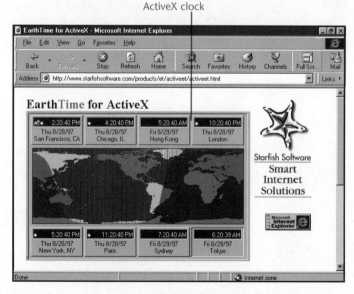

ActiveX clock

Running Java Applets

Internet Explorer runs Java applets while a Web page containing a Java applet is being displayed. There are thousands of Java applets on the Web. Examples include scrolling stock tickers, banners, spreadsheet-like calculators, and many more. Internet Explorer includes a *Just-In-Time* (JIT) Java compiler that speeds up the display and execution of Java applets. The JIT compiler is turned on by default. If you encounter problems with a Java applet, you can turn off the JIT compiler option in the Advanced tab of the Internet Options dialog box.

SEE ALSO

See "Understanding Java and ActiveX" on page 98 for more information on Java.

Run a Java Applet

1 Start Internet Explorer and connect to a Web page containing a Java applet.

Try connecting to *http://home.microsoft.com/exploring/exploring.asp* to locate a Best Of The Web site with a Java applet.

The Java applet downloads and executes.

2 If necessary, enter information or select options associated with the Java applet.

Java applet real-time Score Tracker

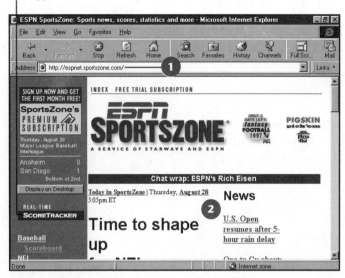

Turn Off JIT Compiler

1 Click the View menu, and then click Internet Options.

2 Click the Advanced tab.

3 Click the down scroll arrow to view Java VM settings.

4 Click the Java JIT Complier Enabled check box to deselect the option.

5 Click OK.

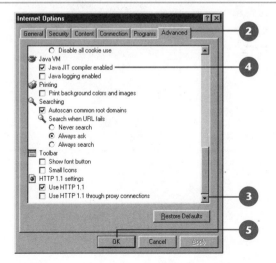

Controlling ActiveX and Java Content

With Internet Explorer you can control exactly how ActiveX controls and Java applets interact with your computer system. Using security zones, users and administrators can decide in advance what capabilities and levels of access to give to ActiveX controls and Java applets. For example, you can give broad access to Java applets from sources you trust, while restricting applets from unknown sources to safe places where they can't harm files.

Change ActiveX Security

1 Click the View menu, and then click Internet Options.

2 Click the Security tab.

3 Click the Custom option button.

4 Click Settings.

5 To set control content, click the Enable, Prompt, or Disable options buttons for each of the following security levels:

◆ Run ActiveX Controls And Plugins

◆ Download Signed ActiveX Controls

◆ Download Unsigned ActiveX Controls

◆ Initialize And Script ActiveX Controls Not Marked As Safe

6 Click OK.

7 Click OK.

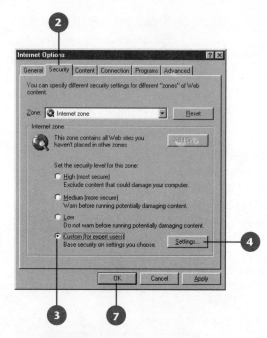

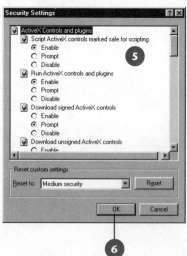

SEE ALSO

See "Understanding Java and ActiveX" on page 98 and "Running Java Applets" on page 101 for more information about Java.

Change Java Security Permissions

1 Click the View menu, and then click Internet Options.

2 Click the Security tab.

3 Click the Custom option button.

4 Click Settings.

5 Click one of the following security option buttons:

- ◆ Low Security
- ◆ Medium Security
- ◆ High Security
- ◆ Disable Java

6 Click OK.

7 Click OK.

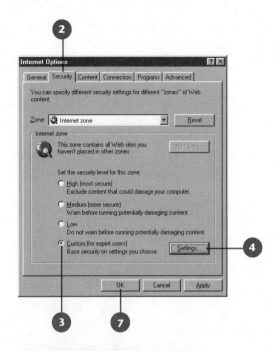

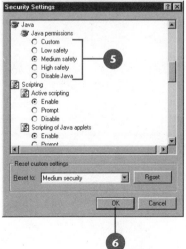

Playing Sounds and Videos

Internet Explorer comes with a built-in sound and video player called *ActiveMovie* that can play most sounds and videos that you'll frequently encountered on the Internet. If you visit a Web site that includes a hyperlink to a sound or video clip, click the hyperlink to download the file. Internet Explorer asks whether you want to save the file to disk or open it. When you play a sound or video, a small control appears containing buttons that enable you to start and stop the media clip. If you visit a Web site that includes a background sound, Internet Explorer automatically downloads and plays the sound, just as it downloads and displays a graphic image.

Play a Sound or Video from the Internet

1 Start Internet Explorer and connect to a Web page containing a sound or video.

2 Click a sound or video link.

3 Click the Open This File From The Internet option button.

4 Click OK.

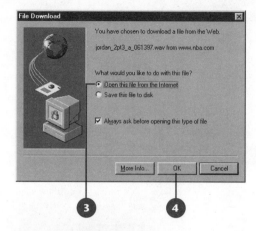

ActiveMovie control

Stop   Slider

Pause/Play

TIP

What multimedia files can ActiveMovie play?
ActiveMovie plays files that are in formats such as MPEG, AVI, WAV, and MOV, among others.

TIP

ActiveMovie supports progressive playback. *This means that you can start playing the sound or movie before it finishes downloading, which enables you to determine if it is worth downloading the entire file.*

TRY THIS

Check out these sound and video Web sites. *Connect to the following sound and video web sites: http://www.nba.com/ theater/ or http://www.loc.gov.*

SEE ALSO

See "Changing Sound and Video Properties" on page 106 for information about playing sound and video with different options.

Play a Sound or Video from Disk

1 Start Internet Explorer and connect to a Web page containing a sound or video.

2 Click a sound or video link.

3 Click the Save This File To Disk option button.

4 Click OK.

5 Specify the location to save the sound or video file, and then click Save.

6 Click OK.

7 Start Windows Explorer, and then double-click the sound or video file.

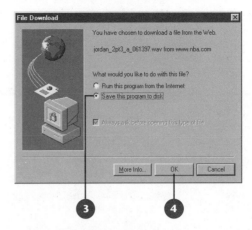

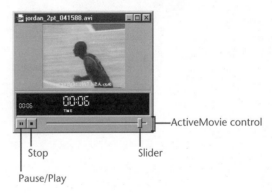

ActiveMovie control

Stop

Slider

Pause/Play

Changing Sound and Video Properties

Internet Explorer gives you control over how a sound or video clip plays. You can change the volume and timing, display size, control panel options and colors, and other advanced settings. If you decide that you do not want to display sounds, videos, or animations in Internet Explorer, you can turn off the corresponding play options. You can also turn off the display option for pictures. When you turn off these options, the Internet Explorer screen display speeds up.

Change Sound and Video Properties

1 Right-click the ActiveMovie control, and then click Properties.

2 Click the Playback tab to change the volume and timing.

3 Click the Movie Size tab to change the display size.

4 Click the Controls tab to change the control panel and colors.

5 Click the Advanced tab to change expert settings.

6 Click OK.

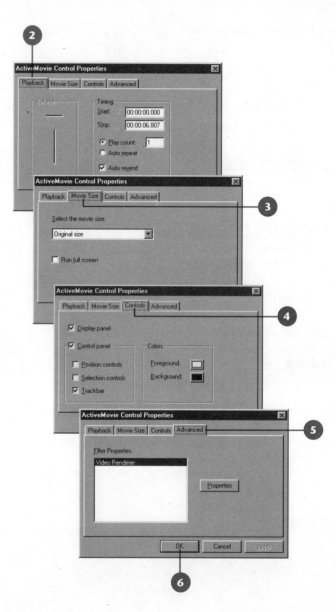

SEE ALSO

See "Playing Sounds and Videos" on page 104 for information about playing sound and video.

TIP

Display video playback by frames. *Right-click the ActiveMovie control, and then click Frames.*

Change Sound and Video Play Options

1 Click the View menu, and then click Internet Options.

2 Click the Advanced tab.

3 Click any of the following check boxes to play or not play the selected media:

◆ Play Animations

◆ Play Videos

◆ Play Sounds

4 Click OK.

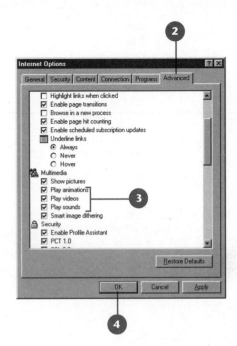

Broadcasting Audio and Video with NetShow

NetShow provides an easy, powerful way to broadcast, or stream, multimedia across the Internet and intranets. *Streaming* allows content to be delivered to the Web site visitor as a continuous flow of data with little wait before the playback begins. NetShow allows users to view and listen to live and recorded broadcasts. NetShow give users the benefit of instant play, and eliminates the frustration of waiting for content to download. With the NetShow Player installed, all you need to do is visit a Web site containing NetShow content and an Active Streaming Format (ASF) file, and then click a NetShow hyperlink to play the streaming content.

Display NetShow Content

1. Start Internet Explorer and connect to *http://www.microsoft.com/netshow/*.

2. Click the Gallery link.

3. Click the Always Live link.

4. Click a link to a Web page containing NetShow content.

5. Click a link to play the NetShow content.

   The NetShow content plays continuously.

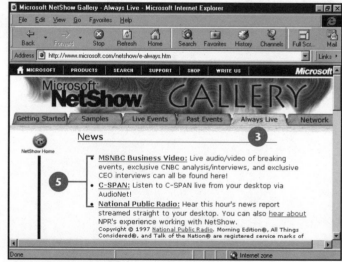

TIP

Change NetShow player properties. *Start the NetShow Player, click the File menu, and then click Properties. Click the Settings tab to change the play count and player appearance. Click the Advanced tab to change buffering—the streaming of the content—and Internet protocols.*

TIP

Create NetShow content. *Connect to the NetShow web site at http://www.microsoft.com/netshow/, and then click the HOW-TO link for complete details.*

TIP

Having trouble playing NetShow content? *Start the NetShow Player, click the Help menu, click Trouble Shooting Guide, and then following the Help information.*

Display NetShow Content with the NetShow Player

1 Click the Start button on the taskbar, point to Programs, and then point to Internet Explorer.

2 Click NetShow Player.

3 For an Internet location, click the File menu, and then click Open Location. For a local file, click the File menu, and then click Open. Click Browse to locate the file.

4 Type the location of the ASF file.

5 Click OK.

The NetShow content plays continuously.

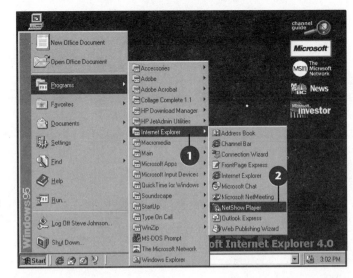

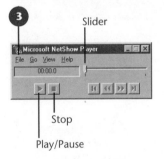

Slider

Stop

Play/Pause

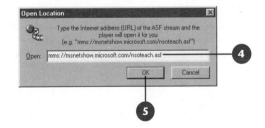

6

Playing a VRML Animation

VRML (Virtual Reality Modeling Language) is a graphic format that places viewers "inside" a scene and allows them to change their point of view and relative location. Microsoft VRML is an Internet Explorer add-on program that displays 3-D interactive animation within Internet Explorer. The VRML viewer doesn't come installed with Internet Explorer, so you will need to install the software before you can view VRML animations.

> **TIP**
>
> **Get more information about VRML.** *Visit Microsoft's Virtual Support Web page at http://www.microsoft.com/vrml/default2.htm.*

Download the VRML Viewer

1. Start Internet Explorer and connect to *http://www.microsoft.com/ie/.*

2. Click the Download link, and then click Internet Explorer 4.0 Components.

3. Read the Web page, and then scroll to the bottom of the page.

4. Click the Internet Explorer 4.0 Components link.

5. Click Yes.

6. Click the Microsoft VRLM 2.0 Viewer check box.

7. Click Next.

8. Click the Component List drop-down arrow, and then select a download site.

9. Click Install Now. Restart your computer if necessary.

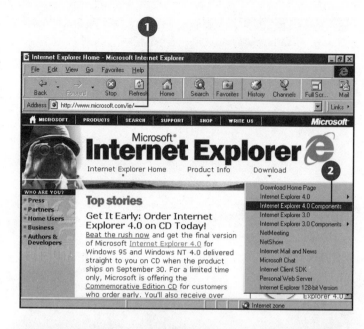

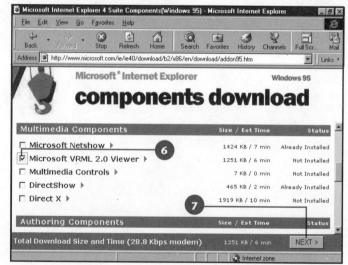

TRY THIS

Check out these VRML web sites. *Connect to the following VRML Web sites: http://www.microsoft.com/vrml/ or http://www.planet9.com.*

Play a VRML Animation

1 Start Internet Explorer and connect to a Web page containing a VRML animation.

2 Click a link to a VRML animation.

3 Click any of the following buttons along the edge of the VRML animation to navigate:

- ◆ W to walk
- ◆ P to pan
- ◆ T to turn
- ◆ R to roll
- ◆ G to go to a location
- ◆ S to study
- ◆ Z to zoom out
- ◆ Up to straighten up
- ◆ V to view right or left
- ◆ R to restore the view

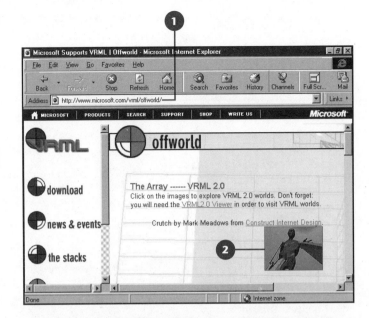

6

Playing an Internet Game

Using Microsoft's DirectX multimedia technology, you can play games over the Internet. For example, the Microsoft Internet Gaming Zone Web site is an easy-to-use and free Internet-based multiplayer gaming service that offers a wide variety of great games. Before you can play over the Internet using DirectX, you need to install the DirectX component from the Microsoft Internet Explorer Download Web site.

SEE ALSO

See "Getting Updates to Internet Explorer" on page 248 for information on installing the DirectX component.

TIP

Check out these Internet gaming Web sites. *Connect to the following Internet gaming Web sites: http://www.zone.com, http://inngames.com, or http://www.mpath.com*

Find a Gaming Web Site and Play a Game Over the Internet

1 Start Internet Explorer and connect to *http://www.microsoft.com/directx/default.asp.*

2 Click the End User Guide link.

3 Scroll down, and then click the DirectPlay Support And Solutions link.

4 Click a link to a Game Service Provider (GSP) Web site. To visit the Microsoft Internet Gaming Zone, click the http://www.zone.com link.

5 Follow the instructions on the Game Service Provider's Web site to play a game.

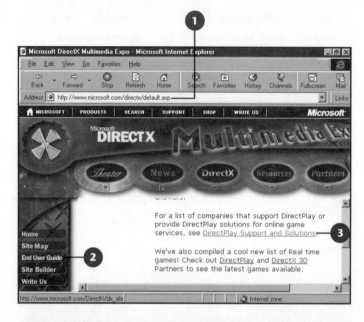

7

Exchanging E-Mail Using Outlook Express

If you're like many people today who are using the Internet to communicate with friends and business associates, you probably have piles of information from names to e-mail addresses that you often need at your disposal. Unless this information is in one convenient place that allows you immediate access to exactly what you need, the information becomes ineffective and you become unproductive. Outlook Express solves these problems by integrating management and organization tools into one simple system.

Using Outlook Express, you can:

◆ Create and send mail messages

◆ Manage multiple mail and news accounts with different Internet service providers

◆ Use the Windows Address Book to store and retrieve e-mail addresses

◆ Create stationery or add a personal signature to your messages

◆ Attach a file to your mail message

◆ Print mail messages

Viewing the Outlook Express Window

Menu bar
The menu bar gives you access to all the menu options. Simply click a menu name to display a list of related menu commands, and then click the command you want to issue.

Title bar
The title bar displays the name of the program, Outlook Express, preceded by the Outlook Express icon.

Toolbar
The toolbar contains buttons for commands you use in Outlook Express. The buttons change depending on which folder of Outlook Express you are using.

Internet Explorer hyperlink
Clicking this hyperlink opens Internet Explorer.

Folder List
The Folder list contains all the folders in Outlook Express. You can customize the folders to meet your needs.

Message List
The Message list displays your e-mail messages.

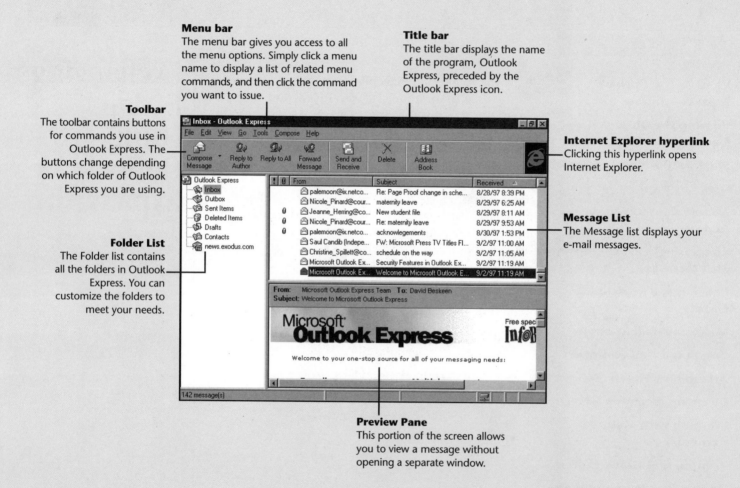

Preview Pane
This portion of the screen allows you to view a message without opening a separate window.

Viewing the Outlook Express Start Page

The Outlook Express Start Page helps you jump to the folders or modules you want to use.

Read News
The Read News link connects you to newsgroups that you can view or subscribe to.

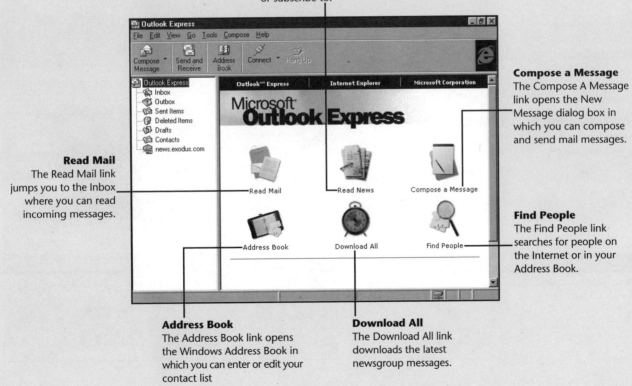

Compose a Message
The Compose A Message link opens the New Message dialog box in which you can compose and send mail messages.

Read Mail
The Read Mail link jumps you to the Inbox where you can read incoming messages.

Find People
The Find People link searches for people on the Internet or in your Address Book.

Address Book
The Address Book link opens the Windows Address Book in which you can enter or edit your contact list

Download All
The Download All link downloads the latest newsgroup messages.

Starting Outlook Express

Once you are at your computer's desktop, you can start Outlook Express. You can start Outlook Express by using the Start menu on the taskbar or the Launch Mail button on the Quick Launch toolbar. Starting Outlook Express with the Launch Mail button is the easiest since it takes only one click.

TIP

Add the Quick Launch toolbar to your screen. *If you do not see the Launch Mail button on the taskbar, right-click the taskbar, point to Toolbars, and then click Quick Launch.*

TIP

Remove your Inbox. *If you are no longer using the Inbox as your default mailbox, you will be asked to remove it from your desktop the first time you open Outlook Express.*

Start Outlook Express from the Quick Launch Toolbar

1. Click the Launch Mail button on the Quick Launch toolbar.

Start Outlook Express from the Start Menu

1. Click the Start button on the taskbar to display the Start menu.

2. Point to Programs to display the Programs menu.

3. Point to Internet Explorer to display the Internet Explorer menu.

4. Click Outlook Express.

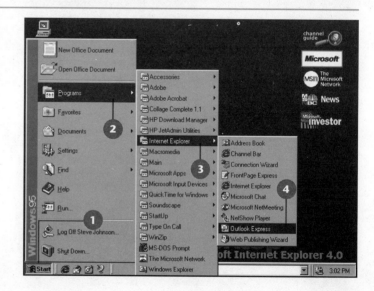

Opening a Folder

As you work, you'll frequently need to switch between Outlook folders and modules to create items such as contacts and mail messages or to join your favorite newsgroups. For example, if you receive a call from a business associate who recommends you e-mail his colleague right away regarding an important business contract, you add the colleague's name to your Address Book and then send her a mail message. When she calls to arrange a meeting, you can move quickly and smoothly between the necessary tasks using the shortcuts on the Outlook Express Start Page.

SEE ALSO

See "Customizing the Outlook Express Window" on page 152 for information on how to customize the layout of the Outlook Express window to display the Outlook Bar.

Open a Folder from the Folder List

1 Click the icon on the Folder list of the folder you want to open.

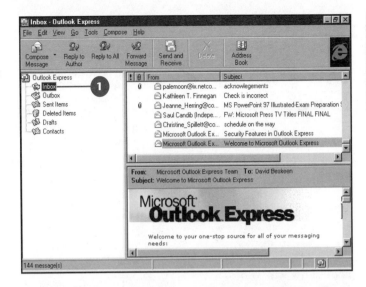

Open a Folder from the Outlook Bar

1 If necessary, click the scroll up button or scroll down button to display additional folder icons.

2 Click the icon on the Outlook bar for the folder you want to open.

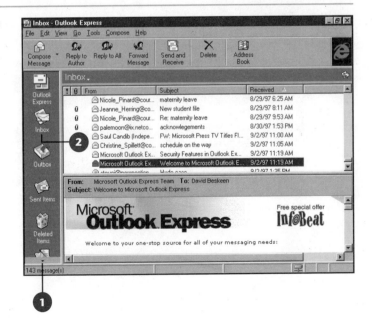

Adding Contacts to the Address Book

A *contact* is a person or company that you communicate with. One contact can often have several mailing addresses, phone numbers, e-mail addresses, or Web sites. You can store this information in the Address Book along with other detailed information such as job title, cellular phone number, and personal Web page address. When you create a new contact or open an existing one, you open the Properties dialog box in which you can enter or change contact information. A contact can also be a part of a *contact group*, which is a group of people you communicate with on a regular basis, such as your colleagues at work.

Add a New Contact to the Address Book

1 Click the Address Book button on the toolbar, or click the Address Book link on the Outlook Express Start Page, and then click New Contact on the toolbar.

2 Fill in the new contact's name and e-mail address, and then click Add.

3 Click the other available tabs to enter additional information about the contact.

4 Click OK to save the contact.

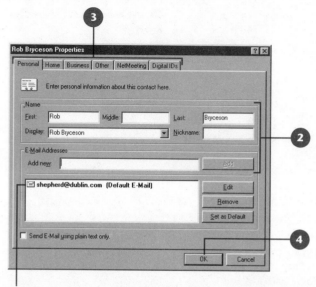

E-mail addresses are not case sensitive (that is, capitalization doesn't matter) and cannot contain spaces.

Update Existing Contact Information

1 Click the Address Book button on the toolbar, and then double-click the contact whose information you want to change.

2 Click the tab containing the information you want to change, and then make your changes.

3 Click OK to save the update.

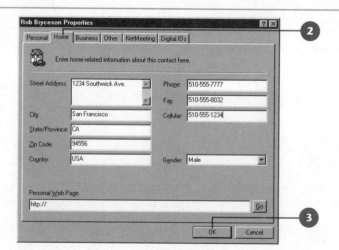

TIP

View a contact's information. *If you want to view the information you have entered for a contact, move the mouse pointer over the contact in the Windows Address Book to display a ScreenTip.*

TRY THIS

Organize your Address Book. *Sort your address book by name, e-mail address, or phone number by clicking on the appropriate column heading. You can switch the sorting method from ascending to descending by clicking the same column heading again.*

Address Book

Create a Contact Group

1 Click the Address Book button on the toolbar, and then click New Group button on the Address Book toolbar.

2 Type a name for the new group.

3 Click Select Members to display your current list of contacts.

4 Click each member in the list of contacts you want to add to the group, and then click Select.

5 To add a new contact to this group, click New Contact to open the Properties dialog box in which you enter the necessary contact information, and then click OK.

6 Click OK.

7 To remove a contact from the group, click the contact, and then click Remove.

8 Click OK.

The new group appears in the Windows Address Book.

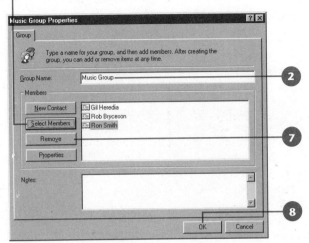

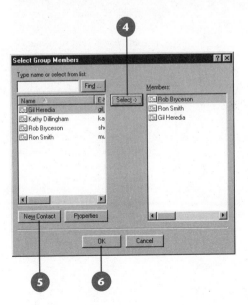

Composing and Sending Mail Messages

Using mail messages as the primary form of written communication is quickly becoming the method of choice for many people—whether it's for business or pleasure. Mail messages follow a standard memo format with lines for the sender, recipient, date, and subject. To send a mail message, you need to enter the recipient's complete e-mail address. You can send the same message to multiple individuals and groups.

Compose Message button

Compose and Send a Mail Message

1 Click the Compose Message button on the toolbar, or click the Compose A Message link on the Outlook Express Start Page.

2 Type the recipient's name in the To box, or click the Select Recipients From A List icon to open the Select Recipients dialog box.

3 Click a recipient's name, and if necessary, press Ctrl while you click other names or groups.

4 If appropriate, click the Cc or Bcc button to send copies of your message to other recipients, and then click OK.

◆ Cc sends a copy of your message including a complete recipient list on the e-mail

◆ Bcc sends your message without displaying a complete recipient list on the e-mail

5 Click in the Subject box, and then enter a brief description of your message.

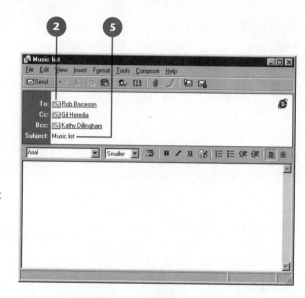

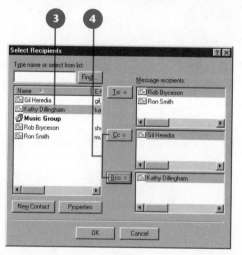

SEE ALSO

See "Attaching a File to Mail" on page 128 for information on how to attach a file to a message.

SEE ALSO

See "Creating and Using E-Mail Stationery" on page 126 for information on how to create a signature and select a business card.

TRY THIS

Send a Web page using Outlook Express. *Open any Web site in Internet Explorer 4. Click the File menu, point to Send, and then click Page By E-Mail or Link By E-Mail. Outlook Express opens with the Web page as an attached file in the Compose Message dialog box.*

Compose A Message

6 Click in the message box, and type the text of your message.

7 If you want, click the Insert File button on the toolbar to attach a file to the message.

8 If you want, use the commands on the Formatting toolbar to format your message.

9 Click the Send button on the toolbar, or click the File menu, and then click Send Later. Your message will be placed in your Outbox folder.

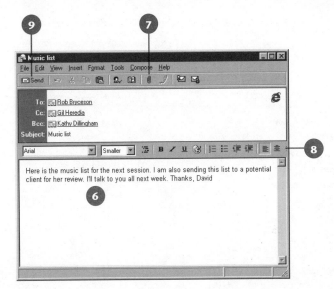

	MAIL MESSAGE ICONS
Icon	**Description**
	This message has been read. The message heading text appears in normal text type.
	This message has not been read. The message heading text appears in bold text type.
	This message has one or more files attached to it.
	The message has been marked as high priority by the sender.
	The message has been marked as low priority by the sender.

Reading and Replying to E-Mail

Mail can be sent to you anytime day or night, even when your computer is turned off. To retrieve your e-mail, you can manually connect to your Internet service provider (ISP) or set Outlook Express to automatically retrieve your messages. New messages appear in the Inbox along with any messages you haven't yet stored elsewhere or deleted. A message flag appears next to any message that has a certain priority or has a file attached to it. A message flag, along with the sender's name and subject information, help you determine the content of a message and which one you want to open, read, and respond to first.

SEE ALSO

See "Diverting Incoming E-Mail to Folders" on page 129 for information on how to route your mail messages.

Retrieve Messages

1. Click the Send And Retrieve button on the toolbar. The Send And Receive button appears in all the Outlook Express folders.

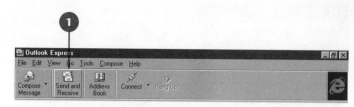

Open and Read a Message

1. Click Inbox on the Folder list or click the Read Mail shortcut on the Outlook Express Start Page.

2. Double-click the message you want to read. The message opens in its own window, making it easier to read.

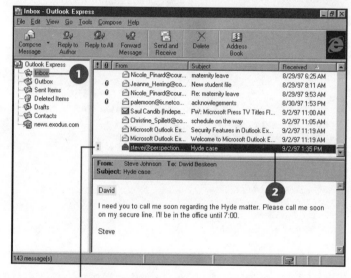

This symbol indicates a high priority message.

Reply to a Message

1. Open the message you want to reply to.

2. Click the Reply To Author button or the Reply All button on the toolbar.

TRY THIS

Get new mail quickly quickly. *You can set up Outlook Express to automatically retrieve new mail messages. Click the Tools menu, click Options, and then set the appropriate retrieval options on the General and Dial Up tabs.*

TRY THIS

Change the mail message status. *Right-click a mail message in any folder, and then click Mark As Read or Mark As Unread.*

TIP

Forward as an attachment. *You can forward any message as an attachment on another e-mail message. Right-click the message you want to attach, and then click Forward As Attachment.*

Forward button

◆ Reply To Author allows you to respond to just the sender.

◆ Reply All allows you to respond to the sender and to all other recipients of the message.

4 Type your message and attach any files you want to send.

5 Click the Send button on the toolbar, or click the File menu and then click Send Later. You will be asked to store your message in the Outbox.

Forward a Message

1 Open the message you want to forward.

2 Click the Forward button on the toolbar.

3 Click the Select Recipients From A List icon, and then select the recipients of the message.

4 Type your message and attach any files you want to send.

5 Click the Send button on the toolbar, or click the File menu and then click Send Later.

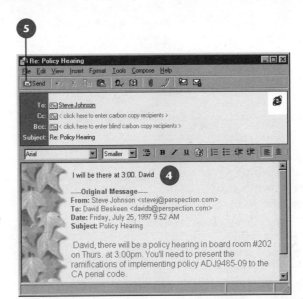

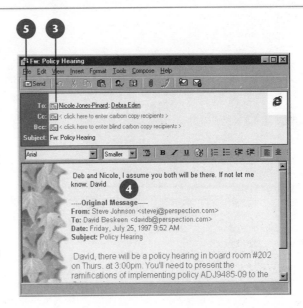

Managing Mail Messages

One problem that can arise as you receive e-mail is an overabundance of messages in your Inbox. To help you manage your mail messages, Outlook Express provides a way to save messages as files, delete messages you no longer want, and move messages to other folders and subfolders, creating new folders as you need them. Storing messages in other folders and deleting unwanted messages make it easier to see the new messages you receive.

TIP

Retrieve deleted messages.
Messages you delete remain in the Deleted Items folder until you empty that folder. To retrieve deleted messages, simply open the Deleted Items folder, and then drag the messages to the Inbox or any other folder.

Save a Mail Message as a File

1 Click the message you want to save.

2 Click the File menu, and then click Save As.

3 Click the Save In drop-down arrow, and then select the drive and folder where you want to store the message.

4 Click the Save As Type drop-down arrow, and then click an available file type.

5 Type a new filename for the message you are saving.

6 Click Save.

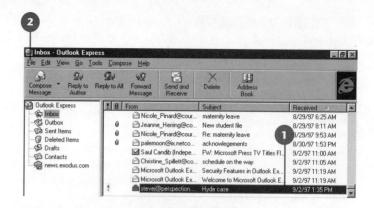

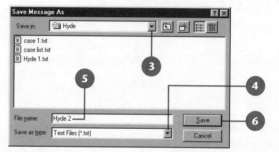

Delete Unwanted Messages

1 Click the folder containing the messages you want to delete.

2 Click the message you want to delete, or press the Ctrl or Shift key while you click other messages you want to delete.

3 Click the Delete button on the toolbar.

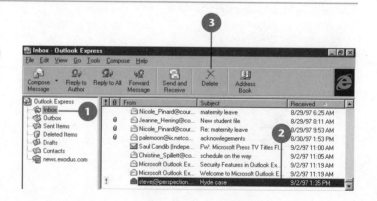

TIP

Delete old and unwanted messages from Outlook Express folders. *Your mail messages are stored in the Outlook Express folders until you manually delete them. To delete an individual message, open a folder and delete the message. To delete all the messages in a folder, right-click a folder, and then click Empty Folder.*

TRY THIS

Automatically empty your Deleted Items folder. *Click the Tools menu, and then click Options. Click the General tab, and click the Empty Messages From the Deleted Items Folder On Exit check box.*

TRY THIS

Use sorting to help manage your messages. *Click the column headings in a folder where your messages are stored, such as your Inbox, to sort your messages by recipient, subject, date received, or date sent. You can sort messages in ascending or descending order.*

Create a New Folder

1. Right-click any folder on the Folder list, and then click New Folder.

2. Type a name for the new folder.

3. Click the folder in which you want to place the new folder.

   ◆ Click Outlook Express to place the folder on the Folder list.

   ◆ Click one of the other folders in the list to make the new folder a subfolder.

4. Click OK.

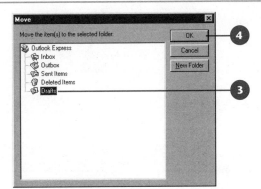

Organize Your Messages in Folders

1. Select the message or messages you want to move or copy, and then right-click.

2. Click Move To or Copy To on the shortcut menu.

3. Click the folder where you want to move or copy the message. If necessary, click New Folder to add your message to a folder not listed.

4. Click OK.

Creating and Using E-Mail Stationery

Tired of the typical bland, unexciting look of e-mail? Well, if so, Outlook Express has the answer—Outlook Express Stationery. This new feature allows you to create colorful e-mail messages and newsgroup postings. Stationery can include background images, different text fonts, a signature, and a personal Business Card. A *signature* is any file, text file with your signature, or photo of yourself you choose to use as your signature. A *Business Card* is your contact information from the Address Book. Any type of computer or digital device can read the Business Card.

TIP

Create a message using other stationery. *Click the drop-down arrow on the Compose Message button, and then select the stationery you want to use.*

Create Stationery

1 Click the Tools menu, and then click Stationery.

2 Click the This Stationery option button, and then click Select.

3 Click a stationery from the list, or click Get More to search the Internet for more options.

4 Click OK, and then click OK again.

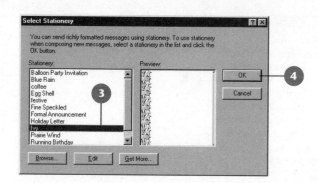

Create a Signature and Select a Business Card

1 Click the Tools menu, and then click Stationery.

2 Click Signature.

3 Click the Text option button and type your name, or click the File option button and select a file that you want to use as a signature. Click Browse to find the file you need, if necessary.

4 Click the Card drop-down arrow, and then click your name in the list. Click the New button to add your name if is not listed.

5 Click OK, and then click OK again.

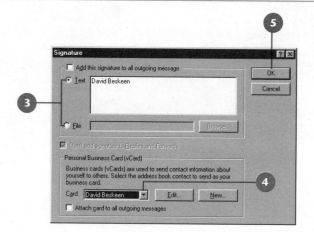

TIP

Add your signature to your message quickly. *Click to place the insertion point in your message, and then click the Insert Signature button on the toolbar.*

Add a Signature to a Message

1 Compose a new message or open an existing message.

2 Click to place the insertion point in your message where you want your signature to appear.

3 Click the Insert menu, and then click Signature to add your signature to the message.

4 Send the message or move it to another folder.

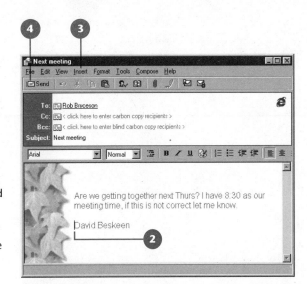

TIP

Having trouble adding a signature or business card? *Before you can add a signature or business card to a message, you need to create a signature or select a business card.*

Business Card icon

Add a Business Card to a Message

1 Compose a new message or open an existing message.

2 Click the Insert menu, and then click Business Card.

3 Send the message or move it to another folder.

A business card icon appears here.

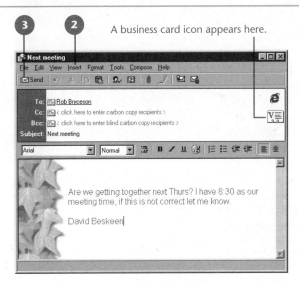

Attaching a File to Mail

In addition to exchanging messages, another powerful feature of e-mail is sharing files. You can attach one or more files, such as a picture or a document, to a mail message. The recipient of the e-mail then opens the file in the program in which it was created. For example, suppose you are working on a report that needs to be presented today by a colleague in another part of the country. After you finish the report, you can attach the report file to a mail message and send the message with the attached report directly to your colleague. Attaching a file to a message becomes very handy when you want the recipient to receive the file promptly.

TIP

Use drag and drop to attach a file quickly. *You can quickly attach a file to a mail message by dragging it from the desktop or Windows Explorer to the message box.*

Attach a File to a Mail Message

1 Compose a new message, or open an existing message.

2 Click the Insert File button on the toolbar.

3 Click the Look In drop-down arrow, and then select the drive and folder that contains the file you want to attach.

4 Click Attach. You can attach more than one file to your e-mail message.

5 Send the message or move it to your Outlook folder.

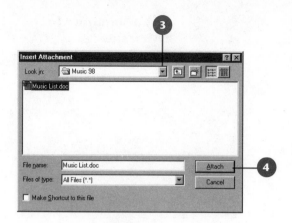

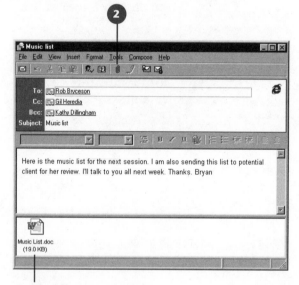

Attached file appears here

Diverting Incoming E-Mail to Folders

Outlook Express can direct incoming messages that meet certain criteria that you specify to specific folders. Let's say that you have a friend that loves sending you funny e-mail, but you often don't have time to read it right away. You can set the Inbox Assistant to send your friend's messages to a folder where the messages are stored until you read them at a later time.

Set Criteria for Incoming Messages

1 Click the Tools menu, and then click Inbox Assistant.

2 Click Add.

3 Click the To button, CC button, or From button, and then enter the name of the appropriate contacts.

4 Fill in the subject box, if applicable.

5 If necessary, click the Account check box, and then click the drop-down arrow to set criteria for another account.

6 Click the appropriate setting for the action you want to perform:

◆ Move To moves the message to another folder

◆ Copy To copies the message to another folder

◆ Forward To forwards the message to another contact

◆ Reply With allows you to choose an e-mail message to reply with

7 Click OK.

8 Click OK.

A description of the criteria appears here.

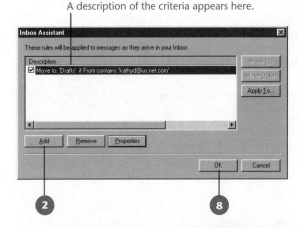

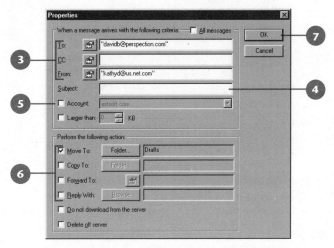

Working with Multiple Accounts

You can set up Outlook Express to receive e-mail from different accounts, or if several people use the same e-mail account, you can set up folders for each person, and then route incoming messages automatically to each individual's folder. For example, if you and a business colleague share an e-mail account, you can set Outlook Express to deliver each of your messages to your own folder.

TIP

Multiple users and different passwords. *If multiple users with different passwords use the same computer, Outlook Express will create separate accounts for each user. Each person must then log on as a different user to use his or her mail account.*

Add a New Mail Account

1. Click the Tools menu, and then click Accounts.

2. Click the Mail tab.

3. Click Add, and then click Mail.

4. Type your name in the Internet Connection Wizard dialog box. Click Next to continue

5. If your e-mail address appears correctly, click Next to continue; otherwise type the correct address.

6. Type the correct information for your mail server. Click Next to continue.

7. Type your logon name and password. Click Next to continue.

8. Type your mail account name. Click Next to continue.

9. Choose the type of connection you want. Click Next to continue, and then click Finish.

10. Click Close to save your new account settings.

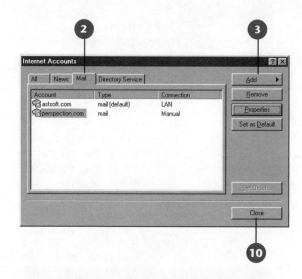

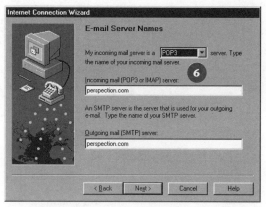

Printing in Outlook Express

You can print your messages from any folder at any time using Outlook Express. You can also open the Address Book and print contact information. Printing styles in the Address Book include Memo, Business Card, and Phone List. The Memo style prints all the information you have for a contact with description titles. The Business Card style prints the contact information without description titles. The Phone List option prints all the phone numbers for a contact.

Print button

Print a Mail Message

1 Open the message you want to print.

2 Click the File menu, and then click Print.

3 Specify a print range, if necessary.

4 Specify the number of copies you want to print.

5 Click OK.

Print Contact Information from the Address Book

1 Open your Address Book.

2 Click the contact whose information you want to print.

3 Click the File menu and then click Print.

4 Specify a print range, if necessary.

5 Click the Print Style option you want to use.

6 Specifiy the number of copies you want to print.

7 Click OK.

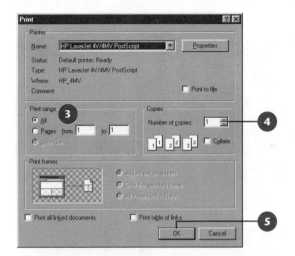

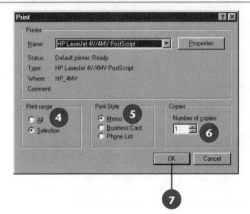

Finding People on the Web

Have you ever tried to search for someone on the Internet? Have you been successful? Outlook Express provides seven popular directory service accounts to assist you to search for people on the Internet. Each directory service accesses different databases on the Internet, which means you have a greater possibility of finding someone. You can also find people in your own Address Book, which is convenient when you have many contact listings.

TIP

Changing directory services. *You can add, remove, or change directory service account properties by opening the Internet Accounts dialog box. Click the Tools menu, click Accounts, and then click the Directory Service tab.*

Locate a Person on the Web

1. Click the Edit menu, and then click Find People.

2. Click the directory service you want to use. Click Visit to jump to a directory services' web site.

3. Type the contact's name or e-mail account, or both if you know them.

4. Click Find Now.

5. Click another directory service, if necessary, and then click Find Now.

6. Click Add To Address Book if a name is found and if you want to keep it for future use.

7. Click Close.

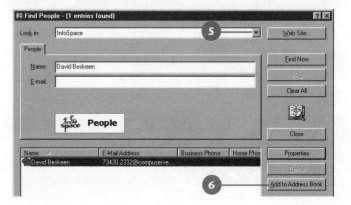

Locate a Contact in Your Address Book

1. Click the Edit menu, and then click Find People.

2. Click Windows Address Book in the Search list.

3. Type the contact's name, e-mail address, or any other information you have available.

4. Click Find Now.

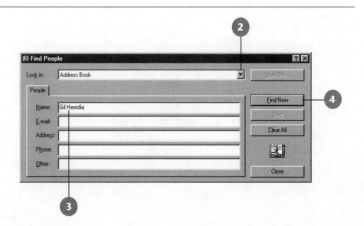

Exploring Outlook Express News

Outlook Express News provides a simple and fun way to participate in ongoing discussions about your hobbies, work, or other topics that interest you. Unlike local clubs or organizations, newsgroups enable you to:

◆ Meet people from around the world with a similar interest

◆ Get answers to questions you might have on a subject

◆ Share your knowledge and expertise with others

◆ Start a new discussion or participate in an existing one

◆ Join the conversation at your leisure—read and reply to messages at your own convenience

Why Newsgroups?

Imagine a conversation with a group of friends about a topic of mutual interest. Now imagine that conversation taking place at two in the morning with people around the world. That's what newsgroups enable you to do. Although joining a newsgroup might seem complicated, if you have exchanged e-mail messages with others, then you already know how to correspond with a newsgroup.

Starting Outlook Express News

Outlook Express News is just a few mouse clicks away, whether you have just started your computer or are working in Internet Explorer. You can always access Outlook Express using the Start button on the taskbar or using the Launch Mail button if you have the Active Desktop installed. Once Outlook Express is open, you can switch quickly to the News window. If you are Web browsing with Internet Explorer, you can just click a toolbar button to switch directly to Outlook Express News.

Start Outlook Express News from the Start Menu

1 Click the Start button on the taskbar.

2 Point to Programs.

3 Point to Internet Explorer.

4 Click Outlook Express.

5 Click the a news server icon on the Folder list, or click the Read News link on the Outlook Express Start Page.

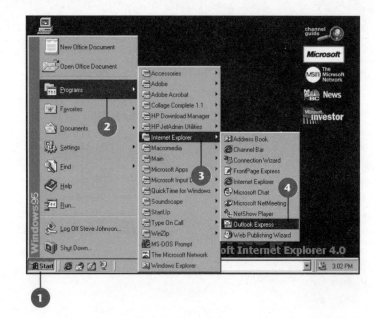

Start Outlook Express News from the Active Desktop

1 Click the Launch Mail button on the Quick Launch toolbar.

2 Click a news server icon on the Folder list, or click Read News link on the Outlook Express Start Page.

Click the Mail icon on the desktop to start Outlook Express.

TIP

Set Outlook Express to start when you start your computer. *Right-click the taskbar, click Properties, click the Start Menu Programs tab, click Advanced, and then drag the Outlook Express shortcut icon from the Internet Explorer folder to the StartUp folder. Click the Close button in the upper right corner of the window, and then click OK.*

TIP

Set your default startup connection. *If you use a dial-up connection, you can set Outlook Express to start without prompting you to select a connection option each time. In Outlook Express, click the Tools menu, click Options, click the Dial Up tab, click one of the option buttons in the When Outlook Express Starts area to select it, and then click OK.*

Start Outlook Express News from Internet Explorer

1. Start Internet Explorer, and then click the Mail button on the Web toolbar.

2. Click Read News.

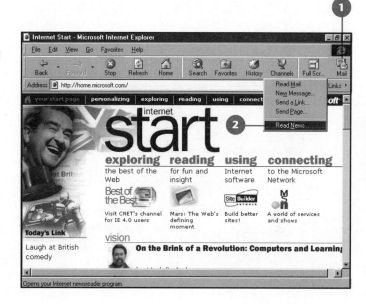

Viewing the News Window

Menu bar
The menu bar gives you access to all the menu options. Simply click a menu name to display a list of related menu commands, and then click the command you want to issue.

Toolbar
The toolbar contains buttons for commands you use in Outlook Express. The buttons change depending on which folder of Outlook Express you are in.

Folder List
The Folder list contains all the folders in Outlook Express. You can customize the folders to meet your needs.

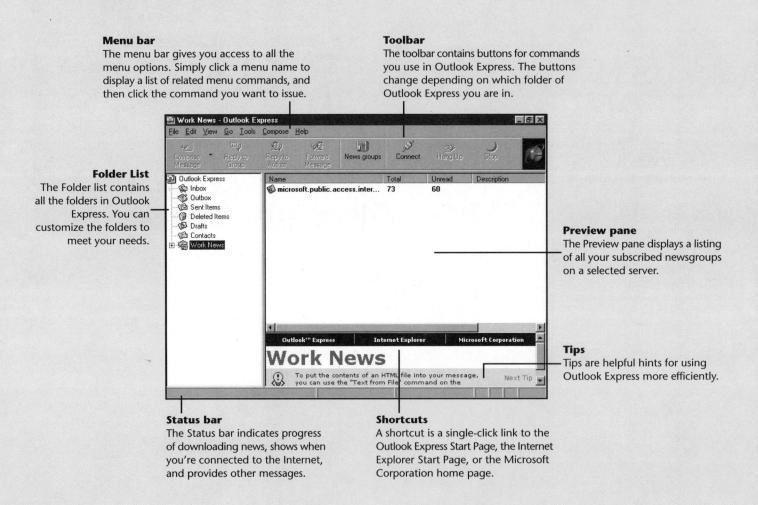

Preview pane
The Preview pane displays a listing of all your subscribed newsgroups on a selected server.

Tips
Tips are helpful hints for using Outlook Express more efficiently.

Status bar
The Status bar indicates progress of downloading news, shows when you're connected to the Internet, and provides other messages.

Shortcuts
A shortcut is a single-click link to the Outlook Express Start Page, the Internet Explorer Start Page, or the Microsoft Corporation home page.

Understanding Newsgroups

To help you understand the concept of a newsgroup, consider the following scenarios:

◆ You're working late to finish a big project for tomorrow morning's deadline, and you can't get Microsoft Excel's PivotTable feature to analyze the data properly. The system administrator left hours ago, and all your computer whiz friends are asleep. What do you do?

◆ It's three in the morning, and you just awoke from a bizarre and complicated dream. You want to tell someone and find out what it means before the images fade. Who can you call?

◆ Buying the old Victorian house was a dream come true. But now you have constant questions about the best way to renovate and restore the house to its previous glory. How can you find people who have advice to give?

◆ The electronic music of a German composer is your latest fascination, but nobody you know listens to that kind of music. Where can you find other fans to share your thoughts with?

In each case, the answer is a newsgroup. Simply, a *newsgroup* is a forum where people from around the world with a common interest can share ideas, ask and answer questions, and comment on and discuss any aspect of a subject.

You can find a newsgroup about almost any topic, from the serious to the lighthearted, from educational to controversial, from business to social. Whatever your interest, there is sure to be a newsgroup where you find others who share it.

In many ways, participating in a newsgroup is similar to sending e-mail messages to and receiving replies from a large number of people. But if 200, 500, or 3,000 people participated, an enormous number of messages would clog the Internet. A newsgroup saves network resources because a message, called an *article*, is sent once and stored on a server where interested parties can download it.

In order to participate in a newsgroup, you need a *news reader program*, such as Outlook Express News, which provides you the ability to subscribe to newsgroups, retrieve the latest conversations, read and reply to messages, save and print messages, and so forth.

Outlook Express News helps you to keep track of the newsgroup or newsgroups to which you belong, or *subscribe*, to organize conversation *threads* (ongoing messages about the same subject), and to clean up your hard drive by getting rid of outdated messages. If you know how to create and send e-mail messages with Outlook Express Mail, you're already familiar with the tools and features you use to compose and post articles to a newsgroup.

8

Configuring the News Reader

Before you can participate in a newsgroup, you must specify a news server. The Internet Connection Wizard walks you though this setup process. This wizard also appears the first time you start Outlook Express Mail or News. To complete it, you'll need the name of the news server you want to use and possibly an account name and password from your Internet service provider (ISP) or system administrator. Unless you plan to install another news reader to access newsgroups, you should set Outlook Express as your primary news reader so that you use it whenever you link to a newsgroup.

SEE ALSO

See "Connecting to the Internet" on page 12 for more Information about setting up your Internet connection using the Internet Connection Wizard.

Add a News Server Using the Internet Connection Wizard

1 Click the Tools menu in Outlook Express, and then click Accounts.

2 Click Add, and then click News to open the Internet Connection Wizard.

3 Type your name. Click Next to continue.

4 Read the information in each wizard dialog box, and then enter the required information. Click Next to continue.

5 In the final wizard dialog box, click Finish.

6 Click Close.

7 Click Yes to download a list of newsgroups available on that server.

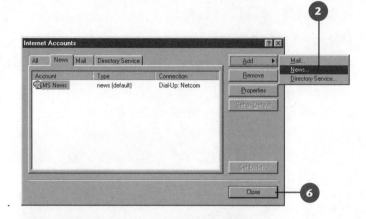

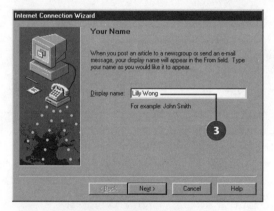

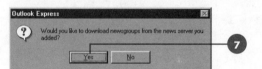

TIP

Name your news servers carefully. *The "friendly name" you assign a news server appears as a shortcut icon on the Outlook bar.*

Make Outlook Express the Default News Reader

1 Click the Tools menu, and then click Options.

2 Click the General tab.

3 Click the Make Outlook Express My Default News Reader check box to select it.

4 Click OK.

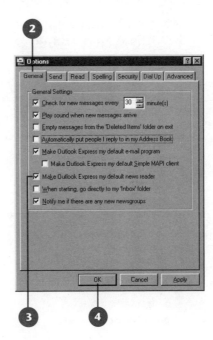

8

Subscribing to a Newsgroup

Subscribing to a newsgroup places a link to the group in the server folder, providing easy access to the newsgroup. You can subscribe to as many newsgroups as you'd like. If you find that you are no longer interested in a newsgroup, you can unsubscribe from it. Before you subscribe to a newsgroup, read some messages (called *articles*) and get a feel for the people and content. If you like what you see and want to regularly read or participate in the conversation threads, you can subscribe to it.

TIP

Why not subscribe now?
Outlook Express News prompts you to subscribe to newsgroups after you complete the Internet Connection Wizard.

View a Newsgroup Without Subscribing

1 Click a news server on the Folder list.

2 Click the News Groups button on the toolbar.

3 Click a newsgroup you want to view.

4 Click Go To.

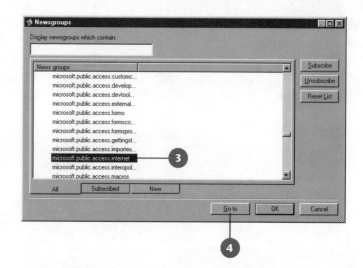

Subscribe to a Newsgroup

1 Right-click the newsgroup you want to subscribe to, and then click Subscribe To This Newsgroup on the shortcut menu.

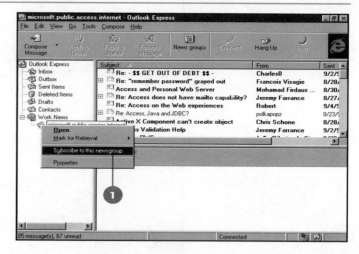

TRY THIS

View a subscribed
newsgroup. *Click a news server icon on the Folder list to access the subscribed newsgroup you want to view. Any message headers and messages stored on your hard drive appear. Note that if you are working offline you will need to retrieve new message headers or messages.*

Unsubscribe from a Newsgroup

1 Right-click the newsgroup.

2 Click Unsubscribe From This Newsgroup on the shortcut menu.

3 If necessary, click Yes to confirm the action.

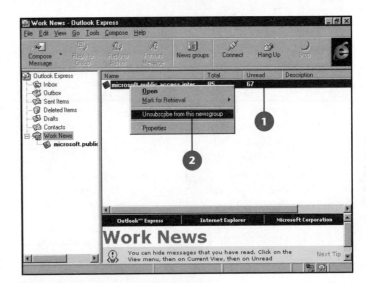

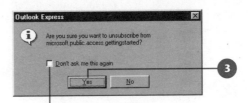

Click to select this check box if you do not want to confirm each time you unsubscribe from a newsgroup.

Reading the News

After retrieving new newsgroup messages or message headers, you need to open the newsgroup to display the messages and read them. In addition to clicking a message, you can use keyboard shortcuts in Outlook Express to move quickly from one message to another. You can save any message to your hard drive for future reference. Periodically, you should clear your hard drive of old messages to free up space.

TIP

Conversation threads. *A thread consists of the original message on a particular topic along with any responses that include the original message title preceded by "RE:".*

SEE ALSO

See "Working Offline" on page 148 for information about reading messages and message headers offline to avoid connect time.

Open and Read News Messages

1 Click the news server icon in the Folder list.

2 Double-click the newsgroup you want to read.

3 If necessary, click + (the plus sign) to the left of a message header to display all the reply headers for that message.

4 When you see a message or reply you want to read, click its header in the message list.

5 Read the message in the Preview pane.

6 Click the next message you want to read, or press a keyboard shortcut.

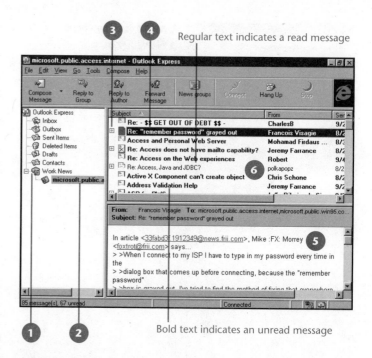

Regular text indicates a read message

Bold text indicates an unread message

MOVING BETWEEN MESSAGES	
Press	**To move to the**
Ctrl+>	Next message
Ctrl+<	Previous message
Ctrl+U	Next unread message
Ctrl+Shift+U	Next unread thread, skipping any remaining unread replies
Ctrl+J	Next unread newsgroup

TRY THIS

View only unread newsgroup messages. *To view only messages you haven't yet read, click the View menu, point to Current View, and then click Unread Messages. Those messages you have already read disappear.*

TRY THIS

Read a message in its own window. *Double-click, rather than single-click, the message header. When you are finished, click the Close button in the upper right corner of the window.*

TIP

Change the message preview time. *To change how long a message appears in the Preview pane before it is automatically marked as read (changed from bold type to regular type), click the Tools menu, and then click Options. Click the Read tab in the Options dialog box, change the value in the Message Is Read After Being Previewed For X Second(s) box, and then click OK.*

Save a Message

1 Click the message you want to save.

2 Click the File menu, and then click Save As.

3 Select a drive and folder.

4 Enter a new file name, if necessary.

5 Specify the file type.

6 Click Save.

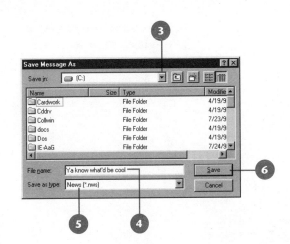

Delete Old News

1 Click the File menu, and then click Clean Up Files.

2 Select the news server or newsgroup that you want to clean up.

3 Click the button for the clean up option you want.

4 Click Close.

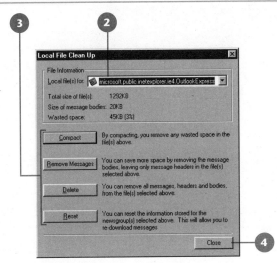

Finding a Particular Newsgroup or Message

When you add a news server account to Outlook Express, it retrieves a list of newsgroups available on that server. Often, this list is quite lengthy. Rather than scroll through the entire list looking for a particular topic, you can search the list for that topic. Similarly, you can look for a particular message or thread from all the messages you retrieved from a newsgroup. After you become familiar with a newsgroup, you might decide to *filter* out (that is, specify that you don't want to read) any message from a particular person, about a specific subject, of a certain length, or older than a number of days.

Search for Specific Types of Newsgroups

1 Click the News Groups button on the toolbar.

2 Type the word or phrase for which you want to search.

3 Click Go To to view the newsgroup.

4 Click Subscribe to suscribe to the newsgroup.

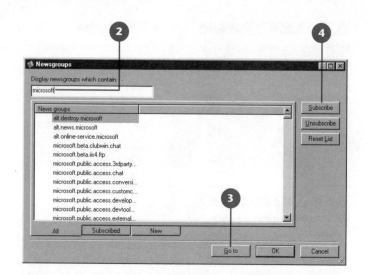

Find a Particular Newsgroup Message

1 Click the Edit menu, and then click Find Text.

2 Type the word or phrase you want to locate.

3 Click Find Next.

4 Click Cancel when you locate the message you want.

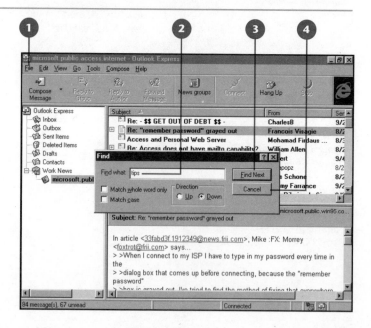

TIP

Can't find a newsgroup. *If the newsgroup for which you are searching doesn't appear, it might be located on another news server.*

TIP

Look and learn. *After you find a newsgroup you find interesting, spend some time getting to know the group before you join in. Read the current threads, and get a sense of the mood and accepted behavior of the group.*

TIP

Don't be filtered. *When you post a message, remember that it might be read by hundreds of people with different cultures and beliefs. Keep this in mind as you compose your messages.*

Filter Unwanted Newsgroup Messages

1 Click the Tools menu, and then click Newsgroup Filters.

2 Click Add.

3 Select the newsgroup or news server you want to filter.

4 Set your filter criteria.

5 Click OK.

6 Repeat steps 2 through 5 for each filter you want to set.

7 Click OK when you're finished.

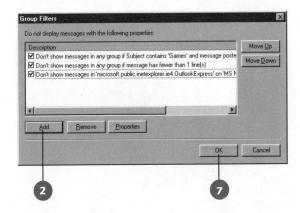

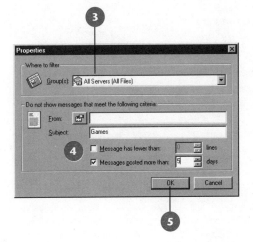

Posting Messages

Part of the fun of newsgroups is that you can participate in an ongoing discussion, respond privately to a message's author, or start a new thread yourself by posting your own message on a topic of interest to you. If you post a message to a newsgroup and then change your mind, you can cancel the message. Keep in mind that if someone has already downloaded the message, canceling the message will not remove it from that person's computer.

TIP

Name your messages carefully. *When you compose a message, choose a subject that accurately reflects the content of your message, so that people can decide whether they want to read it. When you reply to a message, don't change the subject line, so that the conversation will remain threaded.*

Post a New Message

1. Select the newsgroup to which you want to post a message.

2. Click the Compose Message button on the toolbar.

3. Type a subject for your message.

4. Type your message.

5. Click the Post Message button on the toolbar.

6. If necessary, click Yes to confirm your message was posted.

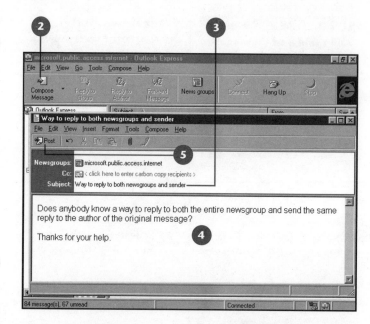

Cancel a Message

1. Select the newsgroup to which you posted the message.

2. Click the Compose menu, and then click Cancel Message.

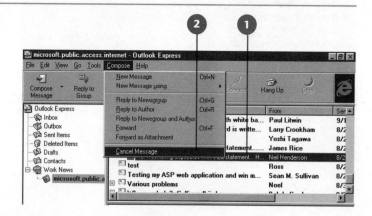

TRY THIS

Post a message to several newsgroups on the server. *You can post the same message to several newsgroups, as long as they are on the same server. When composing your message, click the Tools menu, click Select Newsgroups, click a newsgroup in the list, and then click Add; repeat for each additional newsgroup you want to add. Complete your message as usual.*

TIP

Create stationery for your newsgroup messages. *You can create stationery for your newsgroup messages just as you do for your e-mail messages. Click the Tools menu, click Stationery, click the News tab, set the options you want, such as changing the font or selecting a stationery pattern, and then click OK.*

TIP

Think before you post. *Respond to personal questions posted to a newsgroup directly to the author, not to the entire newsgroup.*

Reply to a Message

1 Click the message to which you want to reply.

2 Select the appropriate command:

◆ Click the Reply To Group button on the toolbar to post your response to the newsgroup.

◆ Click the Reply To Author button on the toolbar to send the message's author a private e-mail message.

◆ Click the Compose menu and then click Reply To Newsgroup And Author to reply to both the entire newsgroup and the message's author at once.

3 Type your message and delete parts of the original message that are unrelated to your reply.

4 Click the Post Message button on the toolbar.

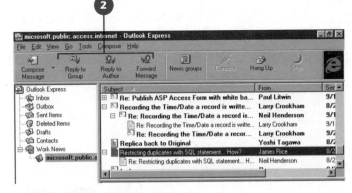

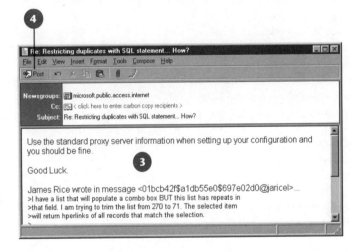

Reading Messages Offline

To keep your phone line free and reduce your Internet connection charges, you can read your newsgroup messages *offline*, while you are disconnected from the Internet. First you set Outlook Express to *download* (transfer to your computer) only the *headers* (message topics, authors, and dates) for newsgroups to which you are subscribed. Second you go online to download only the new message headers, disconnect from the Internet, and then peruse these headers offline. Third go back online to download only those messages that interest you.

SEE ALSO

See "Changing Outlook Express Message Options" on page 150 for more information about changing the number of retrieved message headers.

Set Outlook Express to Retrieve Only Headers

1. Right-click a newsgroup in the Preview pane.

2. Point to Mark For Retrieval on the shortcut menu.

3. Click New Headers.

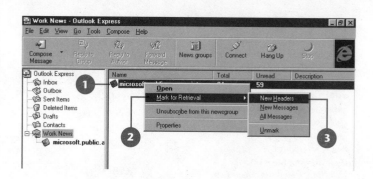

Download Newsgroup Headers

1. If necessary, switch to the News window.

2. Click the Tools menu.

3. Click Download All.

4. Double-click the newsgroup name in the News window to display the message headers.

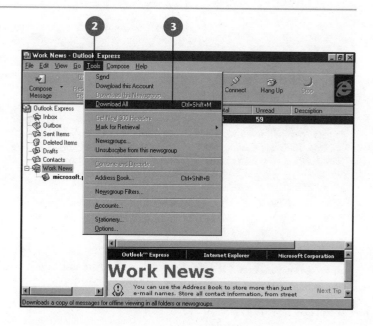

TIP

Read the news online. *If you use a network Internet service provider (ISP) that maintains a constant connection to the Internet, you can read and respond to newsgroup articles online without tying up resources or worrying about your connect time. Go to a newsgroup, read posted articles, and compose and send your responses without disconnecting.*

SEE ALSO

See "Subscribing to a Newsgroup" on page 140 for more information about viewing and joining newsgroups.

Download Interesting Messages

1. Right-click the header of a message you want to read.

2. Click Mark Message For Download on the shortcut menu.

3. Repeat for each message you want to retrieve.

4. Click the Tools menu, and then click Download All.

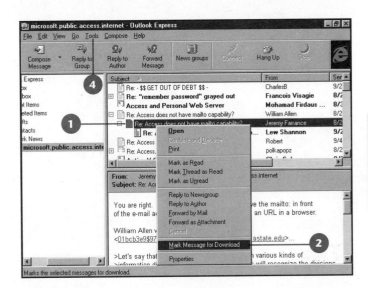

Compose Your Messages and Replies Offline

1. Compose your message or reply as usual.

2. Click the File menu, and then click Send Later.

3. If necessary, click OK.

4. When you are ready to send your messages, click Outbox on the Outlook bar, and then click the Send And Receive button on the toolbar.

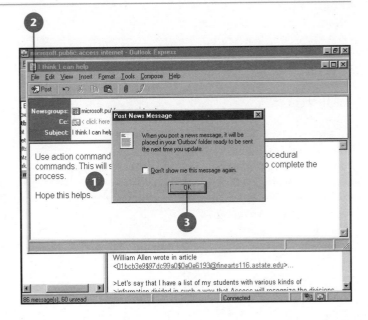

Changing Outlook Express Message Options

As you send and receive newsgroup and mail messages, you might find it easier to adjust some of the default settings. You might want to download a maximum number of newsgroup headers at a time to help control how long you spend online. You might also want to set how long newsgroup messages are stored on your hard drive before being deleted. In addition, you might want to *encode* a message, which compresses and splits a large message into several small ones, reducing the time needed to send and receive messages. Outlook Express can then recombine and decode these messages.

Set the Number of Message Headers to Download

1. Click the Tools menu, and then click Options.

2. Click the Read tab.

3. If necessary, click the Download X Headers At A Time check box to select it.

4. Enter a new value.

5. Click OK.

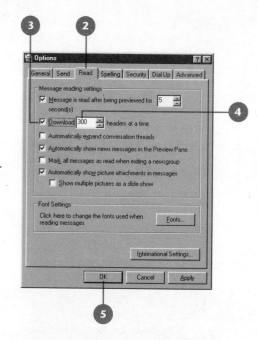

Change Message Storage Options

1. Click the Tools menu, and then click Options.

2. Click the Advanced tab.

3. Change the options in the Local Message Files area as needed.

4. Click OK.

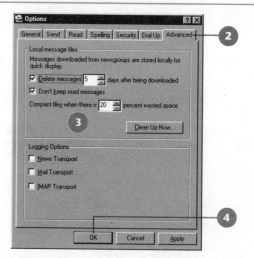

TIP

Size limit for messages.
Many mail and news servers limit each message, including any attachments, to 1 MB per message.

SEE ALSO

See "Reading the News" on page 142 for more information about deleting outdated messages from your hard drive.

Encode Large Messages

1 Click the Tools menu, and then click Accounts.

2 Click the Mail tab or the News tab.

3 Click the account for which you want to set the message size.

4 Click Properties.

5 Click the Advanced tab.

6 Click the Break Apart Messages Larger Than X KB check box to select it.

7 Enter a file size.

8 Click OK.

9 Click Close.

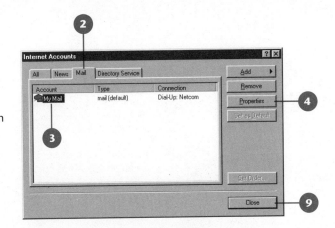

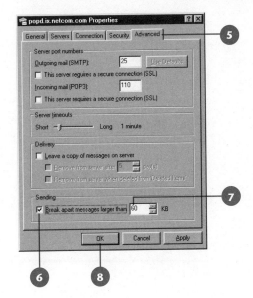

8

Customizing the Outlook Express Window

As you work in Outlook Express, you'll find that you use some commands very frequently and others not so frequently. You can customize the toolbar so that it displays only those buttons you find most useful. Similarly, you can add other columns to the message pane or remove any columns that appear by default. In this way, you can tailor Outlook Express to suit your needs and reflect your style of working.

TRY THIS

Move the toolbar. *You can move the toolbar to any edge of your screen. Right-click the toolbar, point to Align, and then click Left, Right, Top, or Bottom.*

Customize the Toolbar

1. Right-click the toolbar.

2. Click Buttons on the shortcut menu.

3. Double-click a button in the Available Buttons list to add it to the toolbar.

4. Double-click a button in the Toolbar Buttons list to remove it from the toolbar.

5. Click Close.

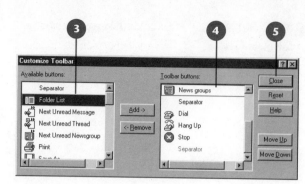

Customize the Columns in the Message Pane

1. From any Mail or News window, click the View menu, and then click Columns.

2. Double-click a column name in the Available Columns list to add it to the pane.

3. Double-click a column name in the Displayed Columns list to remove it from the pane.

4. Click OK.

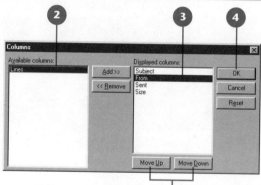

Click to reorder displayed columns.

Customize the Outlook window to display the Outlook Bar. *Click the View menu, click Layout, click the Outlook Bar check box to select it, click the Folder List check box to deselect it, and then click OK.*

Outlook Bar

Customize the Outlook Window Layout

1 Click the View menu, and then click Layout.

2 Click one or more of the check boxes in the Basic area to show or hide elements of the Outlook Express window.

3 Click one of the option buttons in the Toolbar area to position the Outlook toolbar on the screen.

4 Click Customize Buttons to add or remove a toolbar button, or change a toolbar button's position on the Outlook toolbar.

5 Click an option in the Preview Pane area to customize how your Preview pane looks.

6 Click OK.

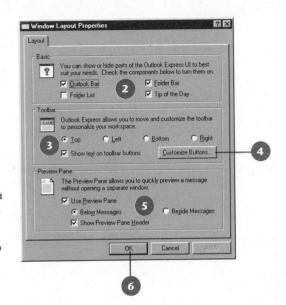

Getting a Personal Certificate

Internet Explorer uses the latest online security so you can securely send information over the Internet. The security system prevents anyone from eavesdropping on your communications as you send e-mail, purchase consumer goods, and conduct personal banking over the Internet. The Internet security is provided through encryption and certificates, or Digitial IDs. You can get a Digital ID to verify your personal identity through a credentials agency such as VeriSign. In Outlook Express, you can encrypt the messages you send and be assured that the e-mail you receive is from a valid source.

TIP

How do you know a Web site is secure? *Internet Explorer displays a lock icon in the Status bar.*

Get a Persoanal Certificate

1. Click the Tools menu, click Options, and then click the Security tab.

2. Click Get Digital ID.

    The Microsoft Digital ID Web page is displayed in Internet Explorer.

3. Scroll down, and then click the VeriSign link.

4. Complete the Digital ID form, read the subscriber agreement, and then click Accept. Click Next to accept the security setting.

5. Select a cryptographic provider. Click Next to continue.

6. Type a name for your personal key, and then click Finish.

7. Start Outlook Express, and check your inbox for a digital e-mail confirmation.

8. Open the confirmation e-mail and then follow the instructions to install your certificate.

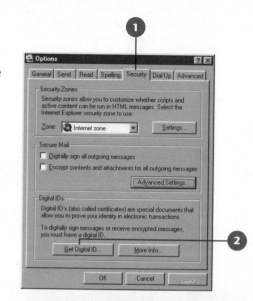

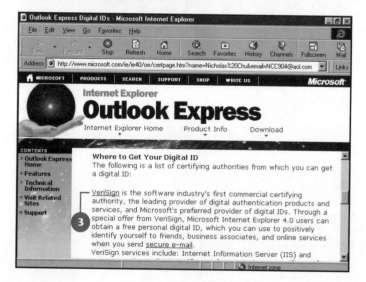

Using NetMeeting to Communicate

NetMeeting delivers solutions right to your desktop computer, bringing group communication and conferencing to a whole new level, for both business and personal purposes. Imagine the following scenarios:

◆ You just received the last quarter's sales figures and want to show them to your company's sales staff, based around the country. Rather than fly everyone to a central location, you host a conference via computer so everyone can see your spreadsheet and ask questions about it.

◆ Your daughter is studying in Italy during her junior year at college. Every month you arrange a video teleconference so you can talk to and see each other, helping to alleviate her homesickness and enabling you to share in her experiences.

◆ You have a brainstorm for a new car for your toy company. You contact your designer, who lives downstate, via computer and sketch your idea on a virtual notepad. He adds other details to the sketch that enhance it even more. Together you've created a top seller.

Understanding Internet User Location Service

What Is ULS?

Microsoft Internet User Location Service, or ULS, enables you to find people who are currently connected to a ULS server or Web site on the Internet or an intranet and to communicate with them in real-time.

You can use ULS on the Internet to find and connect to people around the world, or if you are working on an intranet, you can use it to easily locate and contact your colleagues.

How Does ULS Work?

A ULS server is a computer that keeps track of people who are using NetMeeting. A ULS server compiles a changing database of the correct IP addresses, or computer names, for people who are currently connected to an Internet or an intranet server. An *IP address* is a series of numbers that identifies the unique location of a person's computer on a specific Internet host computer or network server. When you start NetMeeting and connect to a ULS server, the server locates your IP address. To place a call, you just select a name from the NetMeeting Directory or from a Web site that contains links to other people's computers. ULS transfers the needed IP addresses between your computers to establish the connection, and then the call is placed.

Unlike your personal Address Book, which stores on your disk or hard drive a database of unchanging information that you enter, the ULS database is stored in RAM and is constantly updated as people connect to and disconnect from the Web site or service.

NetMeeting Directory   User Location Server

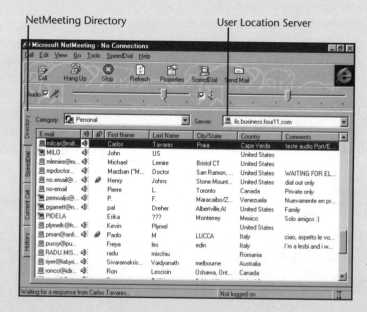

Who Needs ULS?

You do. Although NetMeeting doesn't need an ULS server to work, ULS makes it easier for NetMeeting users to locate and connect to each other so they can exchange sound, images, and data. Without ULS, you could connect directly to someone if you know that person's IP address, but many people don't know their own IP addresses, and those addresses can change every time they restart their computers on the network.

Where Can You Find ULS?

You can view the ULS directory from within NetMeeting or from a Web page and review a list of people currently running NetMeeting.

When you start NetMeeting for the first time, a wizard helps you set up your connection to a Microsoft ULS server or one that you supply. When you start NetMeeting, you can also select another ULS directory from a list of ULS servers.

NetMeeting setup dialog box

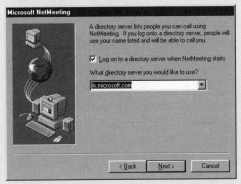

Once you are connected, you can use NetMeeting to communicate with Internet *telephony* (a technology that enables you to transmit voice and data between computers), conduct a video conference, or collaborate on shared applications.

Starting NetMeeting

Like other Windows programs, to start NetMeeting, you use the Start button. The first time you start NetMeeting, a wizard helps you set up your directory listing. You will be asked to supply your name, your e-mail address, your city and state, the type of meetings you will conduct, and the directory server, or User Location Server, you plan to use. This information is listed in the NetMeeting Directory, which others can use to find you, and is visible to those with whom you are meeting.

SEE ALSO

See "Changing Directory Settings" on page 162 for information on changing NetMetting Directory information.

Start NetMeeting

1 Click the Start button on the taskbar.

2 Point to Programs.

3 Point to Internet Explorer.

4 Click Microsoft NetMeeting.

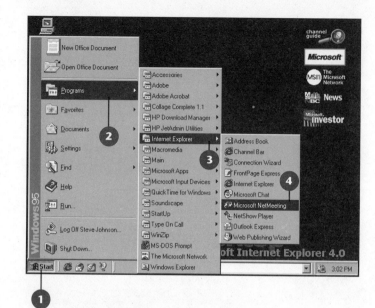

Start NetMeeting for the First Time

1 Click the Start button on the taskbar.

2 Point to Programs.

3 Point to Internet Explorer.

4 Click Microsoft NetMeeting.

5 Click Next to continue.

6 Click the Directory Server drop-down arrow, and then select a User Location Server. Click Next to continue.

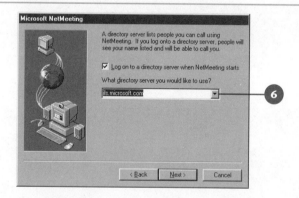

TIP

The faster the better.
*NetMeeting works best with a
fast Internet connection—a
28.8 or faster modem—or a
local area network.*

SEE ALSO

*See "Communicating with
Audio and Video" on page 168
for more information about
setting up NetMeeting.*

7 Fill in your first name, last
name, and e-mail address.
Click Next to continue.

8 Select the option button
for the way you want your
information categorized.
Click Next to continue.

9 Click Next to continue.

10 Specify the speed of your
connection. Click Next to
continue.

11 Click Next to tune your
audio settings.

12 Click Start Recording to
test your audio settings.
Click Next to continue.

13 Click Finish.

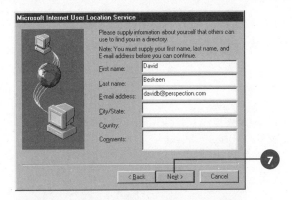

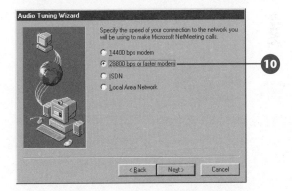

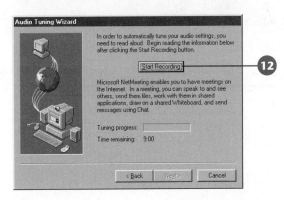

9

Viewing the NetMeeting Window

NetMeeting is a great way to communicate with a group of as many as 32 people, even if they are in a different city, state, or country. Depending on your specific needs and your resources, you can converse, exchange video images, work together on programs, type messages, and even draw together.

To provide you the most flexibility and to meet all of your conferencing needs, the NetMeeting program window is organized by tabs for different kinds of tasks. A menu bar and toolbar keep the appropriate tools and commands available at all times.

NetMeeting

Directory Tab

The Directory tab shows everyone with whom you can meet at any given moment and the resources they have available—voice, video, or file transfer. It's perfect for finding out who is available and who is currently in a call.

SpeedDial Tab

The SpeedDial tab lists the addresses of people who accepted your call and those whose calls you accepted along with any address you saved manually. It's a timesaver for dialing your frequent contacts.

Current Call Tab

The Current Call tab provides information about the person with whom you are meeting at that moment. On this tab you also can send files to others, transmit video and audio with someone, and start the Whiteboard or Chat. This tab helps you keep track of people and resources during a meeting.

History Tab

The History tab logs all the calls you have received by the name of the caller, whether you took the call, and the time the call came in. It's useful for determining how you spend your time.

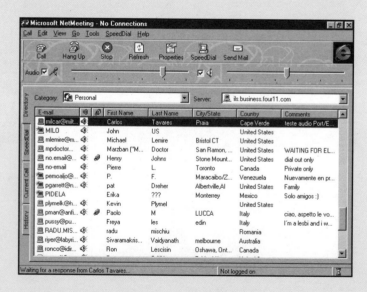

Whiteboard Program

The Whiteboard is a program that provides a place for all meeting participants to write, draw, or type ideas. It's great for showing agendas, brainstorming solutions, or illustrating concepts.

Chat Program

Chat is a program that provides a place where all meeting participants can type and send messages to each other. This tool makes it easy for everyone to contribute to a meeting.

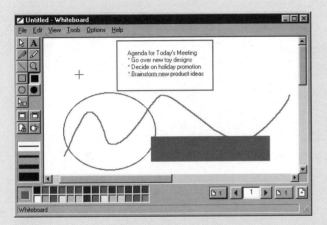

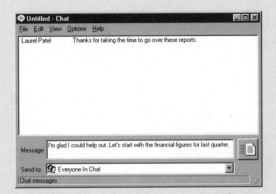

9

Changing Directory Settings

The information you supplied during the NetMeeting setup is listed in the NetMeeting Directory, which others can use to find you, and is visible to those with whom you are meeting. You can easily change or update your directory listing at any time with a new name, address, e-mail address, or other important information. You can also specify that your name not be listed in the directory. You can change whether you connect to the directory server as you start NetMeeting or manually during your session.

Change Your Directory Listing

1 Click the Call menu, and then click Change My Information.

2 If necessary, change your name, e-mail address, or location.

3 Click the option button that describes how you want to categorize your information.

4 Click OK.

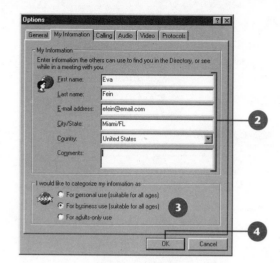

Remove Your Name from the Directory

1 Click the Tools menu, and then click Options.

2 Click the Calling tab.

3 In the Directory area, click the Do Not List My Name In The Directory. People Can Call Me If They Know My E-Mail Name check box to select it.

4 Click OK.

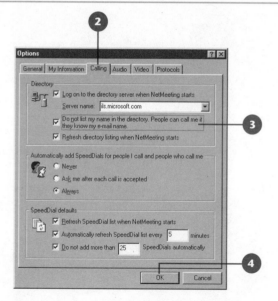

TIP

Going unlisted. *You can still receive calls if you are unlisted, but the person who calls you must know your address.*

TIP

Log on and off manually. *If you communicate using a modem, you might want to log on and off manually. Click the Call menu, and then click Log On To Your Directory Server or Log Off From Your Directory Server.*

Change How You Connect to the Directory Server

1 Click the Tools menu, and then click Options.

2 Click the Calling tab.

3 In the Directory area, click the Log On To The Directory Server When NetMeeting Starts check box to select it if you want to connect automatically.

4 Click the Server Name drop-down arrow, and then click a server.

5 Click OK.

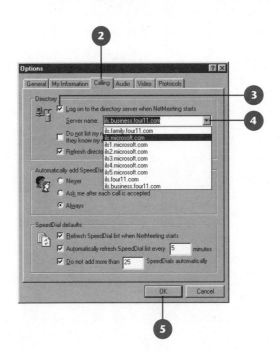

Making and Receiving a Call

NetMeeting makes interacting with people simple. The Directory tab lists everyone who is connected to the selected server and running NetMeeting. You can call someone on that list or switch to another directory server. In addition, you can call anyone for whom you know the e-mail address, network address, modem phone number, or IP address (also known as the *computer name*), indicating the exact location of that person's computer. As long as you are logged onto your directory server, you will receive calls from other people. You can decide to answer these calls on a case-by-case basis or accept all calls. No matter who placed the original call, you can disconnect at any time.

Make a Directory Call

1. If necessary, click the Directory tab.

2. Click the Server drop-down arrow, and then click a server.

3. Double-click the name of the person you want to call.

   A star burst or gleam in the e-mail name computer icon indicates the person is currently in a call.

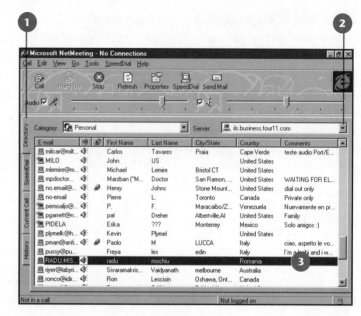

Place a Call Manually

1. Click the Call button on the toolbar.

2. Type the e-mail address, IP address, network address, or modem phone number of the person you want to call.

3. Click the Call Using drop-down arrow, and then click the type of connection you want to use to make the call.

4. Click Call.

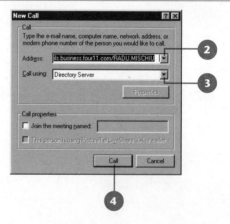

TRY THIS

Place a call quickly. *Double-click the name of the person you want to call from the list on the Directory tab, the SpeedDial tab, or the History tab.*

TIP

Do not disturb. *If you are connected to your directory server but do not want to receive incoming calls, click the Call menu, and then click Do Not Disturb. If necessary, click OK in the dialog box to confirm the block on your line. When you are ready to receive calls, just repeat the process to reverse it.*

TIP

Busy signal? Try e-mail. *If your call does not connect, you can send the person you have called an e-mail message instead. Click Yes in the NetMeeting dialog box, type your message, verify that the address is correct, and then click the Send Mail button on the toolbar.*

TRY THIS

Cancel a call. *If you are placing a call and change your mind, you can hang up before the other person answers by clicking the Stop button on the toolbar.*

Answer a Call

When you receive a call, a dialog box appears. Choose one of the following options:

◆ Click Accept to take the call.

◆ Click Ignore to not take the call.

Accept All Calls

1 Click the Tools menu, and then click Options.

2 Click the General tab.

3 Click the Automatically Accept Incoming Calls check box to select it.

4 Click OK.

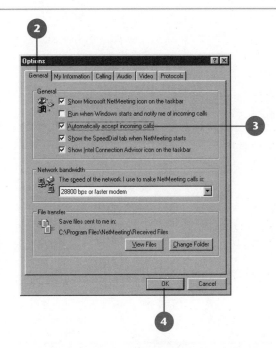

End a Call

1 Click the Hang Up button on the toolbar.

9

Conferencing with People

With NetMeeting you can meet with more than one person at a time. If you host a meeting, each person who attends calls you at the appointed time. If you want to join a scheduled meeting, you simply call the person who is hosting the meeting. A meeting that is hosted by a third party conferencing service, such as a telephone company or a teleconferencing company, is called a *named meeting*. To join a named meeting, you need to know the name of the meeting as well as that of the *conference bridge*, the server where the meeting is held.

TIP

What happens when you hang up? *If you call someone, clicking the Hang Up button on the toolbar simply disconnects you. If you are hosting a meeting, you disconnect everyone who called you.*

Host a Meeting

1 Notify all invitees of the meeting time.

2 Click the Call menu, and then click Host Meeting.

3 If necessary, click OK.

4 Wait for participants to call at scheduled time.

5 Click Accept when each person calls.

Join a Meeting in Progress

1 Click the Call button on the toolbar.

2 Type the address of the person hosting the meeting.

3 Click the Call Using drop-down arrow, and then click the type of connection you want to use to make the call.

4 If necessary, click the Join The Meeting Named check box to select it, and then type the meeting name.

5 Click Call.

Click if you don't want to confirm each meeting.

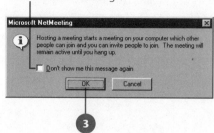

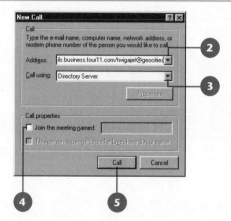

Using SpeedDial Shortcuts

SpeedDial saves the names and computer locations of all the people who accept your calls and those whose calls you accept, plus any entries you add manually. It creates a list, located on the SpeedDial tab, that provides a shortcut for contacting these people. If you don't want names added to your SpeedDial list automatically, you must change the SpeedDial settings.

TIP

Share your SpeedDial shortcut. *Send others your SpeedDial shortcut to make it easier for them to reach you. Click the SpeedDial button on the toolbar, type your IP address, select the connection you want people to use, click the Save On The Desktop option button, and then click OK. Right-click the SpeedDial shortcut on your desktop, click Send To, click Mail Recipient, and then complete and send the message as usual.*

Add People to Your SpeedDial List

1 Click the SpeedDial button on the toolbar.

2 Type the address of the computer you will call.

3 Click the Call Using drop-down arrow, and then click the type of connection you want to use to make the call.

4 Click the Add To SpeedDial List option button to select it.

5 Click OK.

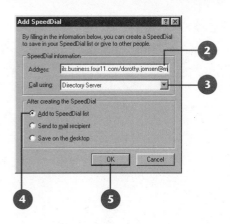

Change Your SpeedDial Settings

1 Click the Tools menu, and then click Options.

2 Click the Calling tab.

3 Click the option button for the Add SpeedDial option you want.

4 Click the check boxes for the SpeedDial defaults you want.

5 Click OK.

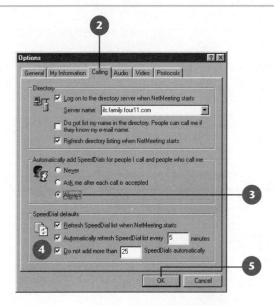

9

Communicating with Audio and Video

The first time you start NetMeeting, the Audio Tuning Wizard will optimize your audio settings to ensure you are heard clearly by having you read aloud. If your audio quality deteriorates, you might need to retune the audio settings. When you make or receive a call, NetMeeting begins to transmit audio and video, providing your computer has the requisite hardware. You can control when you send or receive video during a call by changing the video options to manual. Each person can send and receive audio and video with only one person at a time in a meeting, although several pairs of people can exchange audio and video at once. You can switch the connection from one person to another at any time during a meeting.

Tune Your Audio

1 Click the Hang Up button on the toolbar to ensure you are disconnected from any NetMeeting calls.

2 Click the Tools menu, and then click Audio Tuning Wizard.

3 Read each of the Audio Tuning Wizard dialog boxes. Click Next to continue.

4 Follow the wizard's instructions, and then click Finish.

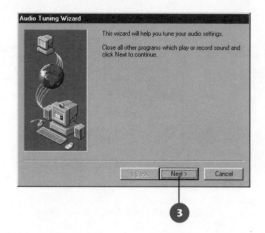

Send and Receive Video Manually

1 Click the Tools menu, and then click Options

2 Click the Video tab.

3 If necessary, click the Automatically Send Video At The Start Of Each Call check box to deselect it.

4 If necessary, click the Automatically Receive Video At The Start Of Each Call check box to deselect it.

5 Click OK.

6 To send or receive video during a call, click the appropriate Play button.

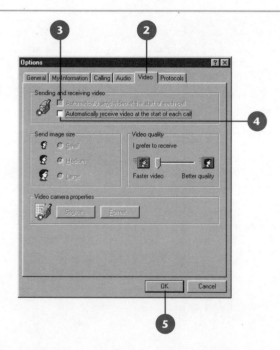

TIP

Preview your video. *Before you place your call, you can see the video you intend to send or verify that your equipment is working. Click the Current Call tab on the NetMeeting window, and then click the Play button in the My Video window. If you are previewing an image while you place or receive a call, the video will immediately be sent.*

TIP

Speaker volume is adjustable. *Drag the Speaker Volume slider on the toolbar to adjust the volume. To mute the speakers, click the Turn On/Off Speaker check box on the toolbar to deselect it. Click the check box again hear the audio again.*

TIP

Microphone volume is adjustable. *Drag the Microphone Volume slider on the toolbar to adjust the volume. To mute your voice, click the Turn On/Off Microphone check box on the toolbar to deselect it. Click the check box again to resume transmitting your voice.*

Switch Your Connection

1 Click the Switch button on the toolbar.

2 Click the person whom you want to talk to and see.

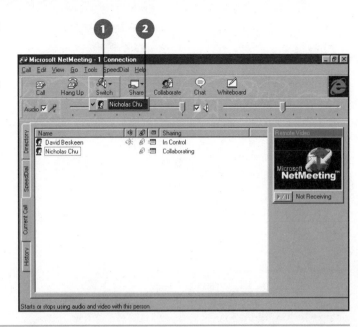

Turn Off Audio or Video

1 If necessary, click the Current Call tab.

2 Click the audio icon or the video icon next to the name of the person to whom you want to stop sending audio or video.

3 Click Stop Using Audio And Video.

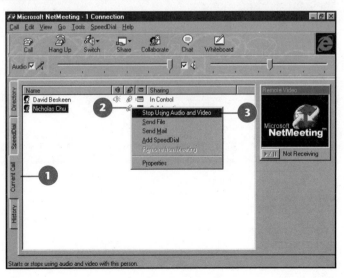

Exchanging Chat Messages

NetMeeting Chat enables all meeting participants to exchange typed messages, which is helpful when more than two people attend a meeting. As soon as one person in the meeting starts Chat, it appears on everyone's screens. Each participant can then type messages to send the others. Every message appears in the Chat window, identified by the sender's name along with the date and time, if you choose. You can also change how a message will display within the Chat window.

TRY THIS

Whisper to a friend. *You can send a message to just one person in a meeting—called a whisper—by clicking that person's name in the Send To list before pressing Enter.*

Start Chatting

1 If necessary, click the Current Call tab.

2 Click the Chat button on the toolbar.

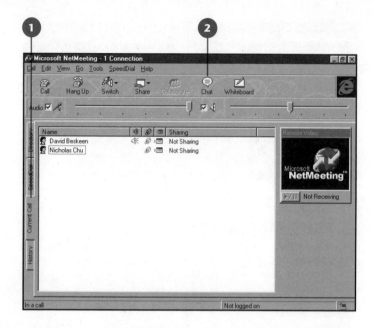

Send a Chat Message

1 Switch to the Chat window.

2 Type your message.

3 Click Send or press Enter to send the message.

TRY THIS

Personalize your chat style. *You can change the font, style, size, and color in which messages are displayed. Click the Options menu in the Chat window, click Font, select the font options and colors you want, and then click OK.*

TIP

Store chat files. *You can save and print all the Chat messages from a meeting by clicking the File menu, and then clicking Save, Save As, or Print. Chat files are saved with a .TXT (text file) extension; you can open them in Notepad, WordPad, Word, or another program that reads text format files.*

TIP

Collaboration and chat. *If you are collaborating in a meeting and if someone has taken control of the shared application, you will not be able to type in the Chat window.*

SEE ALSO

See "Sharing Applications" on page 174 for more information about collaborating in a meeting.

Change the Message Display

1 If necessary, switch to the Chat window.

2 Click the Options menu, and then click Chat Format.

3 Click to select or deselect check boxes next to the options that control how much information appears about your Chat messages.

4 Click the option button next to the format in which you want your Chat messages to appear.

5 Click OK.

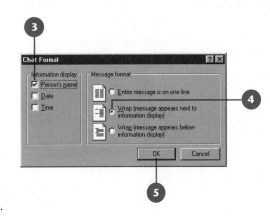

Exit Chat

1 Click the Close button in the upper right corner of the Chat window.

2 Click Yes or No to save or not save the current list of messages.

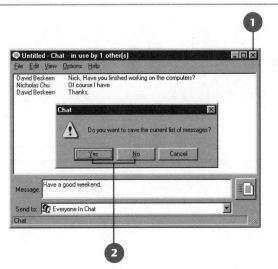

Using the Whiteboard

The Whiteboard is a virtual notepad that everyone in a NetMeeting conference can use for jotting down notes and illustrating ideas during a meeting. As soon as one person in the meeting opens the Whiteboard, it appears on everyone's screen. Each participant can then write or draw on the board, and see what others have contributed. The Whiteboard has a variety of tools that you can use to type text, write with a pen, draw lines and shapes, or highlight objects on the board. If a page becomes filled, you can erase unneeded objects from the board, or insert additional pages.

TIP

Exit Whiteboard. *Click the Close button in the upper right corner of the Whiteboard window, and then click the save option you want.*

Start and Use the Whiteboard

1. If necessary, click the Current Call tab.

2. Click the Whiteboard button on the toolbar.

3. Click the appropriate tool in the toolbox.

4. If necessary, click the Font Options button to change the font, size, or style of text; click a new color in the color palette; or click a different line weight.

5. Click in the Whiteboard, and then type text, or drag the pointer to draw the line or shape you want.

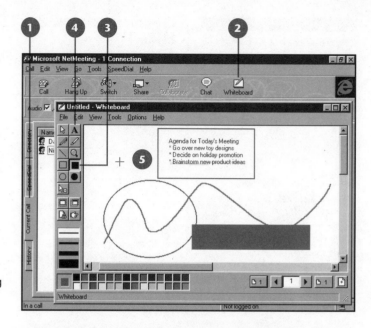

Work with Multiple Pages

◆ To add a page, click the Insert New Page button.

◆ To move to a different page, click the Previous Page button, the Next Page button, the First Page button, or the Last Page button.

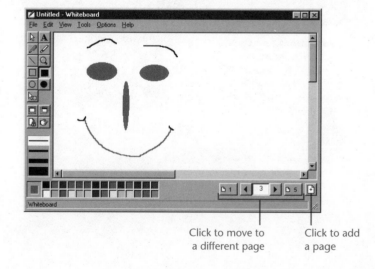

Click to move to a different page

Click to add a page

TIP

Lock the Whiteboard. *You can prevent other meeting participants from changing elements on the Whiteboard by clicking the Lock Contents tool in the toolbox. Click the tool again to allow others access.*

TIP

Erase the current page. *You can completely erase a page on the Whiteboard by moving to the page, and then pressing Ctrl+Del.*

TIP

Make a point. *During a meeting you can point to any object on the Whiteboard. Click the Remote Pointer tool in the toolbox, click the Selector tool, and then drag the pointer to the desired location. Click the Remote Pointer tool again to hide the pointer.*

Erase Elements on the Whiteboard

1 Click the Eraser tool in the toolbox.

2 Click the text block or drawn object you want to delete.

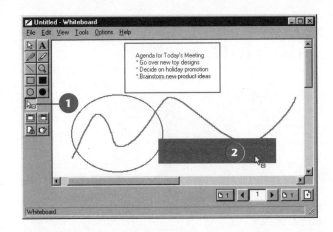

USING WHITEBOARD TOOLS	
Button	**Purpose**
	Select objects
	Type text
	Draw free-form lines with the selected color and line width
	Draw free-form lines with the selected highlight color and line width
	Draw straight lines with the selected line width
	Draw rectangular shapes with the selected line width
	Draw solid rectangular shapes
	Draw elliptical shapes with the selected line width
	Draw solid elliptical shapes
	Select an area and paste the contents into the Whiteboard
	Select the entire window and paste the contents into the Whiteboard

9

Sharing Applications

During a call, whether with one person or several, you can start and then share any program available on your computer. When you share an application, you are the only person who can work on the file—the others can only watch. You can also *collaborate* with other people to enable them to work in your program as well, although only one person at a time can control the cursor. Similarly, you can collaborate to work in someone else's application; however, they retain the results of the file you worked on. If you are sharing one of your applications, you can stop sharing it any time you choose.

> **TIP**
>
> **Three's company.** *Only three people at a time can share an application and collaborate on the work in progress.*

Share an Application

1. During a call, start the application and open document you want to share in the usual way.

2. Click the Current Call tab.

3. Click the Share button on the toolbar, and then click to select the application you want other people to share.

4. If necessary, click OK.

5. Display the application.

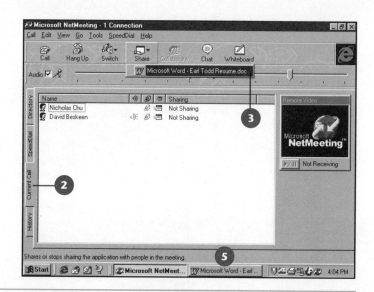

Let Others Work with Your Application

1. During a call, select an application to share.

2. Click the Collaborate button on the toolbar.

3. If necessary, click OK.

4. Start or display the application window to control the cursor.

5. Tell others who want to work in the application to click the Collaborate button on the toolbar.

6. When you are finished, click the Stop Collaborate button on the toolbar.

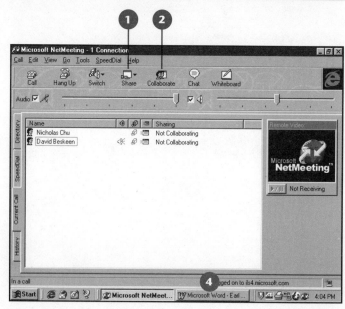

TRY THIS

Share your results. *After collaborating on a file, distribute the final file to all participants, or have the person who shared an application distribute the final file to all participants.*

SEE ALSO

See "Sending and Receiving Files" on page 176 for more information about sending a file to others.

TIP

The Clipboard is fair game. *When you are in a meeting, whether you are sharing an application or not, anything you cut or copy to the Clipboard can be pasted by all those in the meeting into applications on their computers.*

Work with Someone Else's Application

1 During a call, click the Collaborate button on the toolbar.

2 Double-click the application window to control the cursor.

3 When you are finished collaborating, click the Stop Collaborate button on the toolbar or press Esc.

Stop Sharing Your Application

1 If necessary, click the Current Call tab.

2 Click the Share button on the toolbar, and then click the name of the application you no longer want to share.

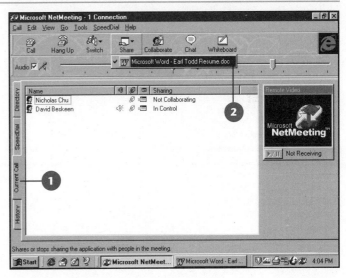

9

Sending and Receiving Files

During a call, all participants can send or receive files with just a few mouse clicks. Any files you send automatically go to everyone who is participating in the meeting. Likewise, other meeting participants can send you files during a meeting. You can specify the exact location on your computer where you want these files sent. With NetMeeting open, you can quickly open any file you have received from someone else during a meeting, whether or not the meeting is still in progress.

TIP
What if you want to send a file to only one person?
Right-click the person's name in the list on the Current Call tab in the NetMeeting window, click Send File on the shortcut menu, and then double-click the file you want to send.

Send a File

1. During a call, click the Tools menu, point to File Transfer, and then click Send File.

2. Locate the file you want to send.

3. Select the file you want to send.

4. Click Send.

5. Click OK.

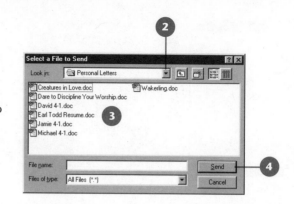

Open a File You Have Received

1. Click the Tools menu.

2. Point to File Transfer.

3. Click Open Received Files Folder.

4. Click any file to open it.

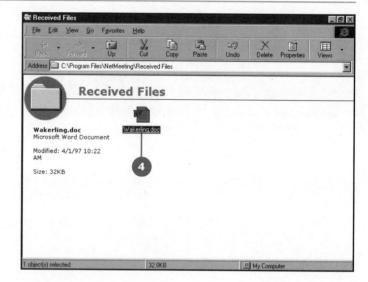

SEE ALSO

See "Browsing the Web and Your Local Hard Drive" on page 16 for more information about opening files with the Active Desktop installed.

SEE ALSO

See "Using the Smart Toolbar" on page 72 for more information about Navigating with the Smart Toolbar.

TIP

Keep Your Files Organized.
You should promptly move any files you receive during a meeting to another folder according to your filing system so you can quickly and easily find material later.

TRY THIS

Assign an official note taker. *Assign someone to take notes during a meeting to record items discussed, decisions made, and actions required. Before any participants hang up, have the person taking notes send the file to everyone.*

Set a Location for Receiving Files

1 Click the Tools menu, and then click Options.

2 Click the General tab.

3 Click Change Folder.

4 Select the folder where you want to save files you receive.

5 Click OK to confirm the new folder location.

6 Click OK.

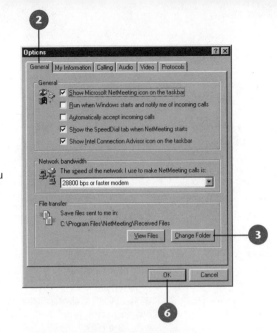

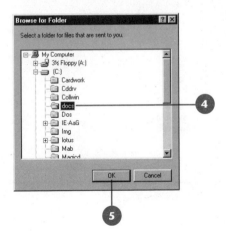

9

Chatting for Fun

Did you ever want to be a part of a real live comic strip? Now you can! Microsoft Chat enables you to converse with others over the Internet, but with a twist—each participant appears in a comic strip as a character. You choose what you want to look like, the nickname you want to be called, and enter other information that your fellow chatters can view. When you're ready, enter a chat room to become part of an existing comic strip. To participate, just type out your remarks, choose a facial expression, and then post your image, text, and even sound to the current comic strip panel.

SEE ALSO

See "Changing Your Chat Character" on page 180 for information on changing Microsoft Chat options.

Start Microsoft Chat and Join a Chat

1 Connect to the Internet, click the Start button on the taskbar, point to Programs, and then click Microsoft Chat.

2 If necessary, enter your nickname, and then click OK.

3 Click the Server drop-down arrow, and then select a comic server.

4 If you know the chat room you want to enter, click the Go To Chat Room option button, and then enter the chat room name.

5 If you want to see a list of available chat rooms, click the Show All Available Chat Rooms option button.

6 Click OK.

7 If you selected the Show All Available Chat Rooms option, double-click the chat room you want to enter.

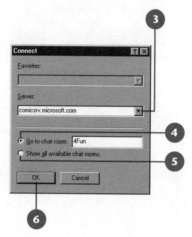

Gesture as you speak. *The words you type can change the pose and expression of your character. Try starting a sentence with I or you, typing in all capital letters, or using e-mail shorthand such as :).*

Record your favorite sayings. *Assign your favorite expressions to a keyboard shortcut so you can quickly send a phrase at the appropriate moment without having to retype it. Click the View menu, click Options, and click the Automation tab. In the Macros area, type your saying in the box, select a Key Combination from the drop-down list, name your saying, click Add Macro, and then click OK. In a chat, press the key combination to send this recorded message.*

Start a Chat

1 If necessary, click the Connect button on the toolbar to connect to the Comic Chat server.

2 If you want to switch rooms, click the Room menu, click Room List, and then double-click a room.

3 If you want, click a character to include in the frame.

4 Click a facial expression in the emotion palette.

5 Type your remarks.

6 Click one of the following buttons:

◆ Say–to insert your remarks in a speech bubble.

◆ Think—to insert your remarks in a thought bubble.

◆ Whisper—to send your remarks to only one character.

◆ Action—to insert your nickname and remarks in a box at the top of the panel.

◆ Sound—to send a sound clip along with your remarks.

9

Changing Your Chat Character

With Microsoft Chat, you choose what your comic strip character looks like and the background of the comic strip. If you want, you can also enter personal information that your fellow chatters can view. Experiment with different characters and backgrounds. Have some fun!

SEE ALSO

See "Chatting for Fun" on page 178 for information on starting Microsoft Chat and joining a chat.

TIP

More panels, please. *To change the number of panels displayed horizontally, click the View menu, click Options, click the Comics View tab, click the Page Layout drop-down arrow, select a new panel width for the comic strip, and then click OK.*

Change Your Comic Strip Settings

1. Click the View menu, and then click Options.

2. Click the Personal Info tab.

3. Enter the information you want others in the chat to know about you.

4. Click the Character tab.

5. Click the character you want to be.

6. Click the Background tab.

7. Click a background for the comic strip.

8. Click OK.

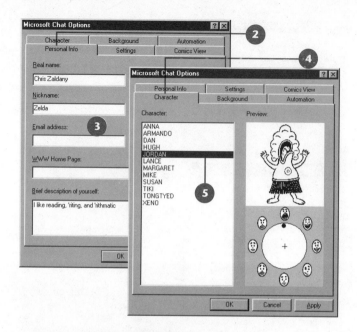

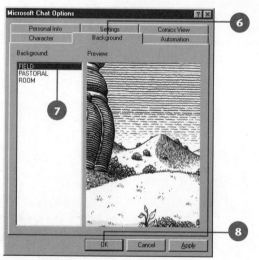

Creating a Web Page with FrontPage Express

W hether you need to create a Web page from scratch or modify an existing one, FrontPage Express can help you produce the results you need quickly and easily.

Introducing FrontPage Express

Microsoft FrontPage Express is a Web page editor that gives you full access to the power of HTML (Hypertext Markup Language) in an easy-to-use interface. With FrontPage Express you can create Web pages from scratch by filling blank Web pages with text, graphic images, hyperlinks, and other information, or from wizards by following step-by-step instructions. When you are done working with your Web pages, you can set them up for printing, and then finally print and save them.

FrontPage Express works very much like a word processing program. So if you've used a word processing program before, particularly Microsoft Word, you'll find FrontPage Express easy to learn and use. If you've used Microsoft FrontPage Editor, you already know how to use FrontPage Express. FrontPage Express offers many of the features of the Microsoft FrontPage Editor in a smaller package.

Starting FrontPage Express

Start FrontPage Express to begin creating your first Web page. You can start FrontPage Express from the Start menu on the taskbar. When FrontPage Express starts, it displays a blank new Web page so that you can begin working immediately.

SEE ALSO

See "Opening a Web Page" on page 188 for information about opening an existing Web page.

SEE ALSO

See "Creating a Web Page Using Templates and Wizards" on page 186 for information about using one of the Web page templates or wizards.

FrontPage Express

Start FrontPage Express from the Start Menu

1. Click the Start button on the taskbar to display the Start menu.

2. Point to Programs to display the Programs menu.

3. Point to Internet Explorer to display the Internet Explorer menu.

4. Click FrontPage Express.

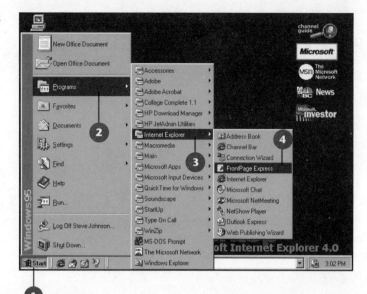

Viewing the FrontPage Express Window

Menu bar
The menu bar gives you access to all FrontPage Express options. Simply click a menu name to display a list of related menu commands, and then click the command you want to issue.

Title bar
FrontPage Express and the name of the Web page appear in the title bar. "Untitled" is a temporary name FrontPage Express uses until you assign a new one.

Standard, Format, and Forms toolbars
These toolbars contain buttons that give you quick access to a variety of commands and features. If you're not sure what a specific button does, move the mouse pointer over it to display the name of the toolbar button.

Insertion point
The blinking insertion point (also called a cursor) shows you where the next character you type will appear.

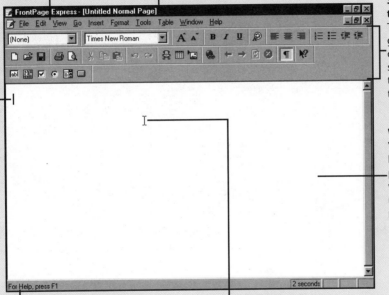

Web page window
You enter text and graphics here. As with all Windows programs, the Web page window can be maximized or minimized independently of the program window.

Status bar
The status bar provides you information about current settings and commands. The time indicated on the status bar is the estimated time it would take to download the current Web page at 28.8 kbs.

Mouse pointer
In the Web page window, the mouse pointer appears as an I-beam. The pointer shape changes depending on where you point in the FrontPage Express window.

Viewing the FrontPage Express Toolbars

To work with entire Web pages and individual Web objects, you will often use buttons and boxes located on the three FrontPage Express toolbars: Standard, Format, and Forms. The Standard and Format toolbars contain common features much like those you find in Microsoft Word or Microsoft Excel. The Forms toolbar contains tools you will need to create electronic forms. The tables shown here display and describe all the FrontPage Express toolbar buttons on the three different toolbars.

STANDARD TOOLBAR	
Button	**Description**
	The New button inserts a new Web page in the Web page window.
	The Open button opens an existing Web page you specify.
	The Save button saves the current Web page to a location you specify.
	The Print button displays the Print dialog box in which you specify settings for printing the current Web page that appears in the Web page window.
	The Print Preview button displays the current Web page in Print Preview.
	The Cut button or the Copy button removes or copies the current selection from the screen and places it on the Clipboard.
	The Paste button inserts the selection from the Clipboard and places it on the screen.
	The Undo button or Redo button cancels or restores the effect of your last action.
	The Insert WebBot Component button adds functionality to your Web page, such as a timestamp or search file, without complex programming.
	The Insert Table button adds a table of the size you specify.
	The Insert Image button displays the Image dialog box and inserts an image.
	The Create Or Edit Hyperlink button displays the Create Hyperlink dialog box in which you create or edit a hyperlink.
	The Back button or Forward button returns or takes you to the previous Web page open in FrontPage Express.
	The Refresh button updates the display of the current Web page.
	The Stop button stops loading the current Web page in the Web page window.
	The Show/Hide¶ button shows or hides special formatting symbols for the current Web page in the Web page window.
	The Help button displays a Help dialog box with options to find Help information about FrontPage Express.

FORMAT TOOLBAR

Button	Description
Normal ▼	The Change Style button changes the style type of the current text selection.
Times New Roman ▼	The Change Font button changes the font type of the current text selection.
A̅ A̅	The Increase Text Size button and the Decrease Text Size button change the font size of the current text selection.
B I U	The Bold button, Italic button, and Underline button change the format of the current text selection.
🖉	The Text Color button displays the Color dialog box to let you change the color of the current text selection.
▤ ▤ ▤	The Align Left button, Center button, and Align Right button change the alignment of the current selection.
▤ ▤	The Numbered List button and Bulleted List button change the current text selection to a numbered or bulleted list.
▤ ▤	The Decrease Indent button and the Increase Indent button move the paragraph text one tab stop to the left or right.

10

FORMS TOOLBAR

Button	Description
abl	The One-Line Text Box button creates a one line text box in a Web page.
▦	The Scrolling Text Box button creates a scrolling text box in a Web page.
☑	The Check Box button creates a check box in a Web page.
◉	The Radio Button button creates a radio option button in a Web page.
▤	The Drop-Down Menu button creates a drop-down menu list in a Web page.
▢	The Push Button button creates a customized button in a Web page.

Creating a Web Page Using Templates and Wizards

FrontPage Express provides predesigned templates and Web page wizards that speed up the creation of Web pages. With the FrontPage Express templates and wizards, you can create a Web page with text and graphics or with forms that users can fill in. Wizards offer you choices in creating a customized Web page, while templates give you an exact copy of the template itself. Specifically, you can create a blank Web page, a personal home page, and a new Web View folder.

SEE ALSO

See "Creating Forms Using Templates and Wizards" on page 226 for more information about using one of the form templates or wizards.

Create a Personal Home Page

1 Click the File menu, and then click New.

2 Click Personal Home Page Wizard.

3 Click OK.

4 Click the check boxes of the major sections you want to include in your home page. Click Next to continue.

5 Type the new page Intertnet adress, Uniform Resource Locator (URL), in the Page URL box, and type the new title in the Page Title box. Click Next to continue.

6 Each major section selected prompts you to select options. Read each dialog box and select the options you want to include in your Home Page. Click Next to continue.

7 Upon completion of the final wizard dialog box, click Finish.

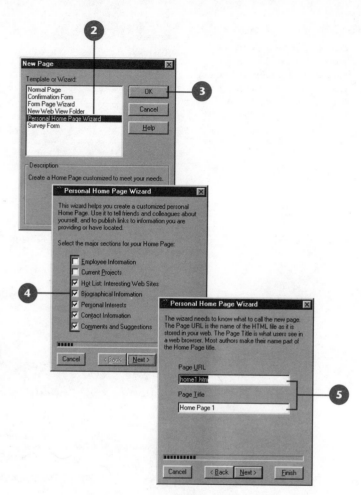

TIP

Create a blank Web page quickly. *Click the New button on the Standard toolbar to create a blank Web page without selecting a template or wizard.*

Create a Blank Web Page

1. Click the File menu, and then click New.

2. Click Normal Page.

3. Click OK.

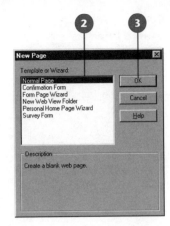

TIP

What is a Web View Folder? *A Web View folder is a folder window where you can create a custom layout and design for the content of your Web page, including background graphics.*

Create a New Web View Folder

1. Click the File menu, and then click New.

2. Click New Web View Folder.

3. Click OK.

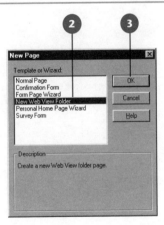

10

Opening a Web Page

To work with an individual Web page, you first need to open the Web page. You can open a Web page from FrontPage Express using the Open command or from Internet Explorer using the Edit button on the Standard toolbar. Which method you choose depends on what application you have open.

SEE ALSO

See "Starting FrontPage Express" on page 182 for information about opening a Web page from Internet Explorer.

TIP

Open a recently used Web page quickly and easily. *If the Web page you want to open is one of the last four Web pages you worked on, you can open the Web page by selecting it from the bottom of the File menu in the FrontPage Express program window. Just click the File menu, and then click the name of the Web page you want to open.*

Open a Web Page from a File

1 Click the Open button on the Standard toolbar.

2 Click the From File option button.

3 Click Browse.

4 Click the Look In drop-down arrow, and then select the drive and folder containing the Web page you want to open.

5 Double-click the Web page you want to open.

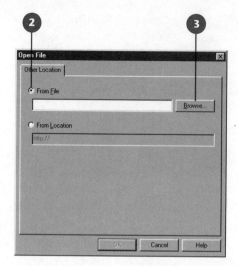

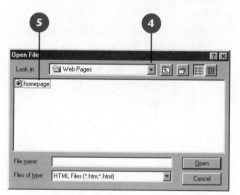

TIP

Save a text file as an RTF file. *When you're creating a document that you plan to use in FrontPage Express, save the document as a rich text format, or RTF, file. You can do this by using the Save As command on the File menu.*

TIP

Open a text file in a Web page. *Click the File menu, click Open, and then click Browse. Click the Files Of Type drop-down arrow, and then specify the format of the file. Click the Look In drop-down arrow, and then specify the location of the file. Double-click the file you want to open, and then select a conversion option.*

Open a Web Page from an Internet Location

1 Click the Open button on the Standard toolbar.

2 Click the From Location option button.

3 Type the Internet address, Uniform Resource Locator (URL), and filename of the Web page you want to open.

4 Click OK.

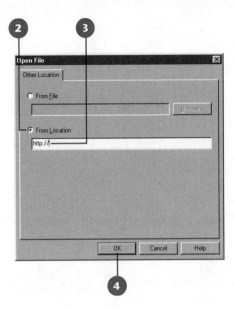

10

Adding and Modifying Text

Once you've created a Web page, you can begin filling your page with text. If you've ever worked with Microsoft Word, you'll find this process familiar. To begin typing, you click a location within the Web page to position the insertion point. To modify the text, you select the text you want to change, and then make your changes. If you make a mistake, you can reverse text entry and editing with the Undo command, and then if necessary, you can restore the action you undid with the Redo command. And to replace text throughout your Web page quickly, you can use the Replace command.

Enter New Text

1 Click to place the insertion point where you want to add new text.

2 Type the new text in the Web page.

3 Press Enter to end one paragraph of text and begin another paragraph.

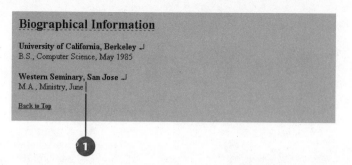

Replace or Delete Existing Text

1 Select the text you want to replace or delete by clicking the first character you want to replace or delete, holding down the mouse button, and dragging to the last character to highlight it.

2 To replace existing text, type the new text you want in the Web page. To delete existing text, press Delete.

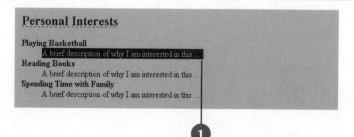

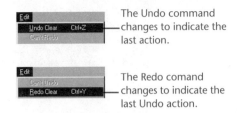

The Undo command changes to indicate the last action.

The Redo comand changes to indicate the last Undo action.

TIP

Use the keyboard to quickly undo your last action. *Press Ctrl+Z to undo your last action. To redo your last action, press Ctrl+Y.*

TIP

Quick ways to select text. *To select a word, double-click it. To select a line of text, click just to the left of the beginning of the line.*

TIP

Insert a text file in a Web page. *Click the Insert menu, and then click File. Click the Look In drop-down arrow, and then specify the location of the file. Click the Files Of Type drop-down arrow, and then specify the format of the file. Then double-click the file to insert its contents in the Web page at the insertion point location.*

TRY THIS

Insert a special symbol. *Click to place the insertion point, click the Insert menu, click Symbol, click the symbol you want to insert, click Insert to place the selected symbol, and then click Close.*

Undo or Redo Edits

◆ Click the Edit menu, and then click Undo to reverse your most recent action.

◆ Click the Edit menu, and then click Redo to restore the last action you reversed.

Replace Multiple Occurrences of Text

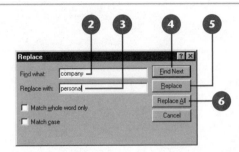

1 Click the Edit menu, and then click Replace.

2 Type the text you want to replace in the Find What box.

3 Type the new text you want to use in the Replace With box.

4 Click Find Next to find the next occurrence of the text in the Find What box.

5 Click Replace to replace the selected occurrence of the text in the Find What box with the text in the Replace With box.

6 Click Replace All to replace the every occurrence of the text in the Find What box with the text in the Replace With box.

10

Inserting and Modifying Images

If you know the location of a graphic image or if you want to use clip art supplied by FrontPage Express, you're ready to insert a graphic image in your Web page. In most cases, you position the insertion point in your Web page, and then you insert the graphic image using the Image command on the Insert menu or the Insert Image button on the Standard toolbar. Once you've inserted a graphic image in a Web page, you can modify its appearance or change its file format type to GIF or JPEG, common Web page graphic file formats.

SEE ALSO

See "Moving and Copying Text and Images" on page 194 for information about inserting a graphic image from another application.

Insert a Graphic Image from a Web Site or Disk

1 Click to place the insertion point where you want to insert your graphic image.

2 Click the Insert Image button on the Standard toolbar.

3 Click the Other Location tab.

4 Enter the Web site location in the From Location box, or enter the path to the graphic image in the From File box. If necessary, click Browse to help locate the file you want.

5 Click OK.

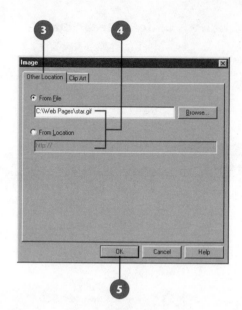

Insert a Graphic Image from Clip Art

1 Click to place the insertion point where you want to insert your graphic image.

2 Click the Insert Image button on the Standard toolbar.

3 Click the Clip Art tab.

4 Click the Category drop-down arrow, and then select a clip art category.

5 Double-click the graphic image you want to insert.

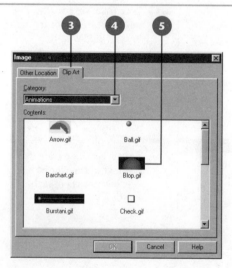

TIP

What's the difference between JPEG and GIF? *JPEG is best used for photographs because it can produce 24-bit files that contain up to 16.7 million colors. GIF is best used for artwork because it can produce 8-bit files that contain only 256 colors.*

TIP

Why change the JPEG quality option? *JPEG reduces the size of an image by compressing like colors. Increasing the value in the Quality box increases the quality of the image because the image is less compressed.*

TIP

Why use the interlaced GIF option? *Interlaced GIF files appear to load one layer at a time, so you can see a representation of the graphic before the entire graphic loads.*

TIP

Why use low-resolution graphic images? *You typically create and use low-resolution graphic images so that users with slow-speed connections to your Web site don't spend a long time waiting for graphic images to load.*

Modify a Graphic Image Appearance

1 Right-click the graphic image, and then click Image Properties.

2 Click the Appearance tab.

3 Modify the Layout options you want to change:

♦ Click the Alignment drop-down arrow, and then select an alignment option.

♦ Enter a value greater than zero in the Border Thickness box to add a border.

4 Click OK.

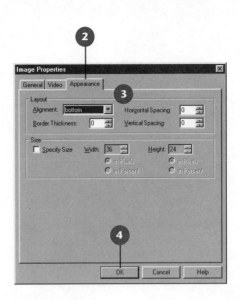

Change a Graphic Image File Format Type

1 Right-click the graphic image, and then click Image Properties.

2 Click the General tab.

3 Click the GIF option button or JPEG option button to convert the graphic image to a new type.

4 If you want, select or modify the GIF or JPEG options.

5 Click OK.

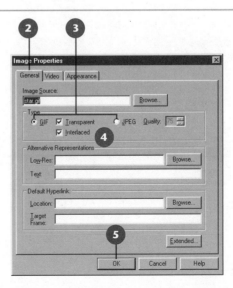

10

Moving and Copying Text and Images

You can move (cut) or copy text and graphic images within a Web page or between Web pages. In either case, the steps are the same. The text or graphic image is stored on the Clipboard, a temporary storage area, until you cut or copy a new selection. You can also move or copy selected text or graphic images to a new location without storing it on the Clipboard using a technique called *drag-and-drop* editing.

> **TIP**
>
> **Selection handles.** *When you click an image, small squares appear along the edge of the image. These are called selection handles.*

Move or Copy and Paste Text or a Graphic Image

1. Select the text or graphic image you want to move or copy.

2. Click the Cut or Copy button on the Standard toolbar.

3. Click where you want to insert the text or graphic image.

4. Click the Paste button on the Standard toolbar.

Drag Text or a Graphic Image

1. If you want to drag text or a graphic image between programs or documents, display both programs or document windows.

2. Select the text or graphic image you want to move or copy.

3. To move the text or graphic image to a new location, position the pointer over the selected text or graphic image, and then press and hold the mouse button.

TIP

Use drag-and-drop editing to copy text or graphic images between other types of documents. *Right-click the Windows taskbar, click Tile Windows Vertically. and then select the text or graphic image. Hold down the Ctrl key while you drag your mouse. A plus sign (+) appears in the pointer box to indicate where you can place the text or graphic image.*

④ To copy the text or graphic image and paste the copy in a new location, also press and hold the Ctrl key. A plus sign appears in the pointer box.

⑤ Drag the text or image to the new location, and then release the mouse button (and the Ctrl key, if necessary).

④ Drag-and-drop pointer

Graphic image copied using drag-and-drop editing

TIP

Change the width or height of a graphic image. *The middle selection handles on the left and right sides of the graphic image let you resize the width of the image, while the middle selection handles on the top and bottom let you adjust the height of the image.*

Resize a Graphic Image

① Click the graphic image you want to resize to select it.

② Drag a corner selection handle outward to increase or inward to decrease the graphic image's size.

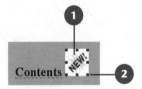

10

TIP

Resize a graphic image proportionally. *Select a graphic image. Position your mouse pointer over the selection handle in the lower right corner of the image. Drag the handle diagonally inward or outward to resize the graphic without distorting the image.*

Creating and Editing Hyperlinks

A *hyperlink* connects Web pages together. A hyperlink can be text or a graphic that you select to represent the information you want linked. Browsers usually underline text hyperlinks and display them in a specific color. Hyperlinks in images are invisible. However, you can tell when the pointer is over a hyperlink because it changes to a pointing hand. You can connect to Web pages on your local hard drive or on the World Wide Web. By a simple click of a mouse button, you can move from Web page to Web page.

> **TIP**
>
> **Test the link.** *Right-click the text or graphic image you want to test, and then click Follow Hyperlink on the shortcut menu.*

Create or Edit a Hyperlink to an Open Web Page

1 Open the Web page in which you want to place a hyperlink or edit an existing hyperlink.

2 Select the text or graphic image you want to use as the hyperlink, or select the hyperlink you want to edit.

3 Click the Create Or Edit Hyperlink button on the Standard toolbar.

4 Click the Open Pages tab.

5 Click the Web page you want to link to or edit a link to.

6 If you want, click the Bookmark drop-down arrow, and then select a bookmark.

7 If you want, enter a frame in the Target Frame box.

8 Click OK.

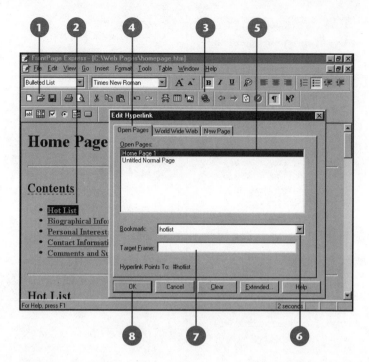

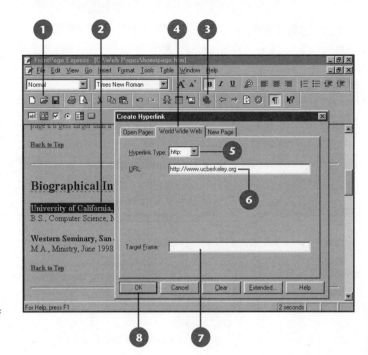

TIP

Create a hyperlink to a new Web page. *Select the text you want to link, click the Create Or Edit Hyperlink button on the Standard toolbar, click the New Page tab, enter the page title of the new Web page, and then type the Internet address, URL, of the new Web page, which is the HTML document's filename and extension without the file pathname.*

TIP

Clear a hyperlink to a Web page. *Select the hyperlink you want to clear, click the Create Or Edit Hyperlink button on the Standard toolbar, click the tab where the link you want to clear is located, and then click Clear.*

TIP

Create a hyperlink to send e-mail. *Select the text you want to link, click the Create Or Edit Hyperlink button on the Standard toolbar, click the World Wide Web tab, click the Hyperlink Type drop-down arrow, select the mailto: protocol, and then type the destination e-mail address following the protocol in the URL box.*

Create or Edit a Hyperlink to an Internet Address

1 Open the Web page in which you want to place or edit a hyperlink.

2 Select the text or graphic image you want to create as the link or the existing link you want to edit.

3 Click the Create Or Edit Hyperlink button on the Standard toolbar.

4 Click the World Wide Web tab.

5 Click the Hyperlink Type drop-down arrow, and then select the protocol of the Internet resource.

6 Type the hyperlink's Internet address, Uniform Resource Locator (URL).

7 If you want, enter a frame in the Target Frame box.

8 Click OK.

Creating a Bookmark

Bookmarks make it easier to move around within a particular Web page or to more precisely control where users land when they move to the page. Bookmarks work as navigation tools you use within a Web page—just as hyperlinks work as navigation tools between Web pages. After you create a bookmark, select the text you want users to click in order to jump to the bookmark, click the Create Or Edit Hyperlink button on the Standard toolbar, click the Open Pages tab, and then select a bookmark from the Bookmark drop-down list.

TIP

You can't move a bookmark. *To move a bookmark, you need to first remove the existing bookmark, and then add it again.*

Create a Bookmark

1. Open the Web page in which you want to place a bookmark.

2. Click to place the insertion point where you want to place the bookmark.

3. Click the Edit menu, and then click Bookmark.

4. Type a name for the bookmark.

5. Click OK.

   A flag icon appears in the Web page to indicate the jump to location of the bookmark.

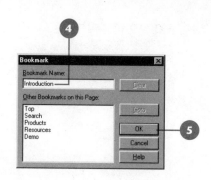

Remove an Existing Bookmark

1. Open the Web page containing the bookmark.

2. Click the Edit menu, and then click Bookmark.

3. Select the bookmark.

4. Click Goto.

5. Click Clear.

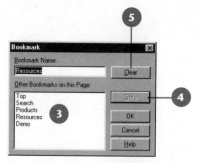

Setting Up a Web Page

When you print a Web page, FrontPage Express uses the Print Page Setup dialog box to control the way text and graphics are printed on a page. In the Header and Footer boxes, you can type text that will appear at the top of a Web page (header) or at the bottom of a Web page (footer) you print. In these boxes, you can also use variables to substitute information about the current page for the variable code and you can combine text and codes. The table shown here describes the variable codes. You can also use the Print Page Setup dialog box to change margin settings.

> **TIP**
>
> **Change the page orientation.** *Click the File menu, and then click Page Setup. In the Print Page Setup dialog box, click the Options button, click the Portrait or Landscape option button, and then click OK.*

Set Up a Web Page

1 Open the Web page you want to set up.

2 Click the File menu, and then click Page Setup.

3 Type the information you want to print at the top of each page in the Header box.

4 Type the information you want to print at the bottom of each page in the Footer box.

5 Specify what size margin you want to use for the printed pages in the Margins boxes.

6 Click OK.

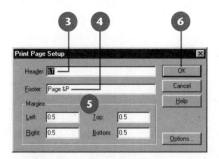

ENTERING HEADER AND FOOTER CODES	
Code	**Description**
&w	Window title
&u	URL or local path of the current web page
&d	Date in short format (m/d/y-10/1/99)
&D	Date in long format (month, day, year-October 1, 1999)
&t	Time of day
&T	Time in 24-hour format
&p	Page number
&P	Total number of pages

10

Printing Your Web Page

You should always *preview* your work before sending it to the printer. A *print preview* is a miniature view of the entire Web page that shows how your document will look when it is printed. To print all or part of a Web page, click the Print button on the Standard toolbar. You can use the Print dialog box to specify several print options, such as choosing a printer, selecting the number of pages you want to print, and specifying the number of copies.

TIP

What if a Print Preview button is grayed out? *Print Preview only enables buttons when they make sense. For example, if there is no previous page, then the Prev Page button is not available.*

Print Preview button

Preview a Printed Web Page

1 Click the File menu, and then click Print Preview.

2 Click the Next Page and Prev Page buttons to move through the Web page you want to print.

3 Click the Zoom In and Zoom Out buttons to magnify or reduce the display size of the Web page you want print.

4 Click the Two Page button to see two pages side by side in the Print Preview window. Click the One Page button to display one page in the Print Preview window.

5 Click the Print button if you decide to print the Web page.

6 Click the Close button if you decide not to print the Web page.

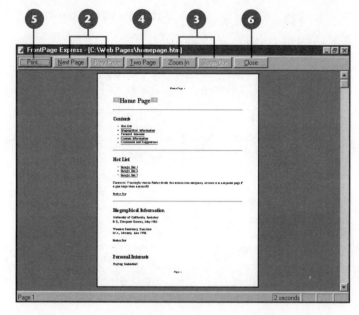

TIP

A Web page can be more than one page of paper. *A single Web page may actually print on several pieces of paper.*

TIP

Change printer properties. *Click the Properties button in the Print dialog box to change general printer properties for paper size and orientation, graphics, and fonts.*

Print button

Print a Web Page

1 Open the Web page you want to print.

2 Click the Print button on the Standard toolbar.

3 If necessary, click the Name drop-down arrow, and then select the printer you want to use.

4 Indicate how many pages of the Web page you want to print using the Print Range option buttons and boxes.

5 Specify how many copies of the Web page you want to print in the Number Of Copies box.

6 Click OK.

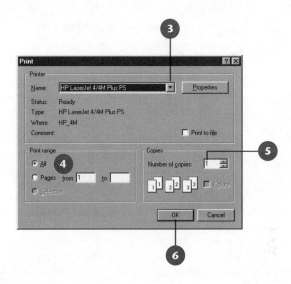

10

Saving Your Web Page

When you open a new Web page in FrontPage Express, the title bar displays a default title such as Untitled. When you save a Web page for the first time, you need to give it a meaningful name and specify where you want to store it. When FrontPage Express saves a Web page, it saves the Web page's HTML source code. The source code controls what a browser, such as Internet Explorer, displays on the screen. Once you have saved a Web page, you must continue to save the changes you've make before closing the Web page or exiting the FrontPage Express program.

SEE ALSO

See "Publishing a Web Page" on page 240 for information on saving a Web page to a Web server.

Save button

Save a Web Page for the First Time to a File

1 Click the Save button on the Standard toolbar.

2 Enter a name for the Web page.

3 Type the filename you want to use for the Web page. You don't need to add the HTM file extension.

4 Click As File.

5 Click the Save In drop-down arrow, and then specify where you want to save the file.

6 Click Save.

7 If necessary, click the Yes, Yes To All, or No button to indicate whether you want the graphic images displayed on the Web page saved with the HTML document.

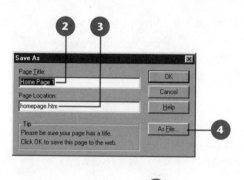

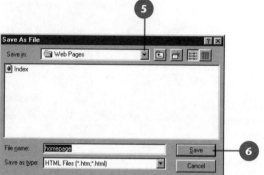

TIP

Save a Web page a second or subsequent time. *Click the Save button on the Standard toolbar, or click the File menu, and then click Save.*

TIP

Save all open Web pages quickly. *Click the File menu, and then click Save All.*

TIP

Use the Save As command to save a Web page with a different name. *To save a Web page with a different name, so that you have the original Web page and a copy with changes you may want, use the Save As command, replacing the current filename with a new filename. You will then have two files: the original and one with the changes.*

SEE ALSO

See "Closing a Web Page and Exiting FrontPage Express " on page 204 for information on what do to after you complete your Web page.

Save a Web Page to a File as a Different Type

1 Click the File menu, and then click Save As.

2 Enter a name for the Web page.

3 Type the filename you want to use for the Web page.

4 Click As File.

5 Click the Save As Type drop-down arrow.

6 Click the file type you want.

7 Click Save.

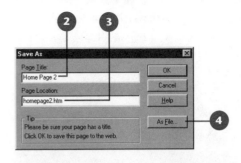

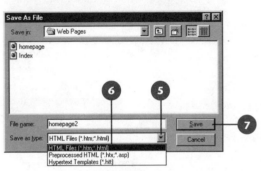

10

Closing a Web Page and Exiting FrontPage Express

After you finish working on a Web page, you can close it. Closing a file make more computer memory available for other processes. Closing a Web page is different from exiting FrontPage Express: after you close a Web page, FrontPage Express is still running. When you're finished using FrontPage Express, you can exit the program. To protect your files, always exit from FrontPage Express before turning off your computer.

Close button

Close a Web Page

1 Click the File menu, and then click Close, or click the Close button on the Web page window title bar.

2 If you have made any changes to the Web page since last saving it, a dialog box opens asking if you want to save changes. Click Yes to save any changes you made to your Web page, or click No to ignore any changes you might have made.

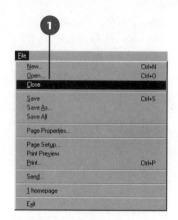

Exit FrontPage Express

1 Click the Close button on the FrontPage Express window title bar, or click the File menu, and then click Exit.

2 If any files are open and you have made any changes to the Web page since last saving it, a dialog box opens asking if you want to save changes. Click Yes to save any changes you made to your Web page, or click No to ignore any changes you might have made. If no files are open or have been changed, the program closes.

Enhancing Web Pages with FrontPage Express

Once you've mastered the basics of creating a Web page with FrontPage Express, you can try some of the more advanced features. In most cases, there's more than one way to perform tasks such as creating tables or forms. To save you time, this book focuses on the fastest and easiest methods.

Enhancing Your Web Page

After you've created your basic Web page, take a moment to consider how you can enhance its appearance and communicate its message more effectively. For example, you could draw attention to important text and data using a table or clarify the details of a complicated paragraph by creating a list. If you want to get feedback from Web page visitors, you'll probably want to include forms you can create using FrontPage Express wizards.

Several FrontPage Express features—among them, WebBots, ActiveX controls, and Java applets—are designed to help you add high functionality to your Web pages in a fast and efficient manner without programming.

Formatting Text

You'll often want to *format*, or change the style, of certain words or phrases to add emphasis to parts of a Web page. Boldface, italics, underline, and other text effects are applied using *toggle switches*, which means you simply click to turn them on and off. For special emphasis, you can combine formats, such as bold and italics. You can also color and resize text. Formatting makes your Web page more interesting and professional looking.

TIP

Quickly remove formatting. *To remove formatting you've added to text, select the text from which you want to remove the formatting, click the Format menu, and then click Remove Formatting.*

Boldface, Italicize, or Underline Text

1 Select the text you want to format.

2 Click the Bold, Italic, or Underline button on the Format toolbar.

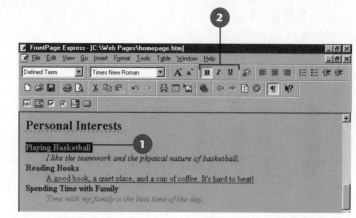

Color Text

1 Select the text you want to recolor.

2 Click the Text Color button on the Format toolbar.

3 Click the color you want to use.

4 Click OK.

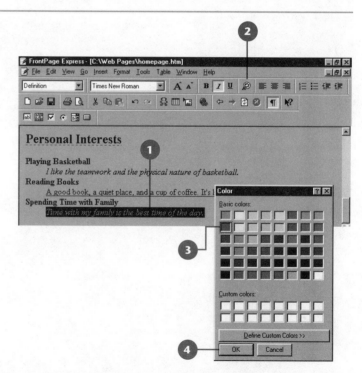

TIP

Quickly change a font style. *Select the text for which you want to specify a font, click the Change Font drop-down arrow on the Formatting toolbar, and then select the font you want to use.*

Increase or Decrease the Text Size

1 Select the text you want to resize.

2 Click the Increase Text Size or Decrease Text Size button on the Format toolbar.

FrontPage Express increases or decreases the font text size to the next higher or lower setting.

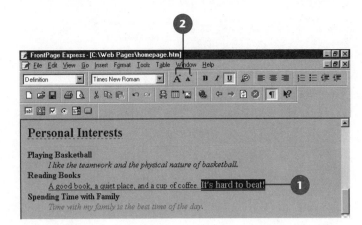

TIP

Create a custom color. *Click the Text Color button on the Formatting toolbar, click Define Custom Colors, select a color range in the color spectrum box, drag the color arrow to select a specific color, click Add To Custom Colors, and then click OK.*

SEE ALSO

See "Formatting Paragraphs" on page 208 for more information about formatting other text in FrontPage Express.

Change Font Attributes and Add Special Styles

1 Select the text you want to format.

2 Click the Format menu, and then click Font.

3 Select the font, font size, color, font style, and font effect you want to use.

4 Click the Special Styles tab.

5 Select one or more of the special styles check boxes you want to use.

6 Click OK.

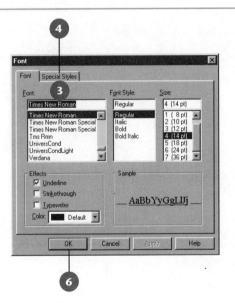

Formatting Paragraphs

You create paragraphs by entering a block of text and then pressing the Enter key. Pressing the Enter key signals FrontPage Express that the text should be considered a paragraph. Once you have created your paragraphs, you can format the paragraph alignment and indenting. *Alignment* moves a selected paragraph to the right margin, left margin, or center of the page. *Indenting* moves a selected paragraph an indent level to the right or left.

TIP

Quickly select a paragraph. *Double-click just to the left of one of the lines of the paragraph.*

SEE ALSO

See "Formatting Text" on page 206 for information about formatting individual characters.

Change Paragraph Alignment

1. Select the paragraph you want to align.

2. Click one of the following Format toolbar buttons:

   ◆ Align Left to align the paragraph against the left edge of the page

   ◆ Center to center the paragraph horizontally

   ◆ Align Right to align the paragraph against the right edge of the page

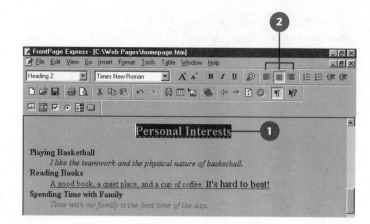

Change Paragraph Indention

1. Select the paragraph you want to indent.

2. Click one of the following Format toolbar buttons:

   ◆ Increase Indent to indent the paragraph one level to the right

   ◆ Decrease Indent to unindent the paragraph one level to the left

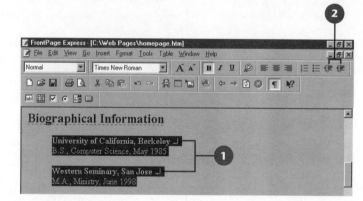

Changing Paragraph Styles

A *style is a* collection of formatting settings you can apply to selected text. Like Microsoft Word, FrontPage Express comes with pre-defined text styles you can use to format your Web page text. To create headings and subheadings within a Web page, you use one of six built-in heading styles: Heading 1 through Heading 6. Besides the heading styles, FrontPage Express also includes other built-in styles: Address, Defined Term, Definition, Normal, Bulleted List(s), Numbered List(s), Directory List, and Menu List.

SEE ALSO

See "Working with Paragraph Lists" on page 210 for more information about creating and formatting lists.

Apply a Heading or Subheading Style

1. Select the text you want to use as a heading or subheading, and then press Enter.

2. Right-click the text, and then click Paragraph Properties.

3. Select a heading style you want to use.

4. Click OK.

   FrontPage Express changes the selected text into a heading or subheading.

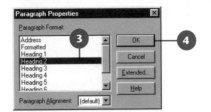

Change a Paragraph Style

1. Select the text whose style you want to change.

2. Click the Change Style drop-down arrow on the Format toolbar.

3. Select a style you want to apply.

   FrontPage Express applies the selected paragraph style to the selected text.

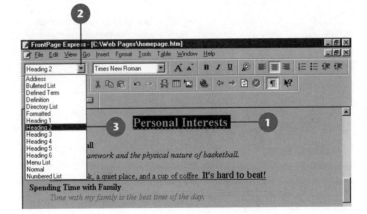

11

Working with Paragraph Lists

The best way to draw attention to a list is to format it with bullets or numbers, or some other special format. Once you've created a list, you can change its character or number style to one of the many predefined formats. For example, you can change a numerical list to an alphabetical list. If you move, insert, or delete items in a numbered list, FrontPage Express will renumber the list sequence for you. FrontPage Express also includes special lists to create a directory, definition, or menu list.

TIP

Remove numbering from a paragraph list. *Select the numbered list, and then click the Numbered List button on the Formatting toolbar.*

Create a Numbered List

1 Select the paragraphs you want to convert to a numbered list.

2 Click the Numbered List button on the Format toolbar.

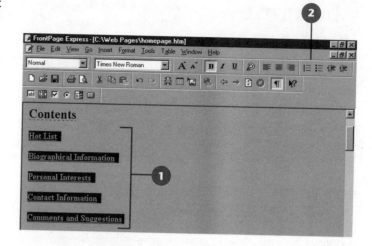

Customize a Numbered List

1 Select the numbered list you want to customize.

2 Click the Format menu, and then click Bullets And Numbering.

3 If necessary, click the Numbered tab.

4 Click the sample box you want your numbered list to look like.

5 Specify the number you want to use for the first paragraph.

6 Click OK.

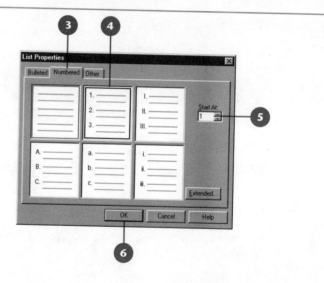

TIP

Remove bulleting from a paragraph list. *Select the bulleted list, and then click the Bulleted List button on the Format toolbar.*

SEE ALSO

See "Changing Paragraph Styles" on page 209 for more information about creating other FrontPage Express special lists: Directory List, Definition List, and Menu List.

TRY THIS

Create other special lists. *Select the text you want to convert into a special list, click the Change Style drop-down arrow on the Formatting toolbar, and then select the Directory List, Menu List, or Definition List style.*

Create a Bulleted List

1 Select the paragraphs you want to convert to a bulleted list.

2 Click the Bulleted List button on the Format toolbar.

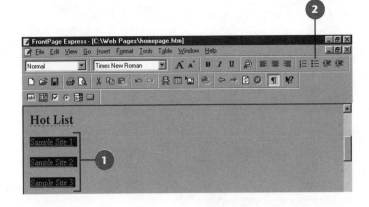

Customize a Bulleted List

1 Select the bulleted list you want to customize.

2 Click the Format menu, and then click Bullets And Numbering.

3 If necessary, click the Bulleted tab.

4 Click the sample box you want your bulleted list to look like.

5 Click OK.

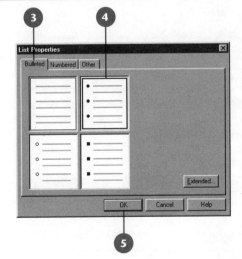

11

Inserting Web Elements

A great way to separate sections, topics, or other elements on a Web page is by using horizontal lines. Adding comments to a Web page gives you the ability to add information without it being viewed on the World Wide Web. Once you place a comment on a Web page, you can't edit the text, but you can select and delete it.

TIP

insert a page break. *Click to place the insertion point where you want a page break, click the Insert menu, click Break, click the Normal Line Break option button, and then click OK.*

TIP

Customize a horizontal line. *Right-click the horizontal line, and then click Horizontal Line Properties on the shortcut menu. Specify the width, height, alignment, and color you want to change, and then click OK.*

Insert a Horizontal Line

1. Click to place the insertion point where you want to insert a horizontal line.

2. Click the Insert menu, and then click Horizontal Line.

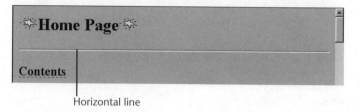

Horizontal line

Insert a Comment

1. Click to place the insertion point where you want to insert a comment.

   The comment won't be part of the actual HTML page that will be viewed on the Web. It only appears when you view the Web page using FrontPage Express.

2. Click the Insert menu, and then click Comment.

3. Type the comment you want to add to the Web page.

4. Click OK.

   The comment text appears in color—generally purple.

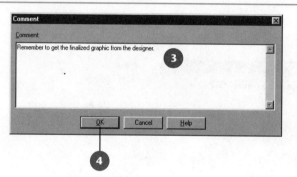

Inserting a Video Clip

A video clip can add a great deal of interest and drama to a Web page. You can insert a video clip in your Web pages and control when and how a visitor sees the video clip. Before you insert a video clip, remember that video clip files can be very large, which means they can increase the time it takes to retrieve a Web page. To play a video's sound, the visitor's computer must have a sound card and speakers.

TIP

Play a video clip over and over. *On the Video tab of the Image Properties dialog box, click to select the Forever check box in the Repeat area.*

TIP

Show the Play and Stop buttons in a browser. *On the Video tab of the Image Properties dialog box, click to select the Show Controls In Browser check box.*

Insert a Video Clip

1. Click to place the insertion point where you want to insert your video clip.

2. Click the Insert menu, and then click Video.

3. Enter the Web site location in the From Location box, or enter the path to the video clip in the From File box. If necessary, click Browse to help locate the file you want.

4. Click OK.

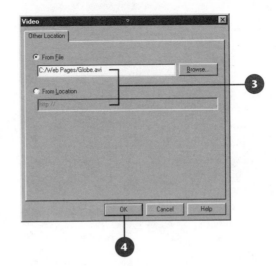

Modify the Way a Video Clip Plays

1. Right-click the video clip, and then click Image Properties.

2. Click the Video tab.

3. In the Loop box, specify the number of times you want the video to play, and specify the delay time in the Loop Delay box.

4. Click the On File Open or On Mouse Over check box to indicate when to play the video.

5. Click OK.

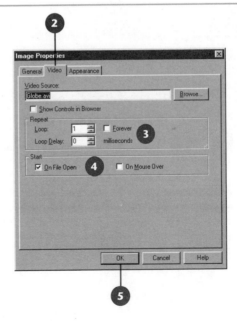

Changing a Background

You can add background graphic images or sound, or change the background color to dramatically improve the audio and visual appeal of your Web pages. Adding a background image can be effective if it adds to the readability of a Web page and does not impair viewing of the text or other images on the page. Background images appear titled in your Web page. Assuming your Web page visitor's computer has a sound card and speakers, the background sound plays when the Web page is loaded or refreshed, and it can play a specified number of times or loop continuously.

TIP

Change hyperlink colors.
Click the File menu, click Page Properties, click the Background tab, click the Hyperlink drop-down arrow, and then select a color you want for your hyperlink.

Insert a Background Graphic Image

1. Open the Web page in which you want to insert a background graphic.

2. Click the Format menu, and then click Background.

3. Click to select the Background Image check box.

4. Click Browse.

5. Click the Other Location tab, and then click Browse, or click the Clip Art tab.

6. Double-click the graphic image or clip art you want to insert.

7. Click OK.

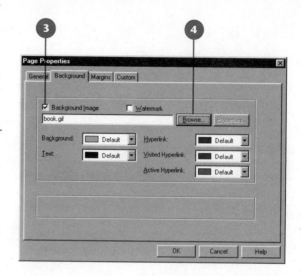

Specify a Background Color

1. Open the Web page whose background color you want to specify.

2. Click the Format menu, and then click Background.

3. Click the Background drop-down arrow, and then select a background color.

4. Click OK.

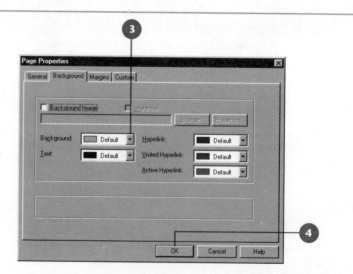

TIP

Delete a background sound. *Click the File menu, click the Page Properties, click the General tab, double-click the Location box to select its contents, and press Delete.*

TIP

Play a background sound more than once. *Click the File menu, click the Page Properties, click the General tab, specify the number of times to play the sound in the Loop box or click to select the Forever check box to play the sound continuously.*

TIP

What is a watermark image? *The Watermark option in the Background tab of the Page Properties dialog box sets the background image so it will not scroll when you scroll the page.*

SEE ALSO

See "Inserting and Modifying Images" on page192 for information on modifying graphic images.

Insert a Background Sound

1. Open the Web page in which you want to insert a background sound.

2. Click the Insert menu, and then click Background Sound.

3. Enter the Web site location in the From Location box, or enter the path to the sound file in the From File box. If necessary, click Browse to help locate the file you want.

4. Click OK.

5. Click the File menu, and then click Page Properties.

   The inserted sound file appears on the General tab of the Page Properties dialog box.

6. Click OK.

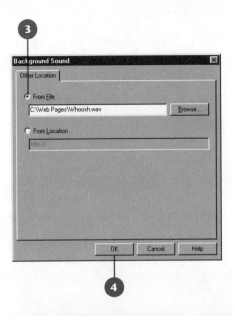

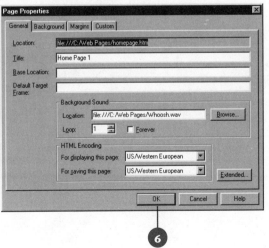

Creating a Marquee

Another way you can add visual interest to your Web pages is by creating a marquee. A *marquee* is a Web element that allows text to move across a Web page. Marquees use moving text for emphasis—the same way that some movie theaters use a marquee to tell you what movie is playing and who's starring in it. But as with any other catchy design element, be careful not to overuse it.

TIP

Convert an existing heading to a marquee.
Select the heading text you want to be a marquee, click the Insert menu, click Marquee—the heading text is automatically set as a marquee text—and then click OK.

Create a Marquee

1. Open the Web page in which you want to add a marquee.

2. Click to place the insertion point where you want to insert a marquee or select the text you want to convert to a marquee.

3. Click the Insert menu, and then click Marquee.

4. Enter the marquee text you want to roll onto and off the Web page.

5. Click OK.

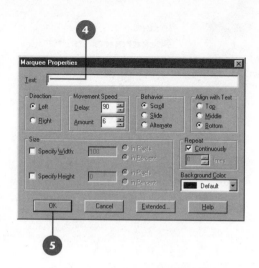

Edit Marquee Text

1. Right-click the marquee, and then click Marquee Properties.

2. Edit the marquee text.

3. Click OK.

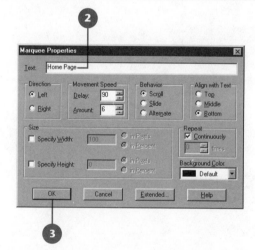

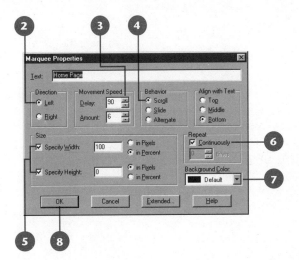

TIP

How does marquee behavior work? *Scroll rolls the marquee onto and off the Web page; Slide rolls the marquee onto the Web page and then stops; and Alternate rolls the marquee onto and off the Web page from alternate directions.*

TIP

How does marquee movement speed work? *The larger the Movement Speed Amount value, the faster the marquee moves.*

TIP

Quickly change marquee width and height. *Click the marquee to select it, and then drag one of its selection handles to resize the marquee.*

TIP

Delete a marquee quickly. *Click to select the marquee, and then press Delete.*

Change Marquee Properties

1 Right-click the marquee, and then click Marquee Properties on the shortcut menu.

2 Click the Left or Right Direction option button to indicate in which direction the marquee should move.

3 Specify the speed of the marquee.

4 Click the Scoll, Slide, or Alternate Behavior option button to indicate the kind of marquee you want.

5 Click to select the Specify Width or Specify Height check box, and then set the width or height in pixels or percentage of the Web page.

6 Click to select the Continuously check box, or set the number of times you want to repeat the marquee.

7 Click the Background Color drop-down arrow, and then select a marquee background color.

8 Click OK.

11

Creating Tables

A table organizes information neatly into rows and columns. The intersection of a row and column is called a *cell*. You use cells to hold the table data. Table cells can hold a variety of data: text, numbers, graphic images, and even other tables. You enter text into cells just as you would anywhere else in a Web page, except that the Tab key moves you from one cell to the next. After you create a table or begin to enter text in one, you might want to add more rows or columns to accommodate the text you are entering in the table.

TIP

Insert a new row at the end of a table. *Click to place the insertion point in the last cell of the table (the lower right corner), and then press Tab.*

Insert a Table

1 Click to place the insertion point where you want to insert a table.

2 Click the Table menu, and then click Insert Table.

3 Specify the number of rows you want.

4 Specify the number of columns you want.

5 Click the Alignment drop-down arrow, and then select an alignment. This alignment affects the position of text and numbers in a cell.

6 Specify the table border thickness (in pixels).

7 Click OK.

Enter Information in a Cell

1 Click the cell to position the insertion point.

2 Type the text or number you want in the cell.

3 Press Tab to go to the next cell.

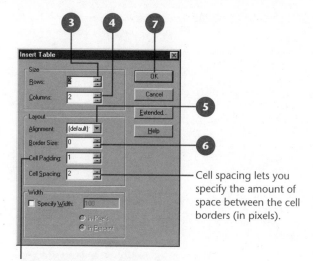

Cell spacing lets you specify the amount of space between the cell borders (in pixels).

Cell padding lets you specify the amount of space between the cell data and the edge of the cell (in pixels).

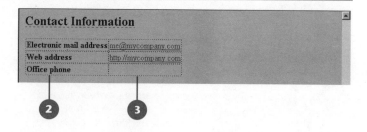

SEE ALSO

See "Inserting and Modifying Images" on page 192 for techniques to insert a graphic image in a table cell.

TIP

Insert a caption in a table. Select a cell in the table you want to label with a caption, click the Table menu, click Insert Caption, and then type a caption.

TIP

Delete a column or row. Click the column or row you want to delete, click the Table menu, click Select Column or Select Row, and then press the Delete key.

TIP

Delete information in a cell. Select the cell's contents by dragging the mouse pointer from the first character to the last character, and then press Delete.

Insert a New Column or Row in a Table

1. Click a cell in the table where you want to insert the new column or row.

2. Click the Table menu, and then click Insert Rows Or Columns.

3. Click the Columns or Rows option button.

4. Specify the number of columns or rows you want to insert.

5. Specify where you want to insert the column (left or right) or row (above or below).

6. Click OK.

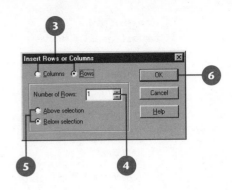

Insert a New Cell in a Table

1. Click a cell in the row or column where you want to insert a new cell.

2. Click the Table menu, and then click Insert Cell.

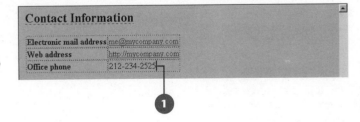

11

Modifying Tables

Once you've created a table and filled it with information, you'll probably want to make changes to the table's appearance. You can change settings for table alignment, border size, cell padding, cell spacing, and overall table width by using the Table Properties command. If your table has borders, you can specify their colors. You can also change some properties for cells, such as the alignment of text within them, their minimum width, the number of rows or columns they span, and their background images or colors.

TIP

Change the width of a table. *Right-click the table, click Table Properties, click to select the Specify Width check box, and then specify the table width in pixels or as a percentage of the Web page width.*

Change Table Properties

1 Right-click the table, and then click Table Properties on the shortcut menu.

2 Click the Alignment drop-down arrow, and then select a table cell contents alignment.

3 Enter a border thickness (in pixels).

4 Enter the amount of space inside the cells (in pixels).

5 Enter the amount of space between the cell border and the cells (in pixels).

6 If you want, click the Use Background Image check box, and then specify a graphic image file or clip art.

7 Click the Background Color drop-down arrow, and then select a table background color.

8 Click the Border, Light Border, or Dark Border drop-down arrows, and then select custom border colors.

9 Click OK.

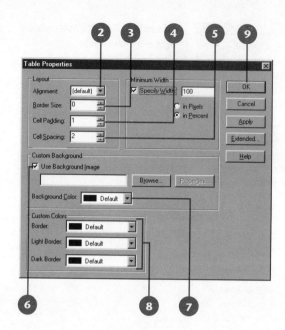

TIP

Combine two or more cells. *Select the two or more cells that you want to combine together, click the Table menu, and then click Merge Cells.*

TIP

Split a cell into two or more cells. *Select the cell that you want to split, click the Table menu, click Split Cells, click Split Into Columns or Split Into Rows, specify how many columns or rows the selected cell should be split into in the Number Of Columns box, and then click OK.*

SEE ALSO

See "Creating Tables" on page 218 for information on inserting columns and rows.

Change Individual Cell Properties

1 Right-click the cell, and then click Cell Properties on the shortcut menu.

2 Click the Horizontal or Vertical Alignment drop-down arrows, and then select a cell contents alignment.

3 Click the Header Cell check box to create a header.

4 Click the Specify Width check box, and then enter a cell width in pixels or as a percentage of the Web page width.

5 If you want, click the Use Background Image check box, and then specify a graphic image file or clip art.

6 Click the Background Color drop-down arrow, and then select a different color.

7 Click the Border, Light Border, or Dark Border drop-down arrows, and then select custom border colors.

8 Specify how many table rows or columns this cell should span.

9 Click OK.

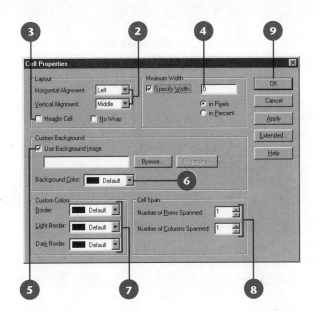

11

Using WebBots

WebBots help people with little or no background in computer programming add functionality to a Web page. For instance, you can add a WebBot to automate tasks such as including the contents of a page on another page, updating the date and time a page was changed, or creating a search page. Keep in mind that in order for WebBots to work properly, the server hosting the Web page must have the FrontPage Server Extensions installed. These extensions are automatically installed with the Microsoft Personal Web Server.

TIP

Delete a WebBot. *Click the WebBot to select it, click the Edit menu, and then click Clear.*

SEE ALSO

See "Setting Up a Personal Web Server" on page 242 for information about installing FrontPage Server Extensions.

Insert the Include WebBot

1 Open the Web page in which you want to place the Include WebBot.

2 Click the Insert WebBot Component button on the Standard toolbar.

3 Click Include from the Select A Component list.

4 Click OK.

5 Type the Internet address, Uniform Resource Locator (URL), for the Web page you want to include.

6 Click OK.

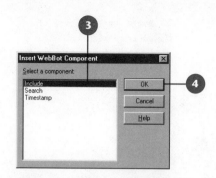

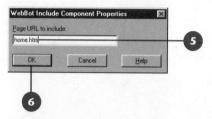

Change the Properties of the Include WebBot

1 Right-click the Include WebBot, and then click WebBot Component Properties on the shortcut menu.

2 Edit or replace the Web page.

3 Click OK.

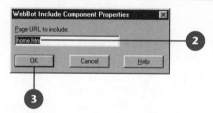

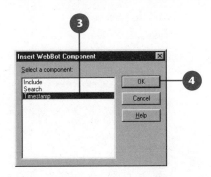

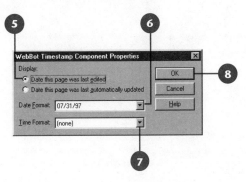

TIP

How does the Include WebBot work? *The Include WebBot is similar to headers and footers used in word processing. When the Web page named by the Include WebBot changes, so do all the pages that use the Include WebBot.*

TIP

Change properties of the Timestamp WebBot. *Right-click the Timestamp WebBot, click WebBot Component Properties, change the WebBot Display, Date Format, and Time Format options, and then click OK.*

TIP

Find the closest match during a search. *Right-click the Search WebBot, click WebBot Component Properties, click the Score check box to return a list of found documents and the scores that show the closeness of the match, and then click OK.*

SEE ALSO

See "Using Interactive WebBots" on page 224 for information about the Search WebBot Component.

Insert a Timestamp WebBot

1. Open the Web page in which you want to place the Timestamp WebBot.

2. Click the Insert WebBot Component button on the Standard toolbar.

3. Click Timestamp from the Select A Component list.

4. Click OK.

5. Select one of the Display option buttons to indicate which date you want to display.

6. Click the Date Format drop-down arrow, and then select a date format.

7. Click the Time Format drop-down arrow, and then select a time format.

8. Click OK.

11

Using Interactive WebBots

FrontPage Express allows you to insert interactive WebBots that provide visitors with the opportunity to interact with your Web page. The Search WebBot, for example, lets you offer Web page visitors the ability to perform quick searches for matching words or phrases in the text of your Web page. For WebBots to work properly, the server hosting the Web page must have the FrontPage Server Extensions installed.

TIP

How to use the Word List To Search field? *You can use the word "All" in the Word List To Search field to search all the pages of the Web site. You can also enter the directory name of a Web site to specify that the Search WebBot should search only that directory.*

Insert a Search WebBot Field

1 Open the Web page in which you want to place the Search WebBot.

2 Click the Insert WebBot Component button on the Standard toolbar.

3 Click Search from the Select A Component list.

4 Click OK.

5 If you want, type a new search label for input.

6 Specify the width (in characters) for the search label.

7 If you want, change the label for the Start Search button.

8 If you want, change the label for the Clear button.

9 Specify how and for what you want the Search WebBot to search.

10 Click OK.

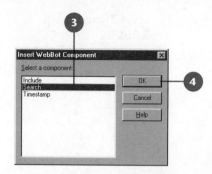

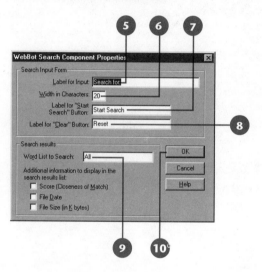

SEE ALSO

See "Using Interactive WebBots" on page 224 for more information about using WebBot components.

SEE ALSO

See "Setting Up a Personal Web Server" on page 242 for information about installing FrontPage Server Extensions.

Change the Properties of the Search WebBot

1 Right-click the Include WebBot, and then click WebBot Component Properties on the shortcut menu.

2 If you want, change the search label for input.

3 Specify the width (in characters) for the search label.

4 If you want, change the label of the Search For button.

5 If you want, change the label of the Clear button.

6 Specify how and for what you want the Search WebBot to search.

7 Click OK.

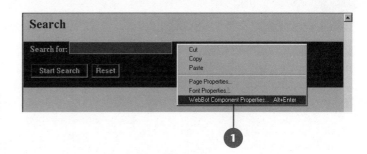

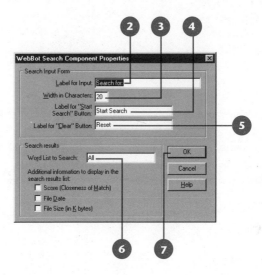

Creating Forms Using Templates and Wizards

Forms let you collect information from your Web page visitors. All forms have several basic elements: questions or requests for information, fields in which visitors type information, Submit Form and Reset Form buttons, and form properties associated with the WebBots that control what happens to the visitor's input. The Form Page Wizard speeds up the creation of a form, and the form templates provide predesigned layouts for certain types of forms. The wizard not only creates a form for you but also inserts the proper WebBots into the properties of the form.

SEE ALSO

See "Working with Forms" on page 228 for information about changing form properties.

Create a Form Using the Form Page Wizard

1. Click the File menu, and then click New.

2. Click Form Page Wizard from the Template Or Wizard list, and then click OK. Click Next to continue.

3. Type the Internet address in the Page URL text box and type the title in the Page Title text box. Click Next to continue.

4. Click Add and then select the type of information you want to collect with this form. Click Next to continue.

5. Select the appropriate option to identify the items to collect. Click Next to continue.

6. Select the appropriate options to describe how your questions should be presented. Click Next to continue.

7. If necessary, select the appropriate output option buttons to describe how the information you collect should be handled. Click Next to continue.

8. Click Finish.

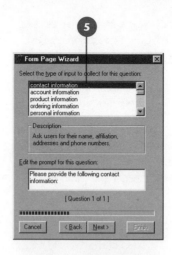

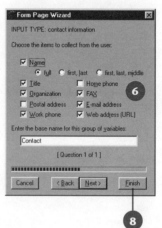

TIP

When to use a confirmation form. *Use a confirmation form to acknowledge a Web visitor's input.*

TIP

What happens to a form when it is submitted? *When a user submits a form, the information from the form is processed by a form handle (WebBot) on the Web server.*

TIP

Where are survey form results stored? *A survey form utilizes the Save Results WebBot to save the survey results. To review the settings, right-click the survey form, click Form Properties, click Settings For The Save Results WebBot, and then click the Results tab. When you are done, click OK.*

SEE ALSO

See "Saving a Web Page" on page 66 for information about saving a Web page for the first time.

Create a New Confirmation Form

1 Click the File menu, and then click New.

2 Click Confirmation Form from the Template Or Wizard list.

3 Click OK.

4 Select and modify the sample text in the form.

5 Click the Save button on the Standard toolbar.

6 Click As File, specify a name and location in which to store the file, and then click Save.

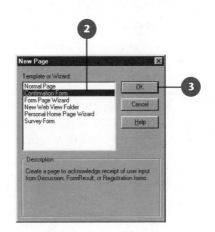

Create a New Survey Form

1 Click the File menu, and then click New.

2 Click Survey Form from the Template Or Wizard list.

3 Click OK.

4 Select and modify the sample text in the form.

5 Click the Save button on the Standard toolbar.

6 Click As File, specify a name for and location in which to store the file, and then click Save.

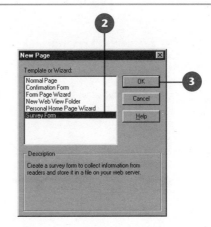

11

Working with Forms

Fields are the building blocks of forms. FrontPage Express provides a variety of form fields that you can use to create a new form or modify one that already exists. You can insert a text box, scrolling text box, check box, radio button, push button, drop-down menu, or image field in your Web page form. Form fields are created in-line with text on the Web page. Once a field is inserted on the Web page, FrontPage Express treats it like a character that you can modify like text.

TIP

Add a choice to a drop-down menu. *Right-click the Drop-Down Menu field, click Form Field Properties, click Add, type the name of the first item in the drop-down menu in the Choice box, click to select the Initial State option button, and then click OK. Using the Height box, change the number of drop-down menu choices shown, and then click OK.*

Insert a Form Field

1. Open the Web page containing the form in which you want to add a form field.

2. Click the Insert menu, point to Form Field, and then click the form field you want to use.

3. If you want, click to reposition the insertion point where you want the title of the form field to appear.

4. Type the title for the form field.

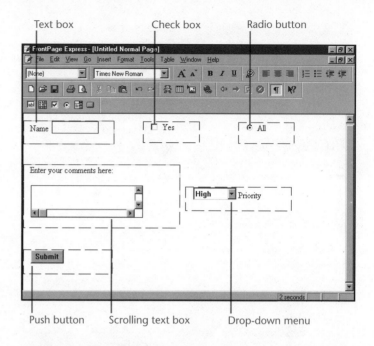

Text box   Check box   Radio button

Push button   Scrolling text box   Drop-down menu

Change the Properties of a Form Field

1. Right-click the form field, and then click Form Field Properties.

2. If you want, type a new name for the field.

3. Choose option buttons and fill in boxes appropriate to the form field. These might include Initial Value, State, Button Type, or Password Field.

4. Click OK.

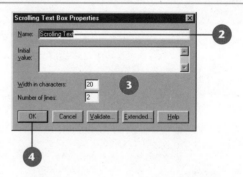

TIP

Quickly insert a form field using the toolbar. *If necessary, click the View menu, and click Forms Toolbar to view the Forms toolbar. Click the form field button you want to insert.*

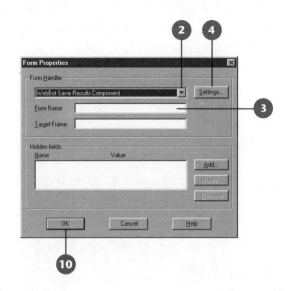

TIP

What is a forms handler? *A forms handler is simply a program that runs on a Web server. The form handler program runs whenever someone submits a form to it. Most form handlers are WebBots.*

Change the Properties of a Form

1. Right-click the form area (inside the dotted rectangle), and then click Form Properties.

2. Click the Form Handler drop-down arrow, and select a form handler.

3. Type a new name for the form.

4. Click Settings.

5. If necessary, click the Results tab.

6. Type the name of the file where the results of the form input will be stored.

7. Click the File Format drop-down arrow, and select a file format.

8. Click to select the Additional Information To Save check boxes to specify the kinds of information you want to store, such as the time and date, in the results file.

9. Click OK to return to the Form Properties dialog box.

10. Click OK.

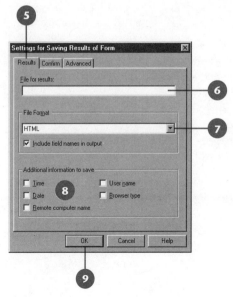

Inserting ActiveX Controls

ActiveX controls are software components that add functionality to your web page that can't be created using standard HTML. Examples of ActiveX controls include a label control that can display text in different sizes and angles, a timer control that can generate timed events, a stock ticker control that can display stock information, and an animation control that can display animations. ActiveX controls are created using programming languages. You can also insert a PowerPoint slide show animation into your Web page as an ActiveX control.

TIP

More information on ActiveX controls. *Check out Microsoft's ActiveX Web site at http://www.microsoft.com/activeplatform/default.asp.*

Insert an ActiveX Control

1 Open the Web page in which you want to insert an ActiveX control.

2 Click the Insert menu, point to Other Component, and then click ActiveX Control.

3 Click the Pick A Control drop-down arrow, and then select the Active X control you want to insert.

4 To change the properties for the ActiveX control, click Properties.

5 Type a name that represents the ActiveX control when it's used along with a script

6 Specify in pixels how you want the ActiveX control to be placed on the Web page.

7 In the Alternative Representation box, enter text to display for browsers that do not support ActiveX controls.

8 Specify a network location that the browser can search for the ActiveX control.

9 Click OK.

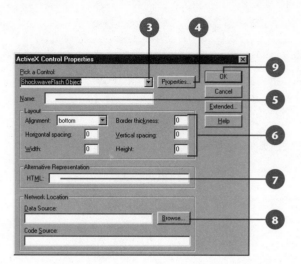

TIP

Create a PowerPoint animation. *In PowerPoint 97, click the File menu, click Save As HTML, and then follow the instructions in the wizard dialog boxes. PowerPoint creates a compressed animation, which has a .PPZ file extension.*

TIP

View a PowerPoint animation. *To view a PowerPoint Animation on a Web page, you must have the PowerPoint Animation Player installed on your computer. You can download it from Microsoft's PowerPoint web site at www.microsoft.com/powerpoint/.*

SEE ALSO

See "Using ActiveX Controls" on page 100 or "Controlling ActiveX and Java Content" on page 102 for information about using ActiveX controls in Internet Explorer.

Insert a PowerPoint Animation

1 Open the Web page in which you want to insert the PowerPoint animation.

2 Click the Insert menu, point to Other Component, and then click PowerPoint Animation.

3 Click Browse.

4 Click Browse again, and then double-click the PowerPoint animation file you want to use.

5 Click the ActiveX Control option button.

6 Click OK.

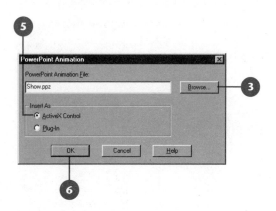

Inserting Java Applets

Java applets are created in a programming language called Java. Like ActiveX controls, Java applets add dynamic functionality to your Web page. You can find thousands of Java applets on the Web. Examples include scrolling banners and stock tickers, real-time sports score tracker, and many more.

TIP

Check out Java applets.
You'll find rating of hundreds of popular Java applets at www.jars.com.

TIP

Where to get applet parameter information.
You need the documentation that came with the Java applet to determine the names and values for the applet.

Insert a Java Applet

1 Open the Web page in which you want to insert a Java applet.

2 Click the Insert menu, point to Other Component, and then click Java Applet.

3 Type the name of the applet source. Source files for Java applets typically have the file extension CLASS.

4 Type the Internet address, URL, of the applet.

5 Type a warning message for browsers without Java support.

6 Click Add.

7 Type the name of the applet in the Applet Name box.

8 Enter the parameter value in the Value box.

9 Click OK.

10 Specify the width and height sizes (in pixels) for the Java applet.

11 Specify the layout spacing (in pixels) and select an alignment.

12 Click OK.

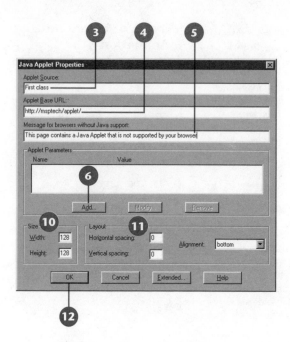

Inserting Plug-Ins

A *plug-in* is an accessory program that extends Netscape's capabilities. If you switched to Internet Explorer from Netscape, you might want to continue using the plug-ins you downloaded and installed.

TIP

Quickly adjust the size of a plug-in. *Select the plug-in on the Web page, and then drag its border controls with the mouse button.*

SEE ALSO

See "Understanding Add-Ons, Plug-Ins, and Viewers" on page 92 for information about plug-ins.

Insert a Plug-In

1 Open the Web page in which you want to insert the plug-in.

2 Click the Insert menu, point to Other Component, and then click Plug-In.

3 Click Browse.

4 Click Browse again, and then double-click the plug-in file you want to use.

5 Type a warning message for browsers without Plug-In support.

6 Specify the width and height (in pixels) for the plug-in.

7 Click the Alignment drop-down arrow, and select a layout alignment.

8 Specify the layout border thickness and horizontal and vertical spacing values (in pixels) in the appropriate boxes.

9 Click OK.

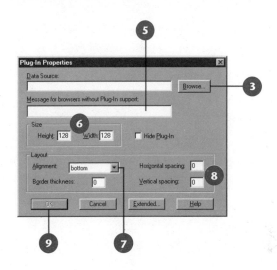

11

Working with Internet Explorer Tools

Internet Explorer tools make it easy for you to publish your Web pages, get the latest version of Internet Explorer, manage Internet Explorer users, and receive online software support, as well as access to free software. The Web Publishing Wizard, which is part of the standard Internet Explorer installation, automates the process of publishing your Web pages to the World Wide Web or a personal Web server. You can even use the Internet Explorer logo in your Web page. You can download the latest version of Internet Explorer right from the World Wide Web and update your Internet Explorer suite with the Update Product program. If you are a software administrator at your company, you can use Internet Explorer's Administrator Kit to help you manage Internet Explorer users.

Because the Internet changes every day, Microsoft helps you keep up to date with software programs and tools—available on the Microsoft Web site. These resources are easy to access and free of charge. If you have questions or need help, Microsoft also provides online software support.

Getting Support and Tools for Web Page Developers

The Microsoft Web site includes online help for Web page developers. For general information about developing Web pages, visit the Site Builder Workshop Web site. The Workshop page includes links to many other useful pages—such as the authoring, design, programming, server and gallery pages—plus news about new development tools for Internet Explorer. The Workshop Gallery provides Web page developers with images, sounds, ActiveX and Java controls, sample style sheets, and dynamic HTML, and data source objects.

Visit the Site Builder Workshop Web Site

1 Start Internet Explorer and connect to *http://www.microsoft.com/workshop/default.asp.*

2 Read the Web page for details about the Site Builder Workshop Web site.

3 Click any of the following links to find out more about these topics:

   ◆ Authoring

   ◆ Design

   ◆ Programming

   ◆ Server

   ◆ Gallery

SEE ALSO

See "Inserting ActiveX Controls" on page 230 and "Inserting Java Applets" on page 232 for information about ActiveX and Java.

TRY THIS

Check out other support Web sites for Web page developers. *Connect to the following online technical support Web sites: http://www.techweb.com or http://www.webreference.com.*

Visit the Site Builder Workshop Gallery

1. Start Internet Explorer and connect to *http://www.microsoft.com/gallery/default.asp*.

2. Click any of the following links to find out more about these topics:

   ◆ Images

   ◆ Sounds

   ◆ ActiveX

   ◆ Java

   ◆ Style Sheets

   ◆ Fonts

   ◆ Tools

   ◆ Dynamic HTML

   ◆ Data Source Objects

Getting Online Support

Microsoft has developed a knowledge database of information for all of its products. This Knowledge Base is the same tool that's used by Microsoft's support engineers. By using specific keywords and a couple of search techniques, you should find the solution to most of your problems in the Knowledge Base. If you want online support for Internet Explorer, you can connect to the Internet Explorer Support Home Page to find the information you're looing for.

TIP

Save Knowledge Base information in a file. *Find the information you want to save in the Knowledge Base, click the File menu, click Save As, click the Save As Type drop-down arrow, select Text File, and then click Save.*

Get Online Support

1. Start Internet Explorer and connect to *http://www.microsoft.com/kb/default.asp/*.

2. Read the technical support instructions.

3. Follow the step-by-step instructions to find the information you want.

4. Click a link generated by the search that contains the information you want to find.

5. If you want, click the Print button on the Standard toolbar.

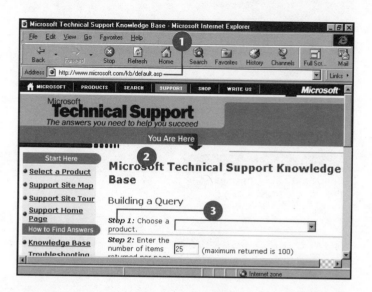

Get Internet Explorer Online Support

1. In the Internet Explorer window, click the Help menu, and then click Online Support.

2. Read the online support instructions, and then click a link to find the information you're looking for.

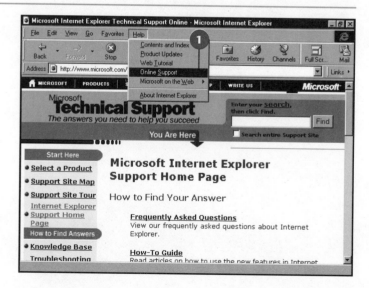

Using the Internet Explorer Logo in Your Web Page

If you want to use the Internet Explorer logo on your web page, you must first register your site with Microsoft and obtain its permission to use the logo. Fortunately, the requirements for using the logo are minimal, and Microsoft doesn't charge a fee for use of its logo. The basic requirement for using the Internet Explorer logo is that your Web page feature at least one of the flashy new features of Internet Explorer. You must submit your Web page to Microsoft for review before getting permission to use the logo. Visit the Internet Explorer Logo Program Web page for more details.

Internet Explorer logo

Visit the Internet Explorer Logo Program Web Page

1 Start Internet Explorer and connect to *http://www.microsoft.com/ie/logo/*.

2 Read the Web page for details about using the Internet Explorer logo on your Web page.

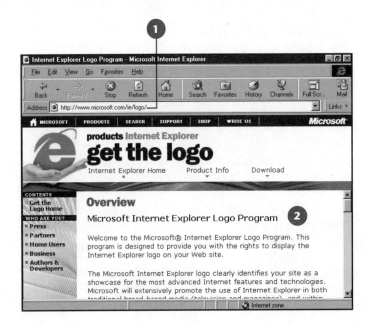

12

Publishing a Web Page

Once you finish creating a Web page, you publish it to a Web server so that people can visit your page. When you publish a Web page, you move the Web page and graphic images to a server. As part of the standard installation of Internet Explorer, a Web Publishing Wizard is included to help you publish your Web page to a Web server. You can start the Web Publishing Wizard from the Start menu or from FrontPage Express. The wizard automates the process of copying files from your computer to the Web server—just follow the step-by-step instructions, and the wizard does the rest.

TIP

If you don't know, call your service provider. *If you don't know what to type or select as you step through the Web Publishing Wizard, call your Internet Service Provider (ISP) for the information you need.*

Publish a Web Page to the World Wide Web

1 Click the Start button on the taskbar, point to Programs, and point to Internet Explorer.

2 Click Web Publishing Wizard. Click Next to continue.

3 Click Browse Folders or Browse Files, and then select the folder or file you want to publish.

4 Click Next to continue.

5 Type or select a name to describe your Web server. Click Next to continue.

6 If necessary, click the Service Provider drop-down arrow, and then select your service provider. Click Next to continue.

7 Type the Internet address, URL you use to access your Web pages. Click Next to continue.

8 Click the option button corresponding to the method you use to access your Web server. Click Next, and then connect to the Internet.

9 Click Next to verify settings.

10 Click Finish.

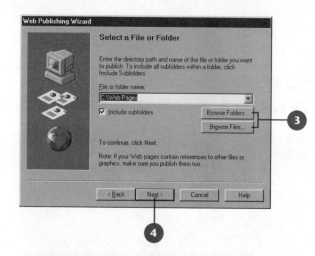

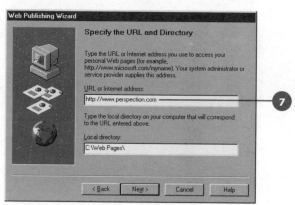

TIP

What is a Web server? *On the World Wide Web, the server is the computer that runs the program that responds to HTTP requests by providing Web pages.*

SEE ALSO

See "Setting Up a Personal Web Server" on page 242 for information on publishing a Web page to a personal Web server.

TIP

Trouble publishing your files? *If you have trouble publishing your files to an HTTP Web site, the Web Publishing Wizard asks you for another location. The best choice is an FTP (File Transfer Protocol) Web site. Select the FTP protocol option and enter a FTP server name. Call your Internet service provider for the FTP server name.*

Publish a Web Page from FrontPage Express

1 Start FrontPage Express and open the Web page you want to publish.

2 Click the File menu, and then click Save As.

3 Enter a name for the Web page.

4 Type the Internet address and filename that you want for your Web page.

5 Click OK.

6 If necessary, click Yes To All to publish the graphic images associated with the Web page.

7 Click Next to continue.

8 Type or select a name to describe your Web server. Click Next to continue.

9 Click the option button corresponding to the method you use to access your Web server. Click Next to continue.

10 Click Next to verify settings.

11 Click Finish.

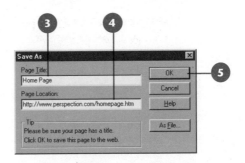

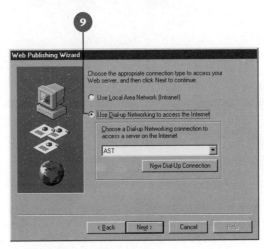

12

Setting Up a Personal Web Server

Microsoft Personal Web Server (PWS) turns any computer running Windows 95 or later into a Web server, enabling easy publication of Web pages onto the Internet or a corporate intranet. Personal Web Server simplifies sharing information for all users on corporate intranets or the Internet. It is designed for small-scale, peer-to-peer Web server usage. Once you've downloaded and installed the Personal Web Server, you need to start it.

SEE ALSO

See "Working with Beta Software" on page 252 for information about installing and removing software on your computer.

Download and Set Up a Personal Web Server

1. Create an empty folder in which to store the downloaded files.

2. Start Internet Explorer and connect to *http://www.microsoft.com/ie/pws/*.

3. Click the Download link, and then click Personal Web Server.

4. Read the Web page, and then follow the download instructions.

5. Click OK to download the Personal Web Server setup files into your new folder.

6. Start Windows Explorer, and then double-click the Personal Web Server setup file in your new folder.

7. Read the Personal Web Server setup wizard dialog boxes, and follow the instructions.

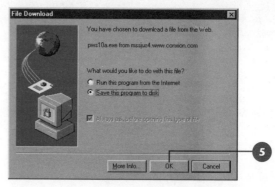

TIP

Quickly access Personal Web Server settings. *Click the Personal Web Server icon on the right side of the taskbar.*

Personal Web
Server

Start the Personal Web Server

1 Click the Start button on the taskbar, point to Settings, and then click Control Panel.

2 Click the Personal Web Server icon.

3 Click the General tab.

4 To find out more about the Personal Web Server, click More Details.

5 Click the Startup tab.

6 Click Start, if necessary.

7 To automatically start the Personal Web Server, click the Run The Web Server Automatically At Startup check box to select it.

8 Click OK.

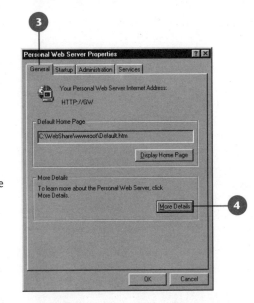

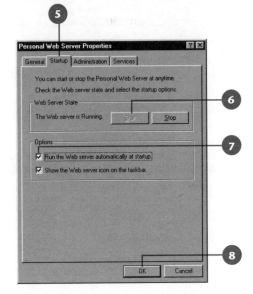

Downloading Internet Explorer

If you haven't installed the latest version of Internet Explorer yet, you can download Internet Explorer from the World Wide Web and set up the software on your computer. To download Internet Explorer, all you need to do is connect to the Internet Explorer Web site, jump to the download page, click the download button, and then specify the location on your computer where you want to copy the software. Once you download the Internet Explorer Setup program, you'll need to start the program and connect to the Internet to complete the downloading process.

SEE ALSO

See "Installing Internet Explorer" on page 245 for information about installing or updating Internet Explorer.

Download Internet Explorer

1 Create an empty folder in which to store the downloaded files.

2 Start Internet Explorer and connect to *http://www.microsoft.com/ie/.*

3 Click the Download link, point to Internet Explorer 4.0, and then select an operating system.

4 Read the Web page, and then follow the download instructions.

5 Click OK, and then download the Internet Explorer setup files into your new folder.

6 Type *C:* in the Address bar, press Enter, and then double-click the setup file in your new folder.

7 Read the Internet Explorer Setup Wizard dialog boxes, and follow the instructions.

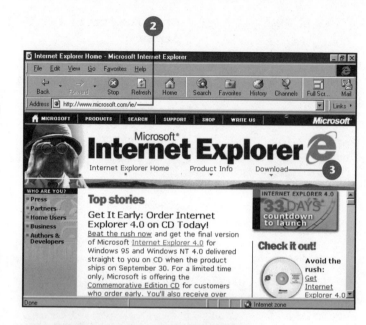

Installing Internet Explorer

Whether you are installing Internet Explorer for the first time or you are upgrading new Internet Explorer components, Microsoft makes it easy to set up the software you need to surf the World Wide Web. Before you can install Internet Explorer, you need to download the software from Microsoft's Internet Explorer Web site or another authorized web site, or contact Microsoft to order the software on CD-ROM.

TIP

How long does it take to set up Internet Explorer over the Internet? *Internet Explorer setup can take two to three hours over the Internet depending on the speed of your Internet connection.*

SEE ALSO

See "Downloading Internet Explorer" on page 244 for information about getting Internet Explorer software.

Install Internet Explorer

1   Click the Start button on the taskbar, and then click Run.

2   Type the path to the Internet Explorer setup program. Click Browse to search your hard disk or CD-ROM to find the program.

3   Click OK. Click Next to continue.

4   Click the I Accept The Agreement option button. Click Next to continue.

5   Select an Internet location to continue the setup over the Internet. Click Next to continue.

6   Click the Installation drop-down arrow, and select an installation option: Full, Standard, or Minimum.

7   Click Next to continue.

8   Use the default installation folder location, or enter a new location. Click Next to continue.

9   If you are upgrading new items, click the Upgrade Only New Items option button, and then click OK.

10   Click OK.

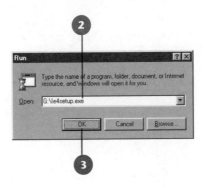

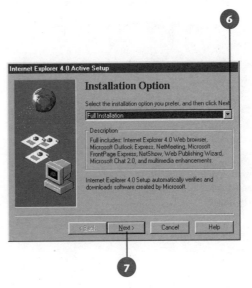

Uninstalling Internet Explorer

Once you have installed Internet Explorer, you can remove the Windows Active Desktop without affecting Internet Explorer, or you can add the Windows Active Desktop from a Web site if it is not already installed. If necessary, you can also uninstall Internet Explorer and any of the installed Internet Explorer components.

TIP

Install the Windows Active Desktop. *Follow the steps for removing, but in step 5 click the Add Windows Desktop Update Component From Web Site option button, and then click OK.*

Remove the Windows Active Desktop Update

1 Click the Start button on the taskbar, point to Settings, and click Control Panel.

2 Double-click the Add/ Remove Programs icon in the Control Panel.

3 Click the Install/Uninstall tab.

4 Click Microsoft Internet Explorer 4.0.

5 Click Add/Remove.

6 Click the Remove Windows Desktop Update Component, But Keep The Internet Explorer 4.0 Web Browser option button.

7 Click OK.

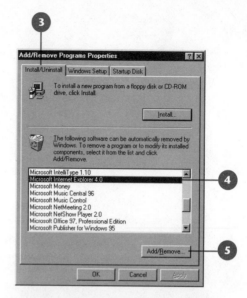

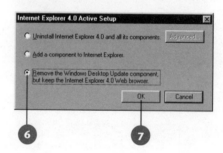

TIP

Add a component to Internet Explorer. *Follow the steps for uninstalling, but in step 5 click the Add A Component To Internet Explorer option button, click OK, select the component you want, and then click OK.*

Add/Remove
Programs

Uninstall Internet Explorer and Its Components

1 Click the Start button on the taskbar, point to Settings, and click Control Panel.

2 Double-click the Add/Remove Programs icon in the Control Panel, and then click the Install/Uninstall tab.

3 Click Microsoft Internet Explorer 4.0.

4 Click Add/Remove.

5 Click the Uninstall Explorer 4.0 And All Its Components option button to select it.

6 Click Advanced.

7 Click the Uninstall Explorer 4.0 And The Components Selected Below option button to select it.

8 Click the check boxes for the components you want to remove along with Internet Explorer.

9 Click OK.

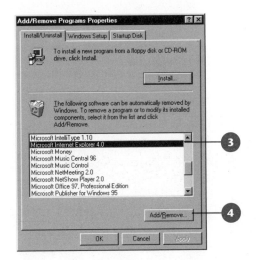

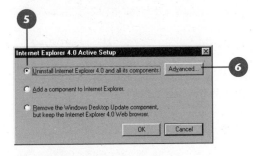

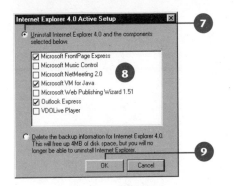

12

Getting Updates to Internet Explorer

Microsoft makes it easy to update Internet Explorer software. All you have to do is start the Update Product program located on the Internet Explorer submenu, and the program does the rest. The Update Product program updates Internet Explorer and its related programs. Besides updating the Internet Explorer software you already have installed, you can install other Internet Explorer components from Microsoft's Web site. Internet Explorer's Active Setup program analyzes your computer to determine what is currently installed and makes it easy to add components.

Get Updates to Internet Explorer Products

1 In the Internet Explorer window, click the Help menu, and then click Product Updates.

A status message appears indicating the progress of the update or telling you that all components are current and do not need to be updated.

2 Click OK.

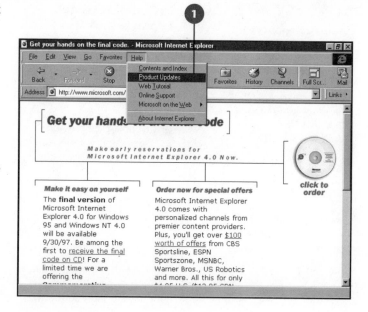

TIP

Use Web fonts and multiple languages in your Web page. *Follow the step-by-step instructions to install additional Internet Explorer components. Click the check boxes for the Multi-Language Pack or the Web Font Pack during the installation.*

SEE ALSO

See "Working with Beta Software" on page 252 for information about installing and removing software on your computer.

Install Additional Internet Explorer Components

1. Start Internet Explorer and connect to http://www.microsoft.com/ie/.

2. Click the Download link, and then click Internet Explorer 4.0 Components.

3. Read the Web page, and then scroll to the bottom of the page.

4. Click the Internet Explorer 4.0 Components link.

5. Click Yes.

6. Click the check boxes of the components you want to add. Click Next to continue.

7. Click the Component List drop-down arrow, and then select a download site.

8. Click Install Now to download the components. Restart your computer, if necessary.

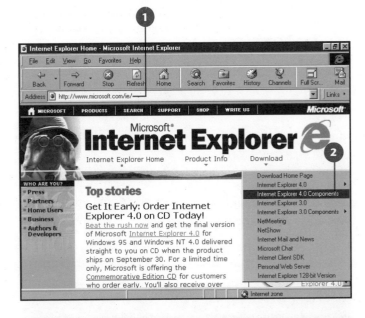

12

Administering to Internet Explorer Users

The Internet Explorer Administration Kit includes all the tools your business needs to deploy Microsoft Internet Explorer company-wide. The administration kit lets you customize Internet Explorer to best meet your needs, and install and manage Internet Explorer from a central network location without having to set up individual computers.

TIP

Read the download instructions carefully. *To avoid problems, read and follow the download and installation instructions carefully.*

SEE ALSO

See "Working with Beta Software" on page 252 for information about installing software.

Download and Set Up the Administrator Kit

1. Create an empty folder in which to store the downloaded files.

2. Start Internet Explorer and connect to *http://www.microsoft.com/ie/ieak/*.

3. Read the Web page, and then follow the instructions to sign up for the kit.

4. Download the Internet Explorer Administration Kit setup files into your new folder.

5. Type *C:* in the Address bar, press Enter, and then double-click the setup file in your new folder.

6. Read the Internet Explorer Administration Kit Setup Wizard dialog boxes, and follow the instructions carefully.

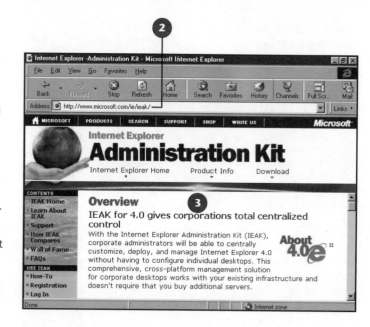

Getting Free Software

Microsoft posts updates, fixes, add-on files, and programs that you can download from the Microsoft Internet Web site. Even though the software is free, downloading software using a modem can sometimes take a long time to complete.

TIP

Read the download instructions carefully. *To avoid problems, read and follow the download and installation instructions carefully.*

Download Free Software

1 Create an empty folder in which to store the downloaded files.

2 Start Internet Explorer and connect to *http://www.microsoft.com/msdownload/default.asp.*

3 Click a link to the software you want to download.

4 Read the Web page, and then follow the download instructions.

5 Download the software setup files into your new folder.

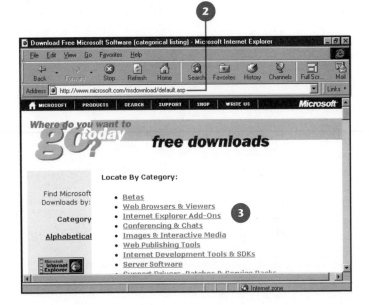

Working with Beta Software

Although the software that's available for download has usually been through a testing program, pre-release, or *beta* software, is software that's still under development, and it has the potential to cause problems. Use Add/Remove Programs in the Control Panel to install or remove a previous version of a software program or to remove beta software that is causing problems, and then install new or updated software.

> **TIP**
>
> **Double-click the setup file to start the installation.**
> *Start Windows Explorer, open the folder where the setup file is located, and then double-click the setup file to start the installation.*

Install Software

1 If possible, back up all your files to a location external to your computer.

2 If you have an earlier version of the beta software installed, remove it.

3 Close all running programs except Windows.

4 Click the Start button on the taskbar, point to Settings, and then click Control Panel.

5 Click the Add/Remove Programs icon.

6 Click Install.

7 Follow the setup or wizard instructions to complete the installation.

8 If the program causes problems, remove the software and wait for the next release.

SEE ALSO

See "Getting Free Software" on page 251 for information about downloading beta software.

Add/Remove
Programs

Remove Software

1 Click the Start button on the taskbar, point to Settings, and then click Control Panel.

2 Click the Add/Remove Programs icon.

3 Select the software program or component you want to remove.

4 Click Add/Remove.

5 Follow the instructions for removing the software.

6 Click OK when the removal process is complete.

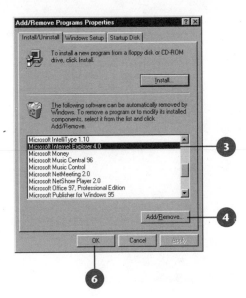

12

Index

drives. *See* hard drives (local)
Drop-Down Menu button
(Forms toolbar,
FrontPage Express
window), 185
drop-down menus (lists)
adding choices to, 228
in dialog boxes, 26
inserting in Web page
forms, 228

e-mail. *See* mail messages
e-mail accounts, multiple, 130
e-mail programs
choosing, 88
See also Outlook Express
editing
hyperlinks, 196-97
marquees, 216, 217
text, 190-91
encoding large Outlook Express
messages, 151
Enter New Nickname dialog
box, 178
entering
Internet addresses, 16, 17
nicknames (for chats), 178
symbols (on Web pages), 191
text (on Web pages), 190
See also inserting
erasing
incorrect characters, 190
Whiteboard elements, 173
error messages, 50
Excel (Microsoft), macro virus
checking, 51
exiting
Chat (NetMeeting), 171
FrontPage Express, 204
Internet Explorer, 27

Whiteboard (NetMeeting),
172
Explorer bar (Internet Explorer
window), 15
finding Web pages, 22
listing available channels, 22

FAQ (Frequently Asked
Questions) page
(Microsoft Web site), 48
favorite files/folders, adding to
the Favorites list, 36-37
favorite Web sites/pages
accessing, 8, 22, 70-71
adding to the Favorites
list, 34
adding to the Links
toolbar, 71
displaying information
on, 35
organizing on your Favorites
list, 35
Favorites button (Standard
toolbar, Internet Explorer
window), 22
Favorites folder, 8, 30
Favorites list
adding folders/files to, 36-37
adding Web sites pages to, 34
adding Web sites/pages to
the Links toolbar
from, 71
organizing, 34, 35
scrolling, 37
Favorites pane, closing, 37
File Download dialog box, 52,
55, 242
file formats (for graphic image
files), 56, 192
changing, 193

file formats (for Web pages),
saving Web pages in
different, 203
"File Not Found" error
message, 50
file repository sites, and
viruses, 51
File Transfer Protocol sites. *See*
FTP sites
files
adding to the Favorites list,
36-37
adding to the Start menu, 9
ASF files, 108
attaching to mail messages,
121, 123, 128
browsing local hard drive
files, 8, 18-19
closing, 204
cookie files, 89, 90
downloading. *See* downloading FTP site files;
downloading Web site
files
inserting text files in Web
pages, 191
moving on the Start menu, 9
opening files received in
meetings, 176
opening local hard drive
files, 7, 18, 36
opening Web pages
from, 188
organizing, 177
receiving during meetings,
176, 177
saving Knowledge Base
information in, 238
saving mail messages as, 124
sending during meetings,
176, 177
temporary Internet files, 20,
86, 87

viewing, 36-37
See also folders (local hard
drive directories); text
files
Filled Ellipse tool (Whiteboard),
173
Filled Rectangle tool
(Whiteboard), 173
filtering news messages,
144, 145
Find dialog box
copying text into, 31
displaying, 31
Find People dialog box, 132
Find People link (Outlook
Express Start Page), 115
finding
add-ons, 93
Address Book contacts, 132
the closest matches, 223
Internet addresses, 115, 132,
156-57
Microsoft All-In-One Search
Web page, 32, 33
news messages, 144
newsgroups, 144, 145
people on the Internet, 115,
132, 156-57
plug-ins, 93
text (on Web pages), 31,
224-25
ULS (Internet User Location
Service), 156-57
viewers, 93
Web information, 22, 29-47
Web sites/pages, 22, 29,
32-33
See also Web site addresses
Folder list (News window), 136
Folder list (Outlook Express
window), 114
opening Outlook Express
folders, 117

sharing programs, 174-75
  and chatting, 171
  maximum participants, 174
  stopping, 175
shopping on the Internet, 80-81
  certificates, 74
shortcut keys
  for links to Web pages, 71
  news message command
    keys, 142
shortcuts
  desktop shortcuts, 7, 71
  See also hyperlinks (on Web
    pages); links (to Web
    pages); shortcut keys
Show Desktop button (Quick
    Launch toolbar), 8
Show/Hide¶ button (Standard
    toolbar, FrontPage
    Express window), 184
Signature dialog box, 126
signatures (for mail messages),
    126
  adding, 121, 127
  creating, 126
Site Builder Workshop Web site
    (Microsoft), 236
  visiting, 236
slash (/), vs. backslash, 18
Smart Toolbar. *See* Standard
    toolbar (Internet Explorer
    window)
software
  beta software, 252-53
  collection site addresses, 93
  downloading free software,
    52, 53, 251
  installing, 252
  removing, 253
  virus checking software, 51
  See also programs
sorting
  the Address Book, 119

drive/directory lists, 19
  mail messages, 125
sounds
  adding to chat comic strip
    characters, 179
  background sounds, 215
  changing properties, 106
  enabling/disabling, 107
  playing, 96, 104-5,
    108-9, 215
  Web site addresses, 105
  See also audio
speaker volume, adjusting, 169
speaking in comic strip
  chats, 179
SpeedDial shortcuts, creating/
    sending/settings, 167
SpeedDial tab (NetMeeting
    window), 160
Standard toolbar (FrontPage
    Express window),
    183, 184
  buttons, 183, 184
Standard toolbar (Internet
    Explorer window) (Smart
    Toolbar), 5, 6, 15, 22-23
  document buttons, 23
  using Microsoft Office-like
    buttons, 73
  Web buttons, 22
Start button (taskbar), adding
    files/programs to the
    Start menu, 9
Start menu
  accessing the Web, 8
  adding files/programs to, 9
  moving files on, 9
  starting FrontPage
    Express, 182
  starting Internet Explorer, 14
  starting NetMeeting, 158-59
  starting Outlook Express,
    116, 134

starting Outlook Express
    News, 134
start page, jumping to, 22
starting
  Chat (NetMeeting), 170
  comic strip chats, 178, 179
  FrontPage Express, 22, 182
  Internet Explorer, 14, 114
  mail servers, 22
  NetMeeting, 156, 158-59
  Outlook Express, 22, 116,
    134, 135
  Outlook Express News,
    134-35
  Personal Web Server, 243
  Web editors, 22
  Whiteboard (NetMeeting),
    172
  See also running
startup, starting Outlook
    Express at, 135
startup connection, setting a
    default, 135
stationery
  for Outlook Express Mail
    messages, 126-27
  for Outlook Express News
    messages, 147
Status bar (FrontPage Express
    window), 183
Status bar (Internet Explorer
    window), 15
  displaying/hiding, 73
Status bar (News window), 136
stock ticker controls
    (ActiveX), 230
Stop button (Standard toolbar,
    FrontPage Express
    window), 184
Stop button (Standard toolbar,
    Internet Explorer
    window), 22

storing
  chat messages, 171
  mail/news messages, 150
streaming audio/video, 96,
    108-9
style sheets (for Web pages),
    62-63
  creating, 62
  displaying Web pages with,
    62, 63
  downloading Microsoft
    style sheets, 63
  effects, 63
styles
  changing paragraph
    styles, 209
  See also style sheets (for Web
    pages)
Subscribe dialog box, 40
subscribing
  to channels, 30, 41
  to newsgroups, 140
  to Web sites, 30, 40
subscription properties dialog
    boxes, 42
Subscription tab (subscription
    properties dialog
    boxes), 42
subscriptions
  modifying, 42
  updating, 42, 43
  See also subscribing
Subscriptions window, 42, 43
Sun Microsystems Java. *See* Java
    (Web browser program-
    ing language)
supervisor passwords, for
    viewing screened-out
    content, 75, 78
survey forms (on Web pages)
  creating, 227
  storing the results, 227
symbols, inserting in Web
    pages, 191

system performance, improving, 86-87

Steve Johnson has written books on a variety of computer software, including Microsoft Office 97 programs, Windows 95, and the Internet. In 1991, Steve founded Perspection, which produced this book. When he is not staying up late writing, he enjoys playing basketball, gardening, leading Bible studies, and spending time with his wife and new born son. When time permits, he likes to travel, which seems unlikely with a new born.

Robin Geller has worked in nearly every type of editorial and production position in the publishing industry since 1986. Today she spends her time editing and writing. In 1992, Robin founded Pale Moon Productions, which provides production and editorial services to many publishers. Whenever she can sever the mouse cord, Robin leaves her computer in San Francisco, and visits family and friends in such places as New York, Texas, and Arizona.

Acknowledgments

I'd like to thank my wonderful wife, Holly, for supporting me during this and other projects. Your understanding, patience, and love seem to never end. I'd also like to thank my son, James Paul, lovingly referred to as J.P., for being a wonderful gift from God and showing me that I can be up in the middle of the night and not be writing.

I'd also like to thank Jane Pedicini for her editorial expertise. Jane, you continue to amaze me. Thanks to Nicholas Chu for his excellent technical review. Nick, I knew your computer expertise would come in handy some day.

Steve Johnson

Acknowledgments

Thank you to David Beskeen and Steve Johnson at Perspection, Inc. for their belief in me and confidence in my writing. Thank you to MT Cozzola, developmental editor, for her invaluable comments and suggestions that honed the text into its final form. And a big thank you to Brian Romer for his constant support.

Robin Geller

Cheryl Kirk has written several Internet-related books and contributed to other Microsoft Office 97 software books. She currently writes columns for the Anchorage Daily News and the Alaska Business Monthly. When not writing, she hosts a computer radio program and teaches as an adjunct lecturer at the University of Alaska.

Acknowledgments

I'd like to thank David Beskeen and Steve Johnson for the great work they did on this book and for allowing me the opportunity to work with them and the whole Perspection Team on what I think is a pretty darn good book. Happy Surfing!

Cheryl Kirk

The manuscript for this book was prepared and submitted to Microsoft Press in electronic form. Text files were prepared using Microsoft Word 97 for Windows 95. Pages were composed by David Beskeen and Gary Bedard using PageMaker 6.5 for Windows, with text in Stone Sans and display type in Stone Serif and Stone Serif Semibold. Composed pages were delivered to the printer as electronic prepress files.

Cover Designer
Tim Girvin Design

Interior Graphic Designer
designlab
Kim Eggleston

Principle Compositior and
Graphic Layout Artist
David Beskeen

Compositor
Gary Bedard

Proofer
Jane Pedicini

Indexer
Michael Brackney

Get quick, easy answers— anywhere!

Microsoft Press® Field Guides are a quick, accurate source of information about Microsoft Office 97 applications. In no time, you'll have the lay of the land, identify toolbar buttons and commands, stay safely out of danger, and have all the tools you need for survival!

Microsoft® Excel 97 Field Guide
Stephen L. Nelson
U.S.A. **$9.95** ($12.95 Canada)
ISBN 1-57231-326-9

Microsoft® Word 97 Field Guide
Stephen L. Nelson
U.S.A. **$9.95** ($12.95 Canada)
ISBN 1-57231-325-0

Microsoft® PowerPoint® 97 Field Guide
Stephen L. Nelson
U.S.A. **$9.95** ($12.95 Canada)
ISBN 1-57231-327-7

Microsoft® Outlook™ 97 Field Guide
Stephen L. Nelson
U.S.A. **$9.99** ($12.99 Canada)
ISBN 1-57231-383-8

Microsoft® Access 97 Field Guide
Stephen L. Nelson
U.S.A. **$9.95** ($12.95 Canada)
ISBN 1-57231-328-5

Microsoft Press® products are available worldwide wherever quality computer books are sold. For more information, contact your book or computer retailer, software reseller, or local Microsoft Sales Office, or visit our Web site at mspress.microsoft.com. To locate your nearest source for Microsoft Press products, or to order directly, call 1-800-MSPRESS in the U.S. (in Canada, call 1-800-268-2222).

Prices and availability dates are subject to change.

Microsoft Press

Take productivity in stride.

Microsoft Press® *Step by Step* books provide quick and easy self-paced training that will help you learn to use the powerful word processor, spreadsheet, database, desktop information manager, and presentation applications of Microsoft Office 97, both individually and together. Prepared by the professional trainers at Catapult, Inc. and Perspection, Inc., these books present easy-to-follow lessons with clear objectives, real-world business examples, and numerous screen shots and illustrations. Each book contains approximately eight hours of instruction. Put Microsoft's Office 97 applications to work today, *Step by Step.*

Microsoft® Excel 97 Step by Step
U.S.A. $29.95   ($39.95 Canada)
ISBN 1-57231-314-5

Microsoft® Word 97 Step by Step
U.S.A. $29.95   ($39.95 Canada)
ISBN 1-57231-313-7

Microsoft® PowerPoint® 97
 Step by Step
U.S.A. $29.95   ($39.95 Canada)
ISBN 1-57231-315-3

Microsoft® Outlook™ 97 Step by Step
U.S.A. $29.99   ($39.99 Canada)
ISBN 1-57231-382-X

Microsoft® Access 97 Step by Step
U.S.A. $29.95   ($39.95 Canada)
ISBN 1-57231-316-1

Microsoft® Office 97 Integration
 Step by Step
U.S.A. $29.95   ($39.95 Canada)
ISBN 1-57231-317-X

Microsoft Press® products are available worldwide wherever quality computer books are sold. For more information, contact your book or computer retailer, software reseller, or local Microsoft Sales Office, or visit our Web site at mspress.microsoft.com. To locate your nearest source for Microsoft Press products, or to order directly, call 1-800-MSPRESS in the U.S. (in Canada, call 1-800-268-2222).

Prices and availability dates are subject to change.

Microsoft Press

Keep things **running** smoothly around the **Office.**

These are *the* answer books for business users of Microsoft Office 97 applications. They are packed with everything from quick, clear instructions for new users to comprehensive answers for power users. The Microsoft Press® *Running* series features authoritative handbooks you'll keep by your computer and use every day.

Running Microsoft® Excel 97
Mark Dodge, Chris Kinata, and Craig Stinson
U.S.A. $39.95   ($54.95 Canada)
ISBN 1-57231-321-8

Running Microsoft® Word 97
Russell Borland
U.S.A. $39.95   ($53.95 Canada)
ISBN 1-57231-320-X

Running Microsoft® PowerPoint® 97
Stephen W. Sagman
U.S.A. $29.95   ($39.95 Canada)
ISBN 1-57231-324-2

Running Microsoft® Access 97
John Viescas
U.S.A. $39.95   ($54.95 Canada)
ISBN 1-57231-323-4

Running Microsoft® Office 97
Michael Halvorson and Michael Young
U.S.A. $39.95   ($53.95 Canada)
ISBN 1-57231-322-6

crosoft Press® products are available worldwide wherever quality computer oks are sold. For more information, contact your book or computer retailer, ftware reseller, or local Microsoft Sales Office, or visit our Web site at press.microsoft.com. To locate your nearest source for Microsoft Press oducts, or to order directly, call 1-800-MSPRESS in the U.S. (in Canada, call 800-268-2222).

ces and availability dates are subject to change.

Microsoft *Press*

Things are looking up!

Here's the remarkable, *visual* way to quickly find answers about Microsoft applications and operating systems. Microsoft Press® *At a Glance* books let you focus on particular tasks and show you with clear, numbered steps the easiest way to get them done right now.

Microsoft® **Excel 97 At a Glance**
Perspection, Inc.
U.S.A. $16.95 ($22.95 Canada)
ISBN 1-57231-367-6

Microsoft® **Word 97 At a Glance**
Jerry Joyce and Marianne Moon
U.S.A. $16.95 ($22.95 Canada)
ISBN 1-57231-366-8

Microsoft® **PowerPoint® 97 At a Glance**
Perspection, Inc.
U.S.A. $16.95 ($22.95 Canada)
ISBN 1-57231-368-4

Microsoft® **Access 97 At a Glance**
Perspection, Inc.
U.S.A. $16.95 ($22.95 Canada)
ISBN 1-57231-369-2

Microsoft® **Office 97 At a Glance**
Perspection, Inc.
U.S.A. $16.95 ($22.95 Canada)
ISBN 1-57231-365-X

Microsoft® **Windows® 95 At a Glance**
Jerry Joyce and Marianne Moon
U.S.A. $16.95 ($22.95 Canada)
ISBN 1-57231-370-6

Microsoft Press® products are available worldwide wherever quality computer books are sold. For more information, contact your book or computer retailer, software reseller, or local Microsoft Sales Office, or visit our Web site at mspress.microsoft.com. To locate your nearest source for Microsoft Press products, or to order directly, call 1-800-MSPRESS in the U.S. (in Canada, call 1-800-268-2222).

Prices and availability dates are subject to change.

Microsoft Press

Register Today!

Return this
Microsoft® Internet Explorer 4 At a Glance
registration card for
a Microsoft Press® catalog

U.S. and Canada addresses only. Fill in information below and mail postage-free. Please mail only the bottom half of this page.

1-57231-740-XA   *MICROSOFT® INTERNET*   *Owner Registration Card*
                          EXPLORER 4 AT A GLANCE

_____
NAME

_____
INSTITUTION OR COMPANY NAME

_____
ADDRESS

_____

_____
CITY   STATE   ZIP

Microsoft *Press*
Quality Computer Books

For a free catalog of
Microsoft Press® products, call
1-800-MSPRESS

NO POSTAGE
NECESSARY
IF MAILED
IN THE
UNITED STATES

BUSINESS REPLY MAIL
FIRST-CLASS MAIL   PERMIT NO. 53   BOTHELL, WA

POSTAGE WILL BE PAID BY ADDRESSEE

MICROSOFT PRESS REGISTRATION
MICROSOFT® INTERNET EXPLORER 4
AT A GLANCE
PO BOX 3019
BOTHELL   WA   98041-9946